Hedge Fund Modelling and
Analysis Using Excel and VBA

For other titles in the Wiley Finance series
please see www.wiley.com/finance

Hedge Fund Modelling and Analysis Using Excel and VBA

Paul Darbyshire and David Hampton

A John Wiley & Sons, Ltd., Publication

Library of Congress Cataloging-in-Publication Data

Darbyshire, Paul.
  Hedge fund modelling and analysis using Excel and VBA / Paul Darbyshire and David
Hampton.
    p. cm.
    ISBN 978-0-470-74719-3 (hardback)
1. Hedge funds–Mathematical models.   2. Microsoft Excel (Computer file)   3. Microsoft Visual
Basic for applications.   I. Hampton, David.   II. Title.
    HG4530.D37 2012
    332.64'5240285554–dc23

                                                                                    2011046750

A catalogue record for this book is available from the British Library.

ISBN 978-0-470-74719-3 (hbk) ISBN 978-1-119-94563-5 (ebk)
ISBN 978-1-119-94565-9 (ebk) ISBN 978-1-119-94564-2 (ebk)

Set in 11/13pt Times by Aptara Inc., New Delhi, India
Printed in Great Britain by TJ International Ltd, Padstow, Cornwall

Mum and Dad
To whom I owe everything.
P.D. and D.H.

Contents

Preface

This book is a practical introduction to modelling and analysing hedge funds using the popular Excel spreadsheet tool and Visual Basic for Applications (VBA) programming language. The structure of the book is as follows. Chapters 1–3 cover the necessary foundations required in order to understand hedge funds and the alternative investment industry. With this fundamental knowledge in place, Chapters 4–7 cover the more quantitative and theoretical material needed to effectively analyse a series of hedge fund returns and extract the relevant information required in order to make critical investment decisions.

Throughout the book there are numerous snapshots of Excel spreadsheets and VBA source code. These are described as follows.

EXCEL SPREADSHEETS

The book assumes a working knowledge of Excel, with an ability to implement simple built-in functions, such as SUM(), AVERAGE() and STDEV(), and build dynamic spreadsheets. The following example schematic explains how to interpret an Excel spreadsheet snapshot within the book:

User-defined formula · User-defined VBA function · Formula copied across these cells · Hidden rows · Built-in Excel formula

	A	B	C	D	E	F
1			Maximum	3.40	=fncMAXIMUM(B4:B75)	
2			Minimum	-2.17	=fncMINIMUM(B4:B75)	
3	Date	RoR (%)	Bins	Frequency	Frequency (%)	
4	Jan-05	0.62	-4.00	0	0	
5	Feb-05	-1.14	-3.75	0	=(D4/$D$37)*100	
6	Mar-05	-1.01	=C4+0.25	0	0	
7	Apr-05	1.89	-3.25	0	0	
8	May-05	1.24	-3.00	{=FREQUENCY(B4:B75,C4:C36)}		
9	Jun-05	-2.17	-2.75			
10	Jul-05	1.40	-2.50	0	0	
18	Mar-06	1.93	-0.50	2	3	
19	Apr-06	-0.90	-0.25	3	4	
20	May-06	0.85	0.00	6	8	
21	Jun-06	0.51	0.25	3	4	
22	Jul-06	0.83	0.50	4	6	
23	Aug-06	1.06	0.75	9	13	
24	Sep-06	1.00	1.00	6	8	
34	Jul-07	0.53	3.50	2	3	
35	Aug-07	3.40	3.75	0	0	
36	Sep-07	-0.28	4.00	0	0	
37	Oct-07	1.80	Sum	72	100	=SUM(E4:E36)
38	Nov-07	1.74		=SUM(D4:D36)		
39	Dec-07	1.33				
74	Nov-10	-0.02				
75	Dec-10	2.51				

Sample Excel spreadsheet

EXCEL AND USER-DEFINED VBA FUNCTIONS

When a built-in Excel function is used in the book, a description of the use of the function is provided, where necessary, in the text or in a footnote. For example, if an Excel spreadsheet makes use of the NORMSINV() built-in Excel function, a brief description is given in a footnote.[1] All user-defined functions are implemented using the VBA programming language available free with all versions of Excel. There is no prior knowledge of VBA required, although a working grasp of the language would be advantageous. The book contains many user-defined

---

[1] The NORMSINV() function returns the inverse of the standard normal cumulative distribution, i.e. a distribution with a mean of zero and a standard deviation of one.

VBA functions (prefixed with the letters 'fnc') which are displayed in a source box, for example:

Source 4.3   User-defined VBA function to calculate the SKEWNESS of a returns array

```
'function to calculate the SKEWNESS of a
returns array
Function fncSKEWNESS(RoR As Range) As Double

    'count number in returns array
    n = RoR.Count

    'the mean of returns array
    avg = (fncMEAN(RoR) / 12) 'monthly
    'the standard deviation of returns array
    std = (fncSTDEV(RoR) / Sqr(12)) 'monthly

    'initialise sum to zero
    sum = 0

    For i = 1 To n
       sum = sum + ((RoR(i) - avg) / std) ^ 3
    Next

fncSKEWNESS = (n / ((n - 1) * (n - 2))) * sum

End Function
```

Sample VBA user-defined function

HYPOTHETICAL HEDGE FUND DATA

Throughout the book there is constant reference to many hedge fund return series and factors. The 10 hedge funds and 15 factors used are all *hypothetical* and have been simulated by the authors as a unique data set for demonstration purposes only. The techniques and models used in the book can therefore be tested on the hypothetical data before being applied to real-life situations by the reader. The hypothetical data set is nonetheless close to what would be expected in reality. The 10 funds are a mixture of several major hedge fund strategies, i.e. commodity trading advisor (CTA), long/short equity (LS), global macro (GM) and market neutral (MN) strategies as described in the table below:

Hedge Fund	Abbreviation
Commodity Trading Advisor	CTA1, CTA2, CTA3
Long Short Equity	LS1, LS2, LS3
Global Macro	GM1, GM2
Market Neutral	MN1, MN2

10 hypothetical hedge funds

The 15 factors are a mixture of both passive and active indices as described in the table below:

No.		Abbreviation
	Beta factors	
1	Passive Global Stock Index	PSDX
2	S&P 500 Equity Index	S&P 500 Index
3	Passive Global Bond Index	PBond DX
4	Passive Long Global Commodity Index	PCom DX
5	Passive Long USD Index	PUSD DX
6	Risk-Free Rate	Rf
	Industry reference alternative beta factors	
7	Commodity Trading Advisor Index	CTA Index
8	Long Short Equity Index	LS Index
	Fama–French–Carhart factors	
9	Value minus Growth	Val – Gr
10	Small Cap minus Large Cap	SC – LC
11	Momentum	Mom
	Active alternative beta factors	
12	Active Global Stock Futures Index	ASDX
13	Active Global Bond Futures Index	ABDX
14	Active Global Commodity Futures Index	ACDX
15	Active Global Foreign Exchange Futures Index	AFDX

15 hypothetical factors

BOOK WEBSITE

The official website for the book is located at:

www.darbyshirehampton.com

The website provides free downloads to all of the hypothetical data, Excel spreadsheets, and VBA user-defined functions as well as many other useful resources.

The authors can be contacted on any matter relating to the book, or in a professional capacity, at the following email addresses:

Paul Darbyshire: pd@darbyshirehampton.com
David Hampton: dh@darbyshirehampton.com

1
The Hedge Fund Industry

The global credit crisis originated from a growing bubble in the US real estate market which eventually burst in 2008. This led to an overwhelming default of mortgages linked to subprime debt to which financial institutions reacted by tightening credit facilities, selling off bad debts at huge losses and pursuing fast foreclosures on delinquent mortgages. A liquidity crisis followed in the credit markets and banks became increasingly reluctant to lend to one another, causing risk premiums on debt to soar and credit to become ever scarcer and more costly. The global financial markets went into meltdown as a continuing spiral of worsening liquidity ensued. When the credit markets froze, hedge fund managers were unable to get their hands on enough capital to meet investor redemption requirements. Not until early 2009 did the industry start to experience a marked resurgence in activity, realising strong capital inflows and growing investor confidence.

This chapter introduces the concept of hedge funds and how they are structured and managed, as well as discussing the current state of the global hedge fund industry in light of the recent financial crisis. Several key investment techniques that are used in managing hedge fund strategies are also discussed. The chapter aims to build a basic working knowledge of hedge funds and, along with Chapters 2 and 3, to develop the fundamentals necessary in order to approach and understand the more quantitative and theoretical aspects of their modelling and analysis developed in later chapters.

1.1 WHAT ARE HEDGE FUNDS?

Whilst working for Fortune magazine in 1949, Alfred Winslow Jones began researching an article on various fashions in stock market forecasting and soon realised that it was possible to neutralise *market risk*[1] by buying undervalued securities and short selling (see Section 1.4.1)

---

[1] *Market risk* (or *systematic risk*) is the risk that the value of an investment will decrease due to the impact of various market factors, such as changes in interest and foreign currency rates.

overvalued ones. Such an investment scheme was the first to employ a *hedge* to eliminate the potential for losses by cancelling out adverse market moves, and the technique of *leverage*[2] to greatly improve profits. Jones generated an exceptional amount of wealth through his *hedge fund* during the 1950s and 1960s and continually outperformed traditional money managers. Jones refused to register the hedge fund with the Securities Act 1933, the Investment Advisers Act 1940, or the Investment Company Act 1940, his main argument being that the fund was a *private* entity and none of the laws associated with the three Acts applied to this type of investment. It was essential that such funds were treated separately from other regulated markets since the use of specialised investment techniques, such as short selling and leverage, were not permitted under these Acts, nor was the ability to charge performance fees to investors.

So that the funds maintained their private status, Jones would never publicly advertise or market the funds but only sought investors through word of mouth, keeping everything as secretive as possible. It was not until 1966, through the publication of a news article about Jones's exceptional profit-making ability, that Wall Street and *high net worth*[3] individuals finally caught on, and within a couple of years there were over 200 active hedge funds in the market. However, many of these hedge funds began straying from the original *market neutral* strategy used by Jones and employed other apparently more volatile strategies. The losses investors associated with highly volatile investments discouraged them from investing in hedge funds. Moreover, the onset of the turbulent financial markets experienced in the 1970s practically wiped out the hedge fund industry altogether. Despite improving market conditions in the 1980s, only a handful of hedge funds remained active over this period. Indeed, the lack of hedge funds around in the market during this time changed the regulators' views on enforcing stricter regulation on the industry. Not until the 1990s did the hedge fund industry begin to rise to prominence again and attract renewed investor confidence.

Nowadays, hedge funds are still considered private investment schemes (or vehicles) with a collective pool of capital only open to a small range of institutional investors and wealthy individuals and

---

[2] *Leverage* is the use of a range of financial instruments or borrowed capital to increase the potential return of an investment (see Section 1.4.2).

[3] A *high net worth* individual (or family) is generally assumed to have investable assets in excess of $1 million, excluding any primary residence.

having minimal regulation. They can be as diverse as the manager in control of the capital wants to be in terms of the investment strategies and the range of financial instruments which they employ, including stocks, bonds, currencies, futures, options and physical commodities. It is difficult to define what constitutes a hedge fund, to the extent that it is now often thought in professional circles that a hedge fund is simply one that incorporates any *absolute return*[4] strategy that invests in the financial markets and applies non-traditional investment techniques. Many consider hedge funds to be within the class of *alternative* investments, along with private equity and real estate finance, that seek a range of investment strategies employing a variety of sophisticated investment techniques beyond the longer established traditional ones, such as *mutual funds*.[5]

The majority of hedge funds are structured as limited partnerships, with the manager acting in the capacity of general partner and investors as limited partners. The general partners are responsible for the operation of the fund, relevant debts and any other financial obligations. Limited partners have nothing to do with the day-to-day running of the business and are only liable with respect to the amount of their investment. There is generally a minimum investment required by *accredited investors*[6] of the order of $250,000 to $500,000, although many of the more established funds can require minimums of up to $10 million. Managers will also usually have their own personal wealth invested in the fund, a circumstance intended to further increase their incentive to consistently generate above average returns for both the clients and themselves. In addition to the minimum investment required, hedge funds will also charge fees, the structure of which is related to both the management and performance of the fund. Such fees are not only used for administrative and ongoing operating costs but also to reward employees and managers for providing above average positive returns to investors. A typical fee basis is the so-called *2 and 20* structure which consists of a 2% annual fee (levied monthly or quarterly) based on the amount of *assets under management* (AuM) and a 20% performance-based fee, i.e.

---

[4] *Absolute return* refers to the ability of an actively managed fund to generate positive returns regardless of market conditions.

[5] *Mutual funds* are similar in structure to hedge funds but are subject to much stricter regulation and limited to very specific investments and strategies.

[6] An *accredited investor* is one who has a net worth of at least $1 million or has made $200,000 each year for the past two years ($300,000 if married) and has the capacity to make the same amount the following year.

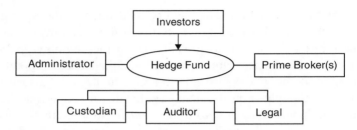

Figure 1.1   A schematic of the typical structure of a hedge fund

an incentive-oriented fee. The performance-based fee, also known as *carried interest*, is a percentage of the annual profits and only awarded to the manager when they have provided requisite returns to their clients. Some hedge funds also apply so-called *high water marks* to a particular amount of capital invested such that the manager can only receive performance fees, on that amount of money, when the value of the capital is more than the previous largest value. If the investment falls in value, the manager must bring the amount back to the previous largest amount before they can receive performance fees again. A *hurdle rate* can also be included in the fee structure, representing the minimum return on an investment a manager must achieve before performance fees are taken. The hurdle rate is usually tied to a market benchmark, such as LIBOR[7] or the one-year T-bill rate plus a spread.

1.2   THE STRUCTURE OF A HEDGE FUND

In order for managers to be effective in the running of their business a number of internal and external parties covering a variety of operational roles are employed in the structure of a hedge fund, as shown in Figure 1.1. As the industry matures and investors are requiring greater transparency and confidence in the hedge funds in which they invest, the focus on the effectiveness of these parties is growing, as are their relevant expertise and professionalism. Hedge funds are also realising that their infrastructure must keep pace with the rapidly changing industry. Whereas in the past some funds paid little attention to their support and administrative activities, they are now aware that the

---

[7] LIBOR is the *London Interbank Offered Rate*, a rate at which banks borrow from other banks in the London interbank market.

effective operation of their fund ensures the fund does not encounter unnecessary and unexpected risks.

1.2.1 Fund Administrators

Hedge fund administrators deal with many of the operational aspects of the successful running of a fund, such as compliance with legal and regulatory rulings, financial reporting, liaising with clients, provision of performance reports, risk controls and accounting procedures. Some of the larger established hedge funds use specialist in-house administrators, whilst smaller funds may avoid this additional expense by outsourcing their administrative duties. Due to the increased requirement for tighter regulation and improved transparency in the industry, many investors will only invest with managers who can prove that they have a strong relationship with a reputable third-party administrator and that the proper processes and procedures are in place. The top five global administrators in 2010 were CITCO, HSBC, Citigroup, GlobeOp and Custom House.

Hedge funds with offshore operations often use external administrators in offshore locations to provide expert tax, legal and regulatory advice for those jurisdictions. Indeed, it is a requirement in some offshore locations (e.g. the Cayman Islands) that hedge fund accounts must be regularly audited. In these cases, administrators with knowledge of the appropriate requirements in those jurisdictions would fulfil this requirement.

1.2.2 Prime Brokers

The prime broker is an external party who provides extensive services and resources to a hedge fund, including brokerage services, securities lending, debt financing, clearing and settlement, and risk management. Some prime brokers will even offer incubator services, office space and *seed* investment for start-up hedge funds. The fees earned by prime brokers can be quite considerable and include trade commissions, loan interest and various administration charges. Due to the nature of the relationship between the prime broker and hedge fund, in particular being the counterparty to trades and positions, only the largest financial institutions are able to act in this capacity. The top five global prime brokers in 2010 were Goldman Sachs, JP Morgan, Morgan Stanley, Deutsche Bank and UBS.

For this reason the prime brokerage market is relatively small and each prime broker tends to service a large number of hedge funds and therefore takes on an extremely high degree of risk. Some major restructuring occurred amongst prime brokers in 2008 and 2009, for example the acquisitions of Bear Stearns by JP Morgan, Merrill Lynch by Bank of America, and Lehman Brothers by Barclays Capital. This resulted in a shift in market share from some former investment banks to commercial banks and saw the prime brokerage industry begin to consolidate. In order to alleviate investor concerns since the collapse of several major financial institutions, many fund managers are cautious in employing a single prime broker and prefer to subscribe to multiple prime brokers.

1.2.3   Custodian, Auditors and Legal

Hedge fund assets are usually held with a custodian, including the cash in the fund as well as the actual securities.[8] The custodian is normally a bank that will offer services, such as safekeeping of hedge fund assets, arranging settlement of any sales or purchases of securities and managing cash transactions.

The general structure of a hedge fund precludes them from the requirement to have their financial statements audited by a third party. However, in order to satisfy investors, many hedge funds have their accounts and financial reviews audited annually by an external audit firm. It is important that the auditing firm is seen to be independent of the hedge fund to give credence to their reports and services.

The legal structure of a hedge fund is designed to provide investors with limited liability, so that if a fund suffers a severe loss the maximum amount an investor can lose is only the level of capital invested in the fund. That is, an investor cannot be made liable for losses over this amount or any other outstanding debt or financial obligation of the hedge fund. In addition, the legal structure is also chosen to optimise the tax status and legal liability of the hedge fund itself. To facilitate this, there are a small number of standard hedge fund structures, such as the master–feeder structure, which is adopted by a large number of funds. These comply with the legal requirements of the various jurisdictions

---

[8] This is true except when the assets are used as *collateral* for gaining leverage. In these cases, the assets used as collateral are held by the prime broker. As most hedge funds use some degree of leverage, it is common for assets to be held by both custodians and prime brokers.

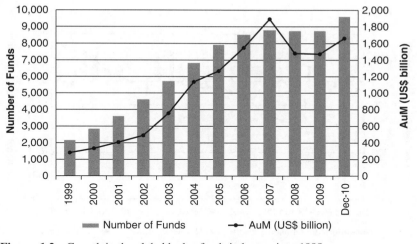

Figure 1.2   Growth in the global hedge funds industry since 1998
Source: *Eurekahedge*

where the hedge funds operate and obtain the optimal tax treatment. The master–feeder structure is a two-tier structure where investors invest through a feeder vehicle which itself invests in the hedge fund. There can be a number of feeder vehicles, located and domiciled in a number of different jurisdictions. Each can have a different legal form and framework. Depending on their tax status, investors can decide which feeder vehicle they wish to invest in. As a general rule the tax regime of an investor will depend on the location of the investor, i.e. *on-* or *offshore*.[9]

1.3   THE GLOBAL HEDGE FUND INDUSTRY

After exceptional growth since 1998, total assets managed by the hedge fund industry peaked at $1.97 trillion in 2007. After the credit crunch and financial crisis of 2008, with well-publicised frauds and scandals as well as the collapse of several major financial institutions, the hedge fund industry suffered severe losses and investor loyalty. Not until early 2009 did the industry start to experience a marked resurgence in activity, realising strong capital inflows and growing investor confidence, as shown in Figure 1.2.

---

[9] *Onshore* (or *domestic*) locations include the US and UK, and to a lesser degree Switzerland and some other European countries. *Offshore* locations include the Cayman Islands, Bahamas, Bermuda, Luxembourg and Ireland.

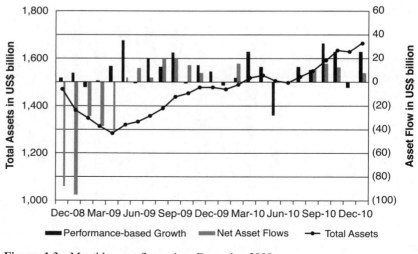

Figure 1.3 Monthly asset flows since December 2008

Source: *Eurekahedge*

It is estimated that the total amount of AuM in the industry at the end of 2010 stood at over $1.60 trillion, with a strong stream of asset flows into hedge funds over the past several years (see Figure 1.3). It is widely assumed that the industry will cross the all-time high set in 2007 and exceed $2 trillion by the end of 2011.

Over the last decade, the global hedge fund industry has consistently outperformed the underlying equity markets, as can clearly be seen in Figure 1.4.

North American funds still remain the most important global hedge fund market, making up around two-thirds of the global industry, followed, quite a long way behind, by Europe and then Asian sectors (see Figure 1.5).

1.3.1 North America

Despite periods of high volatility and market swings, North American hedge funds have consistently posted record returns since reaching their lowest point in early 2009. The total size of the industry at the end of 2010 was estimated at $1.08 trillion, managed by over 4,500 funds (see Figure 1.6). This is a clear indication of the confidence investors began to show in North American funds after the fallout from the global financial crisis

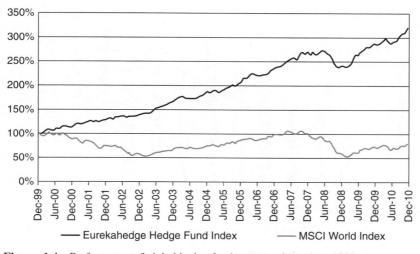

Figure 1.4   Performance of global hedge funds over equities since 1999
Source: *Eurekahedge*

of 2008, when billions of dollars were redeemed and funds suffered massive performance-based losses. Since then, hedge fund managers have provided significant protection against market downturns as well as addressing investors concerns over counterparty risk by engaging multiple prime brokers instead of the usual singular relationship. Moreover, managers have increased redemption frequencies, allowing investors better access to their capital, allowed for more transparency across investment

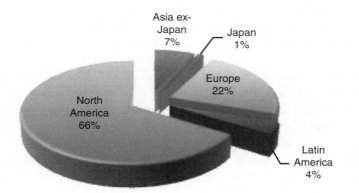

Figure 1.5   Geographical location of hedge fund
Source: *Eurekahedge*

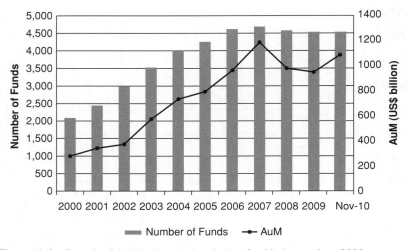

Figure 1.6   Growth of the North American hedge fund industry since 2000
Source: *Eurekahedge*

strategies and implemented more stringent risk management controls. Such changes, together with a much improved outlook on the US economy and the introduction of *quantitative easing*,[10] have led to increased investor confidence and substantial asset flows into North American hedge funds, a situation which looks set to continue well into 2011.

1.3.2   Europe

The rapid growth of the European hedge fund industry over the first seven years of the last decade was eventually slowed by the onset of the financial downturn in 2008. As with North American hedge funds, the European sector experienced huge losses and increased pressure for redemptions from investors which continued until early 2009 when the global economy began to see a potential recovery (see Figure 1.7).

The European sector has shown some interesting trends with regard to fund launches since the market began to rebound in 2009. Although

---

[10] *Quantitative easing* is a monetary policy that has been employed by the US, the UK and the eurozone since the financial crisis of 2008. When a country's interest rate is either at or close to zero, normal expansionary monetary policy fails so the central bank creates new money which it uses to buy government bonds and increase the money supply and excess reserves of the banking system. A further lowering of interest rates follows and it is anticipated that this will lead to a stimulus in the economy.

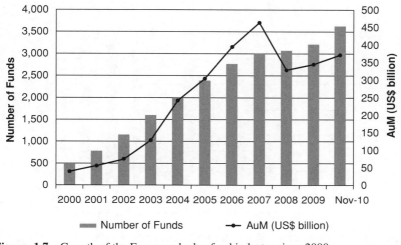

Figure 1.7   Growth of the European hedge fund industry since 2000
Source: *Eurekahedge*

attrition rates have been relatively high, launches have gained strength on the back of the new UCITS III regulation.[11] The popularity of UCITS III has seen the launch of many new start-ups seeking investment capital in the increasingly competitive hedge fund arena. Many new hedge fund launches have suffered from the investment bias towards allocating to much better-known and larger hedge fund names. However, it is anticipated that this trend is likely to change as a result of the increased diversification offered by European hedge funds and a new regulatory environment over the coming years.

1.3.3   Asia

Like the European hedge fund sector, Asian funds have seen tremendous growth over the last decade up until the slowdown during the financial crisis starting in 2008. After the second half of 2009, the Asian sector has shown a steady improvement, with over 1,200 active funds; however, the sector has not seen a repeat of the growth experienced before 2008. This is mainly due to speculation that the Asian markets may suffer

---

[11] UCITS III is the *Undertakings for Collective Investment in Transferable Securities*, an EU investment regulation for the creation and distribution of pooled investment funds, such as mutual funds and hedge funds (see Section 1.5.1).

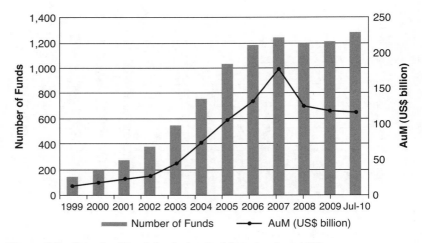

Figure 1.8   Growth of the Asian hedge fund industry since 1999

Source: *Eurekahedge*

from a possible double-dip recession as a result of the debt contagion passing from Europe (see Figure 1.8).

In the Asian sector, hedge fund managers have struggled to generate asset flows and this, together with the highly volatile markets, has led investors to be extremely cautious about investing in the current climate. However, the desire for Asian governments to attract global hedge fund managers to the region, reductions in hedge fund set-up costs compared to other Western locations, the availability of a growing range of financial products and the easing of access and market restrictions in regions such as China and India should see an increased growth in the sector through 2011 and beyond.

1.4   SPECIALIST INVESTMENT TECHNIQUES

1.4.1   Short Selling

A *short sale* is the sale of a security that a seller does not own or that is completed by delivery of a borrowed security. The short seller borrows the securities from a prime broker in return for a daily fee, and promises to replace the borrowed securities at some point in the future. The transaction requires the prime broker to borrow the shares from a securities lender and make delivery on behalf of the short seller. Prime brokers can borrow securities from custodians who hold large institutional investments, e.g. mutual and pension funds, or from their own proprietary trading accounts. The cash from the transaction is held in an *escrow account*[12] until the short seller is in a position to replace the borrowed shares (or until they are called back by the lender). Since the short seller borrows the securities from the prime broker and has a future commitment to replace them, collateral must be posted in the form of cash, securities or other financial assets. The collateral, in addition to the fee for borrowing the securities, provides the prime broker with additional income in the form of interest until the shares are returned.[13] In addition, the short seller must cover any dividends paid on the shares during the period of the loan, and in the event of any stock splits, e.g. a two-for-one split, the short seller must pay back twice as many shares.

The eventual buyer of the shares from the short seller is usually unaware that it is a short sale, so the seller must make arrangements to cover the delivery obligations. The shares are transferred to the buyer with full legal ownership, including voting rights, which can pose a severe problem for the short seller if the prime broker requires the securities back (or *called away*), for example, if the original securities lender requires them for a company shareholder meeting. Although this rarely happens in practice, short selling does carry a great deal of risk, especially if the shares are held over a long period of time and the stock fails to decline as expected, making it necessary to post further margin and eventually forcing the short seller to close out their position at a significant loss. However, when stock prices fall, short sellers make a profit from the short sale, and usually between 60% to 90% of the interest income charged by the prime broker on the cash deposit (the *short rebate*).

It is often the case that hedge funds do not disclose the names of companies they are selling short for fear of a *short squeeze*. Unexpected news on short selling activity can cause share prices to suddenly rise due to potential price manipulation through long investors buying additional shares or forcing securities lenders to recall loaned shares. In this case, short sellers' demand for stocks to cover their short positions can cause a mismatch in the availability of shares and thus drive prices up further. To avoid short squeezes, hedge funds employing short selling only normally invest in large cap companies which have a greater amount of liquidity and volume of shares available from prime brokers. In the

---

[12] An *escrow account* is an account set up by a broker for the purpose of holding funds on behalf of the client until completion of a transaction.

[13] Borrowing money to purchase securities is generally known as *buying on margin*. It is usually necessary for a hedge fund to open a margin account with a prime broker and maintain the margin with available cash reserves when market prices move adversely against them in order to meet a *margin call*.

US, hedge funds are only allowed to engage in short sales with those securities whose recent price change was an upward movement.[14] Such restrictions are used to prevent hedge funds investing in stocks that are already declining so as to avoid the possibility of sending the market into free fall. Nevertheless, short sellers are often thought of as providing efficient price discovery as well as market depth and liquidity. It is important to investors that they are confident that prices represent fair value and that they can get easy access to liquid markets in which they can readily convert shares into cash. Through short selling, hedge funds provide this level of confidence by forcing down overvalued stocks and generating liquidity within the markets.

1.4.2 Leverage

Leverage is using borrowed cash, or a margin account, to increase purchasing power and exposure to a security (or investment) with the aim of generating higher returns. Financial instruments, such as options, swaps and futures (i.e. derivatives), are also used to create leverage. A premium is paid to purchase a derivative in the underlying asset which gives various rights and obligations in the future. This premium is far less than the outright price of the underlying asset and thus allows investors to buy an economic exposure to considerably more of the asset than would otherwise be possible.

Although generally misunderstood, leverage is an extremely widespread investment technique, especially in the hedge fund industry. A great deal of confusion often arises from the various definitions and measurements of leverage. In terms of hedge fund leverage, the debt-to-equity ratio or percentage is often the preferred indicator. For example, if a hedge fund has $50 million equity capital and borrows an additional $100 million, the fund has a total of $150 million in assets, with a debt-to-equity ratio of 2 and a leverage of 67% (=$100 m/$150 m). Leverage ratios are typically higher than traditional investments and generally more difficult to measure due to the sophisticated use of various financial instruments, such as derivatives and investment strategies. Since adding leverage to an investment inherently increases risk, investors often equate a highly leveraged hedge fund with a high

---

[14] The *up-tick* rule was introduced in the US by the Securities and Exchange Commission (SEC) in 1938 to restrict the short selling of stocks unless there was an upward movement in the price. The restriction was lifted in 2007, but there has since been a growing debate on reinstating the ruling to prevent the potential for market manipulation through short selling (see Section 1.5.3).

risk investment. However, this is not normally the case since hedge funds often use leverage to offset various positions in order to reduce the risk on their portfolios.[15] For this reason, it is not advisable for investors to solely rely on leverage ratios as proxies for hedge fund risk. It makes more sense to correctly analyse the nature of the strategy in more detail before making a decision on the riskiness of the hedge fund.

1.4.3 Liquidity

Although hedge funds can generate abnormal returns by exploiting the value from investing in *illiquid*[16] assets, there is always a need to access market liquidity. Liquidity is the degree to which an asset can be bought or sold without adversely affecting the market price or value of the asset.[17] Liquidity plays a critical role in the financial markets, providing investors with an efficient mechanism to rapidly convert assets into cash. During the recent financial turmoil, hedge funds experienced an unprecedented volume of requests from investors to withdraw their capital, creating a serious liquidity problem.

As already mentioned, the recent credit crisis was a result of the bursting of the growing bubble in the US real estate market which led to an unprecedented level of mortgage defaults linked to subprime debt. In reaction, many financial institutions began tightening credit facilities, selling off bad debts at huge losses and pursuing fast foreclosures on failing mortgages. The resultant liquidity crisis that followed made credit much harder to source and, when available, extremely expensive. Eventually financial markets around the globe went into free fall as the worsening liquidity position escalated. Hedge funds with assets linked to the debt disaster suffered massive losses which were further exacerbated when investors tried to withdraw capital from their funds. As credit markets froze, hedge fund managers found it increasingly difficult to source available capital to meet investors' redemption requirements.

Hedge funds that had assets linked to the subprime debt disaster and other related securities suffered huge losses. Problems were amplified further when investors tried to withdraw capital from their funds, to which it subsequently became apparent that there was a liquidity

---

[15] The amount of leverage that hedge funds can take on is usually limited by margin supplied by the prime broker and by certain restrictions set by regulators or other organisations. In circumstances where the amount of leverage rises above a certain limit, the lender can take possession of the hedge fund investments, sell them and use the proceeds to offset any losses on the debt financing.

[16] *Illiquid* assets include low volume traded stocks, real estate and other capital holdings.

[17] A highly liquid market can also be considered a *deep* market.

mismatch between assets and liabilities. When the credit markets froze, hedge fund managers were unable to source sufficient capital to meet investor redemption requirements. This forced managers to restructure their liquidity terms and impose further *gated provisions*,[18] increase the use of *side-pocketing*[19] and enforce *lock-ups*.[20] This had a negative effect on investor relations which was exacerbated by the selective and insufficient disclosure of performance being made by hedge fund managers. For example, many managers were seen to be reporting side-pocket performance only to investors while relaying much better liquid performance in publications with only a passing note of disclosure about the exclusion of side-pockets. In the case of lock-ups, there exists a clear conflict of interest between locking up investors' capital and continuing to charge management fees. Investors have since argued that it would be more acceptable for gated provisions and the issue of involuntary side-pockets to be tied to deferrals or a reduction in management fees until the hedge fund returns to an appropriate liquid position. The aftermath of the financial crisis has clearly highlighted many of the shortcomings of the hedge fund industry and heightened the debate over the need for increased regulation and monitoring. Nevertheless, it has since been widely accepted that hedge funds played only a small part in the global financial collapse and suffered at the hands of a highly regulated banking system. Indeed, many prominent institutional and economic bodies argue that their very presence provides greater market liquidity and improved price efficiency whilst aiding in the global integration of the financial markets.

1.5 NEW DEVELOPMENTS FOR HEDGE FUNDS

1.5.1 UCITS III Hedge Funds

One of the major developments in the hedge fund industry over the past several years has been the exceptional growth in UCITS III hedge funds in comparison to the global industry. As of September 2010, the UCITS

---

[18] *Gated provisions* are a restriction on the amount of capital that can be withdrawn from a fund during a redemption period. Such provisions are subject to management discretion and normally referred to in the hedge fund prospectus.

[19] A *side-pocket* (or *designated investment*) is an account used by hedge funds to separate illiquid assets from more liquid ones. Holding illiquid assets in a hedge fund can cause a great deal of complexity when investors try to withdraw their capital.

[20] A *lock-up* is a period of time designated by the hedge fund manager in which an investor may not withdraw any investment in a fund.

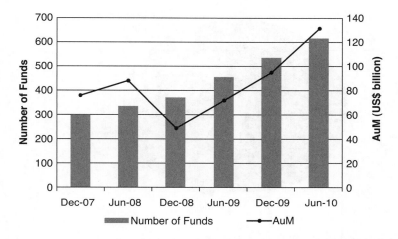

Figure 1.9   Growth in number of UCITS III hedge funds since December 2007
Source: *Eurekahedge*

hedge fund industry stood at an estimated $131 billion managed by over 600 individual funds (see Figure 1.9). UCITS is a set of directives developed by the EU member states to allow cross-border investments. The aim of the directive is to improve the financial opportunities offered to UCITS-compliant hedge fund managers whilst addressing the needs of investors in terms of effective risk management procedures, and increased transparency and liquidity, especially in light of the recent financial crisis.

The original version of the directive was introduced in 1985 with the goal of establishing a common legal framework for open-ended funds investing in transferable securities set up in any EU member state i.e. developing a pan-European market in collective investment schemes. Unfortunately, the framework suffered from many obstacles, such as the extent of different marketing rules and taxation allowed across member states. Not until December 2001 was a directive formally adopted under the UCITS III banner which has since undergone several further amendments with a view to including the use of additional asset classes (e.g. hedge fund indices) and a more diverse range of derivative products (see Figure 1.10). Such inclusions have allowed UCITS III funds to pursue a number of different investment possibilities, such as absolute return strategies, in ways that were simply not possible under previous UCITS frameworks.

The increased number of eligible asset classes and available use of derivatives has led to a greater number of multi-strategy funds being

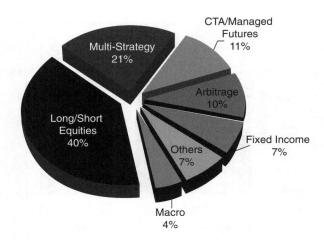

Figure 1.10   UCITS III hedge funds by investment strategy
Source: *Eurekahedge*

launched in the UCITS III sector in comparison to that of the European multi-strategy industry. Despite this, however, almost half of UCITS III funds over the last two years have adopted the long/short equity strategy for several reasons:

1. Long/short equity is by far the largest global hedge fund strategy and therefore those existing managers launching new UCITS III vehicles would naturally prefer this strategy.
2. Operating the long/short equity strategy under the UCITS III framework is relatively straightforward.
3. The simplicity of the long/short equity strategy lends itself well to marketing and liaising with retail investors who may not have the knowledge and understanding of the markets like a typical hedge fund client.

Despite the strong link in the use of the long/short equity strategy, the regulatory constraints within the UCITS III framework mean that there are very few similarities elsewhere across industry sectors. For example, there are very few event-driven UCITS III hedge funds and practically no distressed debt based funds primarily due to the liquidity restrictions placed on UCITS III compliance. Nevertheless, a major advantage of UCITS III funds is the ability of managers to utilise their experience in a proven investment strategy whilst offering potential investors the added incentive of investing in a regulated market. The key features of UCITS III hedge fund regulation and fund structure are as follows:

1. Only investment in liquid securities is permitted, i.e. those that can be sold within 14 days without substantial loss of value.
2. Funds cannot have exposure to more than 10% in one stock.
3. Managers can utilise leverage up to 100% of the *net asset value*[21] of the fund.
4. Managers can employ shorting techniques through the use of derivatives.
5. The ease of marketing such funds across the EU and registering them in member states.
6. The implementation of effective risk management procedures and processes.
7. Funds must be domiciled in an EU member state as opposed to offshore locations.

The development of UCITS III funds has also opened up the sector to new sources of capital, e.g. from retail investors wishing to make use of the alternative investment market but with the assurance of stricter regulatory controls. In addition, improved redemption rules and transparency have helped in building investor confidence, especially after the much debated issue surrounding the use of gated provisions that stopped investors withdrawing large amounts of capital from their funds during the period of huge losses following the financial crisis in 2008. Indeed, the much anticipated release of UCITS IV and the development of other European directives, such as the new EU passport (see below), which will give hedge funds marketing rights throughout the EU, will broaden the investment appeal of UCITS-compliant funds even further.

1.5.2 The European Passport

In November 2010 the European Union passed a new set of laws governing the use and regulation of the alternative investment industry, named the Alternative Investment Directive (AID). The AID aims to provide hedge funds (and private equity funds) with a so-called *passport* to allow funds that meet EU standards access to all EU markets. The passport gives hedge funds the opportunity to market to investors throughout the

---

[21] *Net asset value* is used to put a value on a hedge fund and is the total of all the hedge fund assets minus all the hedge fund liabilities.

EU with only a single authorisation. In addition, the AID will subject hedge funds to increased supervision, regulation and transparency, providing pan-European investors with the confidence to invest and operate in a stable European financial market.

The newly formed Paris-based European Securities and Markets Authority (ESMA) will act as the EU financial supervisory authority and issue passports, especially to non-EU funds that wish to operate in the EU markets under a single authorisation. The ESMA will also demand that non-EU funds are granted outside the EU the same rights that their funds will enjoy in the European markets. However, the controversial passport scheme will not come into effect for EU funds until 2013, and even later for non-EU funds, so the established framework that allows each EU country to decide which funds they will allow access to their market will remain in place until then.

1.5.3 Restrictions on Short Selling

Short selling can result in unlimited losses if the hedge fund incorrectly anticipates the direction of movement of share prices. Moreover, short selling can also be used to manipulate market prices. It has been argued for some time that hedge funds can engage in collective short selling to create an imbalance in supply and force down the price of a security. During the recent financial turmoil and substantial falls in stock prices, hedge funds were often accused of short selling to exacerbate and profit from the declining markets. During 2008 and 2009, regulators announced several actions to protect against abusive short selling and to make short sale information more readily available to the public.

One of the main methods of market abuse was the use of *naked* short sales, i.e. the activity of selling short without having borrowed or arranged to borrow the securities to make delivery to the buyer. Such a *failure to deliver* is a gross violation of ethical market practice and something the regulators were determined to address. New temporary rulings forced prime brokers to first ascertain, before undertaking a short sale transaction, if the securities were available for short selling or could be borrowed against delivery. Market participants were also required to provide detailed information on short sale activity and their overall short positions. Although the rulings curbed short sale abuses during the financial crisis of 2008, many hedge fund managers have since argued that such regulation hinders the efficient workings of the financial markets and causes a negative effect on liquidity. Restrictions and other regulation on short sales are a contentious area of debate amongst market professionals and regulators and under continual review. Nevertheless, regulators are keen to address issues associated with short selling and the provision of detailed information on short sale activity for public disclosure and may certainly impose further restrictions on the practice in the near future.

In this chapter we have provided an introduction to the concept of hedge funds, how they are structured and the key players within such an investment vehicle. Each of the major markets within the global hedge fund industry has been reviewed with focus on the current financial crisis and how hedge funds have performed over this period. In fact, it has been publicly stated that hedge funds have played only a minimal part in the global financial collapse and have instead suffered at the hands of a highly regulated financial system. Nevertheless, some of the specialist investment techniques employed by hedge fund managers have since come under increased scrutiny and regulatory pressures.

2

Major Hedge Fund Strategies

Hedge funds can be classified in a number of different ways, e.g. by particular asset, geographical location of strategy or industrial sector. The most common hedge fund classification is by strategy and then by style within that strategy. There are three major hedge fund strategies, namely relative value, event-driven and tactical, each with its own individual strategy styles.

This chapter introduces the most common investment strategies within each of the major hedge fund strategy styles. Emphasis is placed on equity related strategies since these will be the focus of more detailed quantitative modelling and analysis in later chapters.

2.1 SINGLE- AND MULTI-STRATEGY HEDGE FUNDS

Hedge funds are a private investment vehicle with a collective pool of money designed to exploit superior manager skills in order to make above average returns for investors. Single-strategy funds rely heavily on the expertise and knowledge of the hedge fund manager(s) to provide such returns using a specific investment strategy (see Figure 2.1). Considerable and effective due diligence is required when attempting to select top (or *star*) managers in single strategy funds. Such research can be very time-consuming and costly along with the additional problems associated with gaining access to a professional network of top managers.

Although fund managers are usually willing to discuss the general structure of a particular chosen strategy, they are unlikely to divulge sensitive or potentially profitable information. Those involved in single-strategy hedge fund investing will usually have a high degree of experience in qualitative and quantitative analysis. There are obvious drawbacks to single-strategy hedge fund investing and the investor needs to accept a suitable trade-off between ongoing exhaustive research and the return expected on their investment. There is also the problem of investing in a fund that offers no diversification, making the investor extremely vulnerable to the success of a single strategy.

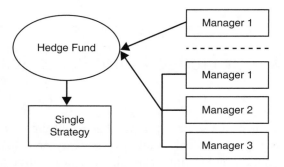

Figure 2.1   A schematic of the single-strategy, single- and multi-manager hedge fund

Multi-strategy hedge funds can provide an attractive alternative to single-strategy funds. Their objective is to provide positive returns regardless of the directional movement in a variety of asset classes and sectors, such as equity, fixed income and currency markets. The general multi-strategy fund is based on a selection of hedge fund strategies in a single portfolio operated by a team of managers in a single hedge fund (see Figure 2.2). Such a strategy can prove lucrative to investors who have strong knowledge of, or confidence in, a particular hedge fund management team as well as the added benefits of diversification of investing across a range of asset classes and sectors. This can, however, also be the most convincing argument against multi-strategy hedge funds since the majority of failures are related to operational inefficiencies within the hedge fund. Multi-strategy hedge funds are also faced with the problem of retaining and employing highly skilled managers that have expertise

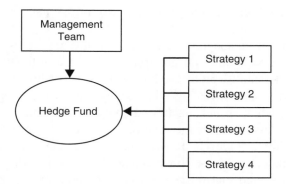

Figure 2.2   A schematic of the multi-strategy hedge fund

across a range of different investment strategies and sectors. It is often thought that the best managers concentrate on a single or limited group of hedge fund strategies and these can be difficult to source and locate without the necessary experience and network of contacts.

2.2 FUND OF HEDGE FUNDS

A common investment vehicle for an inexperienced investor or one who has had limited exposure to the alternative investment market is the fund of hedge funds (FoHFs) strategy. Of course, this strategy is not necessarily only for inexperienced investors. If an investor does not have the time or resources to design an efficient hedge fund, select qualified managers for each strategy, determine optimal weightings of investable assets, negotiate the legal documents and then monitor monthly performance, a FoHFs strategy may be a more realistic approach to investing. Such investments are also ideal for individual investors who may not be able to attract the interest of leading hedge fund managers.

Funds of hedge funds allocate their capital by investing in hedge funds with different strategies, or investing in multiple hedge funds with the same strategy (see Figure 2.3). A FoHFs manager will usually construct a portfolio of hedge funds (on average 10–20 hedge funds) in order to achieve a certain risk–return profile and level of diversification that is suitable to a range of investors. The manager is responsible for all the due diligence and qualitative and quantitative analysis of potential hedge funds and the termination of poorly performing ones, as well as deciding the management fee structure. Since there are fees associated with each individual hedge fund making up the FoHFs and an additional fee for

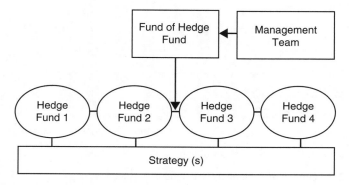

Figure 2.3 A schematic of the FoHFs structure

the FoHFs manager, such investments are normally more expensive than standard hedge fund investing.

Despite the additional layer of fees, there are clear advantages to investing in FoHFs when considering the extent of the skills and expertise offered by the fund manager as well as the expected higher risk-adjusted returns. It is often the case that gaining access to the hedge fund arena can be very expensive with prohibitively high initial minimum investments, whereas FoHFs investors can get involved in the market with much lower minimums whilst accessing the same potential underlying hedge funds. Another advantage of FoHFs is that the manager will also have access to a professional network of individual hedge funds and information usually not available to normal investors along with detailed market knowledge. They will also be highly trained in sourcing talented and often undiscovered star managers whom the general investment community would be much less likely to reach.

This well-diversified portfolio of hedge fund investments can protect an investor from suffering large losses due to the poor performance or failure of a single strategy. However, over the past several years, AuMs in global FoHFs have experienced a dramatic downturn since peaking in early 2008. During the financial crisis, FoHFs suffered massive losses and record redemptions (see Figure 2.4).

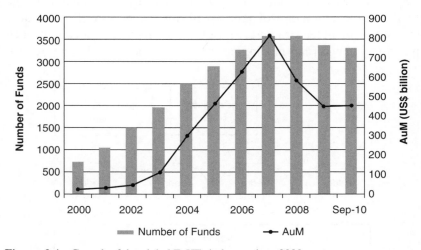

Figure 2.4   Growth of the global FoHFs industry since 2000
Source: *Eurekahedge*

The poor asset flows into the FoHFs industry over the past several years are mainly a result of investors preferring to allocate capital to a single hedge fund rather than multiple managers. As a result of single hedge funds outperforming FoHFs in 2008 and 2009, and the use of gated provisions during the financial crisis, investors have had a change of sentiment towards investing in multi-manager structures. Investors are also unwilling to pay an additional layer of fees to FoHFs managers without the level of returns expected from similar investments. Managers have since begun to address these issues by offering investors lower fee structures, more frequent redemptions and increased transparency. Despite these changes, FoHFs managers need to show improved performance and consistently higher returns in order to entice investors back to investing in the FoHFs industry.

2.3 HEDGE FUND STRATEGIES

Hedge funds can be classified in a number of different ways, for example by particular asset, geographical location of strategy or industrial sector. The most common hedge fund classification is by strategy and then by style within that strategy. As can be seen in Table 2.1 there are three major hedge fund strategies, namely relative value, event-driven and tactical, each with its own individual strategy styles. However, it is important to note that there is no definitive hedge fund strategy classification and the boundaries between them are very blurred.

In addition to classifying hedge funds by strategy and individual strategy styles, they can also be categorised in terms of their risk–return characteristics and the volatility of each strategy. Figure 2.5 is a schematic diagram of the relationship between each major hedge fund strategy and the associated risk, return and volatility. Tactical strategies offer the

Table 2.1   The major hedge fund strategies and their individual strategy styles

Relative value	Event-driven	Tactical
Equity market neutral	Distressed securities	Global macro
Convertible arbitrage	Risk arbitrage	Long/short equity
Fixed income arbitrage		Managed futures
Capital structure arbitrage		
Swap-spread arbitrage		
Yield curve arbitrage		

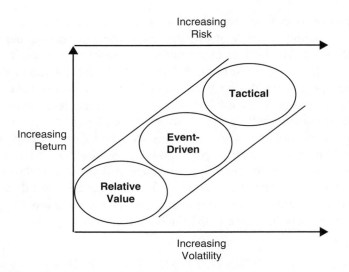

Figure 2.5   The major hedge fund strategies in relation to increasing return, volatility and risk

highest return but for the greatest risk and are generally highly volatile strategies requiring exceptional skills, ability and experience from the fund manager. On the other hand, relative value strategies offer a much lower return but with the added incentive of lower risk and volatility.

2.3.1   Tactical Strategies

2.3.1.1   Global Macro

The global macro strategy attempts to make superior returns based on leveraged trades on price movements in the equity, currency, interest rate and commodity markets. Fund managers make use of macroeconomic[1] analysis to identify price inefficiencies across a range of asset classes, markets and geographical locations (both *developed*[2] and *emerging*[3]

---

[1] Macro events are changes that take place across global economies, typically brought on by shifts in government policy and political events which impact on interest rates that, in turn, affect all financial instruments, including currency, stock, and bond markets.

[2] *Developed* markets are those countries thought to be the most advanced, offering higher levels of liquidity and a lower investment risk, among them the US, Australia, Hong Kong, UK, Germany and France.

[3] *Emerging* markets are those that are in the process of rapid growth and industrialisation, such as Brazil, China, Chile, South Africa, and Russia. A subset of the emerging markets is the *frontier*

markets). In researching investment opportunities, macro managers will analyse geopolitical issues, economic indicators (e.g. GDP, balance of trade, public deficit), capital markets and the flow of liquidity, i.e. undertake a *top-down*[4] approach to investing. Global macro managers have the widest and most flexible mandate of all the hedge fund strategies, allowing them to take positions in any instrument (including derivatives) across any market whilst also making use of leverage to further increase potential returns. Macro investing can be broken down into two main trading styles: the directional trade where the manager focuses on discrete price movements in the markets, e.g. short S&P 500 index or long French bonds; and the relative value trade where the manager will pair two similar securities together to exploit a price mismatch, e.g. long the 10-year Japanese bond and short the 30-year Japanese bond. In addition to the two main trading styles, global macro managers will also be classified as to whether they are *discretionary* or *systematic* traders. Discretionary trading involves using the manager's subjective beliefs on market conditions to arrive at a suitable investment, while systematic trading utilises a quantitative or rule-based approach to investing. When the sentiments of investors on market dynamics differ widely from the actual economic fundamentals, a noticeable price trend (or *spread*) can develop in the market. Such a situation is tailor-made for the global macro manager who will aim to identify when and where the market has moved furthest from the equilibrium point and make their play before markets correct themselves. Clearly, market timing is paramount to a successful global macro hedge fund strategy.

As already mentioned, global macro managers are not limited to a specific market or instrument which constrains other hedge fund strategies. This allows managers to efficiently allocate resources across global opportunities and take advantage of multiple potential profitable investments in highly liquid markets. Although global macro traders have been criticised in the past for doing nothing but place huge speculative bets causing considerable swings in profits and losses, the global macro hedge fund strategy has consistently produced above average returns. Macro managers also employ a large amount of leverage and use

---

market, i.e. a country expected to increase in liquidity and investable opportunity over time, such as Argentina, Bulgaria, Nigeria, Pakistan and the United Arab Emirates.

[4] The opposite to *top-down* investing is the *bottom-up* approach in which an investment is sought based on fundamentals of an individual investment rather than industrial or macroeconomic analysis. A *stereoscopic* approach combines the top-down and bottom-up investment styles.

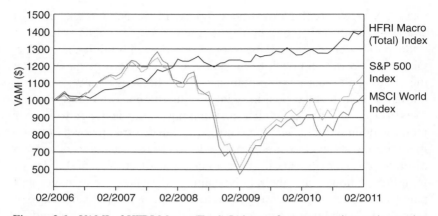

Figure 2.6   VAMI of HFRI Macro (Total) Index performance against major market indices over the past five years

Source: *Hedge Fund Research*

derivatives to further enhance returns. It is the use of such leverage on these so-called *directional bets*, which are often not hedged, that has the greatest impact on the performance of macro funds whilst also adding to the high volatility that they attract. Figure 2.6 shows the *value-added monthly index* (VAMI)[5] for the HFRI Macro (Total) Index performance against several major marker indices over the past five years.

In the 1990s the global macro hedge fund strategy was by far the most popular of all the strategies and accounted for almost 70% of hedge funds by AuM. One of the most famous of all global macro hedge funds was that developed by George Soros: the Quantum Fund. This fund hit the headlines and gained instant infamy by betting that the UK would exit the European Exchange Rate Mechanism (ERM) in 1992, forcing sterling to be devalued. Soros sold short around $10 billion in sterling (making use of extensive leverage) and on Black Wednesday (16 September, 1992), when sterling was eventually devalued, made a profit estimated in excess of $1 billion. Nevertheless, during the recent financial crisis, global macro funds weathered the storm but their popularity has waned. Nowadays, the global macro strategy accounts for a much smaller percentage of all hedge funds assets.

---

[5] The VAMI is an index that tracks the monthly performance of a $1,000 investment: VAMI = Previous VAMI × (1 + Current Rate of Return).

2.3.1.2 Managed Futures

The thirty-year-old managed futures – or commodity trading advisors (CTAs)[6] – industry comprises professional money managers that specialise in investing in commodity futures (see Box 2.1) and their derivatives through discretionary trades on a client's behalf. The managed futures strategy is similar to the global macro strategy in that they are both directional strategies. Managed futures funds generally employ sophisticated trading rules and implement them on computerised trading platforms that can span over 100 different futures markets across a variety of time zones. Managed futures take long or short positions in futures contracts across a range of asset classes, such as equity indices

---

Box 2.1 Commodity futures

In the nineteenth century, with the establishment of a central market for grain, farmers could sell their products either for immediate (i.e. cash or spot) or forward delivery. These *forward* contracts between buyers and sellers became the forerunners of today's exchange traded *futures* contracts. Both forward and futures contracts are legal agreements to buy or sell an asset on a specific date. Forward contracts are negotiated directly between buyer and seller and settlement terms may vary from contract to contract. Futures contracts are facilitated through a futures exchange and are standardised according to quality, quantity, delivery date and location. The only remaining variable is the price which is discovered through an auction-like process that occurs daily at the exchange. Exchange traded futures cover a huge range of assets, including metals, energy, currencies, equities indices, treasuries and interest rates, the majority of which are now traded electronically. Futures provide a fast, easy and cost-effective way for investors to access financial and commodity markets around

---

[6] *Commodity trading advisors* are a type of professional money manager and trader who deal exclusively with managed futures investments and are usually registered with the National Futures Association (NFA), a self-regulated organisation. CTAs give advice on the buying and selling of commodity futures and options and trade the managed futures for which they earn a fee. A *commodity pool operator* (or CPO) is an individual or organisation that assembles public funds or private pools of capital for investing in managed futures. A CPO usually employs a CTA to make investment decisions on behalf of the CPO. A *futures commission merchant* is a brokerage firm that executes CTA-directed trades and also acts like a CPO and generates reports on investment performance.

the clock. The diagram below shows the profit and loss (P&L) profiles for buying and selling commodity futures.

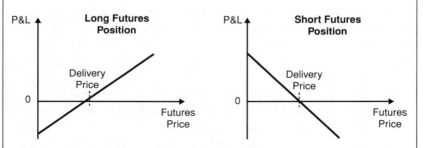

Leverage on futures contracts is created through the use of performance bonds, often referred to as margin, i.e. the amount of money deposited by both the buyer and the seller to ensure the performance of the terms of the contract. The performance bond may represent only a fraction of the total value of the contract (usually between 3% and 12%), making futures a highly leveraged trading vehicle.

Consider a portfolio of E-mini S&P* with a value of $65,500 in which the exchange sets a performance bond of 7.0%. In this case, the investor would only have to post $4,585 (=0.07 × $65,500) in order to hold the portfolio position.

The ability to leverage may seem similar to buying stocks on margin. However, in equity markets buying on margin implies borrowing from a securities lender to purchase stocks. In the futures market the performance bond is not partial payment for the future contract but a *good faith* payment to ensure you are able to meet the day-to-day obligations of the positions held. The amount of capital that needs to be deposited against open futures positions may vary from day to day, depending on the performance of the futures contract. Due to the use of leverage and holding such large futures positions, only a small movement in the futures price can lead to huge gains and losses. Leveraged opportunities provide the trader with more flexibility and capital efficiency, but also require a well-thought-out risk management process that addresses the amount of leverage used.

---

*The E-mini S&P 500 is a stock index future contract traded on the Chicago Mercantile Exchange Global electronic trading platform. One E-mini S&P 500 is 50 times the value of the S&P 500 index value.
Source: *CME Group*

(e.g. S&P futures and NASDAQ 100 futures), currency futures, government bond futures, hard commodities (e.g. gold and silver), grains (e.g. soybeans, corn, wheat) and soft commodities (cotton, cocoa, coffee, sugar). Managed futures have for some time been classified separately from other hedge fund strategies due to their unique structure and characteristics; however, the distinction has become blurred over the years and they are now generally considered an integral part of the hedge fund industry.

Due to the low historical correlation between managed futures and traditional asset classes, CTAs are extremely valuable in lowering portfolio risk. Adding a managed futures fund to a portfolio of stocks and bonds can greatly reduce the portfolio volatility and in many cases enhance performance. Managed futures also offer the increased opportunity of diversification since they can be traded on many regulated financial and commodity exchanges around the globe. By using such a broad investment strategy, a fund manager can simultaneously profit from movements in stock, bonds, currencies and commodity prices in a variety of economic and market environments. Indeed, CTAs can profit in both increasing and decreasing markets, due to the ease with which managed futures can go both long and short in anticipation of market movements across a range of asset classes and exchanges.

Managed futures investment strategies fall into two main categories, namely trend followers and market-neutral traders. Trend-following strategies make use of proprietary trading systems which provide buy, hold and sell signals in anticipation of upward and downward moves in the futures markets.[7] Trend followers often focus on commodities which show a stronger tendency to trend, as opposed to stocks which are more likely to show *mean reversion*.[8] Other trend followers use discretionary systems based on fundamental analysis, e.g. economic and industrial factors, as well as fund manager discretion. In either case the majority use fully automated trading systems that eliminate human emotion and rely only on rule-based trading strategies. Computer-based models[9] will

---

[7] A market that is neither trending upwards or downwards is said to be a *flat* or *sideways* (or *deer*) market.

[8] A *mean-reverting process* is one in which the underlying asset, e.g. a stock price, will tend to move back towards its average (or mean) value over time. Another type of process is one that shows a persistent trend upwards or downwards known as *momentum* and gives rise to momentum trading strategies.

[9] Computer-based trading (or *algorithmic* trading) involves building trading platforms that are automated by mathematical and quantitative models (so called *black-box* models) that take input signals in the form of time series of prices (including volume and open interest) and subsequently

search for a trend in over 100 different futures across the global financial markets and follow a trend (long-, medium- or short-term) until it
appears to fade away. The models will first be *back-tested*[10] using historical data, and then implemented on a test portfolio, and once the fund
manager is satisfied with the results, the strategy will be run in real time.
In order that the strategy makes a steady profit, the model must take into
account the frequency and timing of trades so as to reduce transaction
costs and brokerage fees as well as avoid *slippage*.[11] Pattern recognition
may also be employed in managed futures strategies to try and identify
trends across different time horizons, e.g. to search for a trend in monthly
gold futures, or a six-hour trend in stock index futures (see Box 2.2).
Market-neutral traders use non-discretionary trading strategies aiming
to seek profit by taking spreads between different financial and commodity markets or different futures contracts in the same market. There
is also a subset of market-neutral traders called option premium sellers
who use *delta-neutral* trading strategies.[12]

Box 2.2   Trends and moving averages

Hedge fund managers who employ trend-following strategies do not
aim to forecast or predict price movements but simply jump on a
realised trend and ride it until it fades away. Trend followers will
usually enter the market when they are convinced the trend has properly established itself and will often ignore the initial turning point
into profit. Identifying such trends relies heavily on moving averages (MAs)* to determine the general direction of the market and to

---

filter out the any background noise, detect a market signal, and generate buy, hold and sell signals
automatically. The trading platform will also have an integrated risk management system built in
to ensure that losses are minimised through *stop-loss* orders and other trade-specific parameters.

[10] *Back-testing* involves the analysis of a particular model against a large historical database in
order to test and evaluate the profitability of the trading strategy before risking any capital. Care
must be taken when considering the validity and accuracy of a back-testing model, especially since
the results are based only on historical data, i.e. the past may necessarily not be a good indicator
of the future.

[11] *Slippage* occurs when there is a change in the spread whilst a market order is being placed so
that the executed trade may not go though at the desired (or expected) price.

[12] The *delta* of an option is the rate of change of the value of an option with respect to a unit
change in the price of the underlying asset. For example, if an option has a delta of 0.35 and
the price increases by $1, the option value should increase by 35 cents (known as *35 deltas* in
market jargon). *Delta-neutral* trading strategies involve taking positions with offsetting positive
and negative deltas, i.e. a total delta of zero, so as to neutralise the response of the portfolio to
market movements.

generate trade signals. MAs provide a *lag* to the price time series and help smooth out any *background noise* in order to form a trend-following indicator. The figure below shows the closing price of gold (2007–2010) and the relationship between the 50-day and 200-day MA. Notice how the 50-day MA changes faster than the 200-day MA.

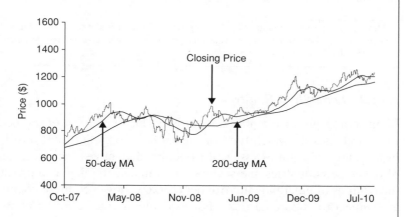

A common use for MAs is to develop a simple trading system based on MA crossovers. For example, a trading system would generate a buy signal when the shorter-term MA crosses above the longer-term MA. A sell signal would be generated when the shorter-term MA crosses below the longer-term MA. The response time and number of signals generated will depend on the length of the individual MAs. The figure below shows a simple trading strategy based on the signals generated using 20-day and 100-day MA crossovers.

Care must be taken when using such trading strategies since volatile markets can cause rapid trend reversals or countertrend, i.e. one day a trading system may signal a buy order due to a bullish crossover and the next day signal an exit due to a sudden market downturn.

---
*Moving averages also form the basic building blocks for other useful trend-following techniques, such as Bollinger bands, moving average convergence/divergence and the relative strength index.

2.3.1.3 Long/Short Equity

Long/short equity (or equity hedge) is by far the largest of the hedge fund strategies, in which fund managers hold long and short positions in a variety of equities (as well as equity derivatives) across a range of developed countries and sectors. Fund managers may also invest in the equities of emerging and frontier markets; however, these countries are subject to additional risks. For example, a change in the political climate in such a country, along with a lack of a stable government and restrictions on foreign trade, can cause share prices to move rapidly and adversely. The sudden lack of liquidity can also be devastating for such long/short equity funds and so the manager must possess a certain level of experience and skill to operate in such market environments. Figure 2.7 shows the VAMI for the HFRI Equity Hedge (Total) Index performance against several major marker indices over the past five years.

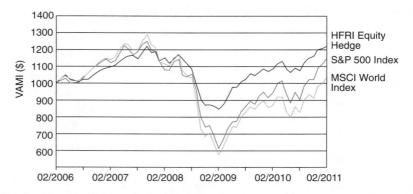

Figure 2.7   VAMI of HFRI Equity Hedge (Total) Index performance against major market indices over the past five years

Source: *Hedge Fund Research*

Table 2.2 An example of a long/short equity portfolio

Equity	Country	Sector	Position	Amount ($ million)	% of Portfolio
1	UK	Retail	Short	45	(26.2)
2	France	Pharmaceuticals	Long	22	12.8
3	USA	Banking	Long	35	20.3
4	France	Engineering	Short	38	(22.1)
5	UK	Pharmaceuticals	Long	32	18.6
			TOTAL	**172**	**3.4**

An example long/short equity portfolio is shown in Table 2.2 in which five different equities across a range of countries and sectors have a total AuM of $172 million. The net long position is 3.4%, i.e. the long/short equity strategy has a 3.4% *long bias* exposure.[13] Some managers prefer to maintain an overall short position in their portfolio by taking advantage of the limited restrictions on short selling and looking for shares that they consider overvalued in the marketplace.[14] In a long/short equity portfolio, the short positions have a double effect: they provide a negative exposure to overvalued shares whilst reducing the exposure of the portfolio to market risk. Usually the manager will focus on the shares of companies with large market capitalisation that provide high liquidity with ease of securities lending. However, there are few strategies that maintain a long-term short bias due to the fact that equity markets are generally assumed upward trending over time. Regardless of the long or short position maintained, long/short equity strategies are clearly directional strategies.

Long/short equity strategies rely heavily on the manager having exceptional skill in *stock selection* as well as the knowledge to accurately determine an equity's true value in relation to the market price. With a long/short equity strategy the fund manager will buy stocks they assume are *undervalued* and sell those they consider *overvalued*. Ideally, the long position will increase in value and the short position decline so that a profit is made regardless of the directional movement of the stock

---

[13] A common example of a *long bias* strategy is the 130/30 strategy in which the manager invests 130% in long positions and 30% in short positions.

[14] Hedge funds that rely solely on short selling to maintain a short bias strategy are generally known as *dedicated short bias* strategies.

market, i.e. the goal of the strategy is to minimise exposure to *market risk*[15] and gain from the spread between different stocks.

2.3.1.4 Pairs Trading

Pairs trading (or statistical arbitrage) is closely related to long/short equity and involves simultaneously buying and selling two similar equities (or exchange traded funds)[16] from the same industry that are expected to have a strong correlation. By entering and exiting long and short positions in the two equities at the correct time it is possible to make a positive return regardless of the direction of the market. However, this relies heavily on market timing, and a risky situation can arise when two equities begin to drift apart from each other, i.e. start to trend, rather than converge. Coping with such adverse market movements requires a strict risk management procedure that forces a trader to exit an unprofitable trade as soon as the original strategy has been invalidated so as to minimise losses. In most cases, a pairs trader will thoroughly analyse the two stocks being considered and aim to buy the overvalued stock and sell the undervalued one whilst exiting the market at the time the two stocks converge to a predetermined level (usually the mean of the closing price ratio).[17] The two stocks will normally be chosen after a detailed analysis of their statistical correlation, market capitalisation, valuation and company reports (price–earnings ratio, dividend yield etc.). Typical examples of strongly correlated equities that would make suitable pairs trades include Coca-Cola and Pepsi, Ford and General Motors, and WalMart and Tiger. Pairs traders will also trade in equal dollar amounts on both the long and short side making such a trade dollar-neutral.

Consider Figure 2.8, which shows the previous year's historical prices for companies A and B which are from the same industrial sector and expected to have a strong correlation with each other. Figure 2.9 shows the closing price ratio (i.e. the closing price for company B divided by

---

[15] *Market* (or *systematic*) risk is the risk that the value of a portfolio will decline due to movements in *market factors*, such as stock prices, interest and currency rates and commodity prices. *Unsystematic* (or *idiosyncratic*) risk is uniquely associated with a particular security and can be practically eliminated through diversification.

[16] An exchange traded fund (or ETF) is a security traded on an exchange that tracks an index, a commodity or a basket of assets like an index fund. Its price changes throughout the day as it is bought and sold in the market.

[17] Pairs trading can also be thought of as a *mean-reverting* strategy.

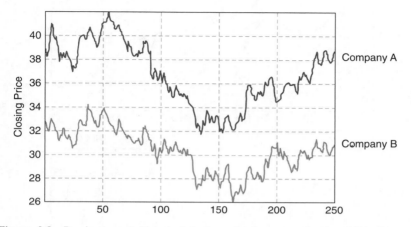

Figure 2.8   Previous year's historical closing price for companies A and B

the closing price for company A) for the same historical data, along
with markers for the mean and 1σ, 2σ and 3σ (i.e. standard deviations).
Clearly showing that the closing price ratio is mean-reverting, and indicating that companies A and B are ideal candidates for a successful
pairs trading strategy. A close inspection of Figure 2.9 also shows that
there were many occasions when the price ratio moved above or below

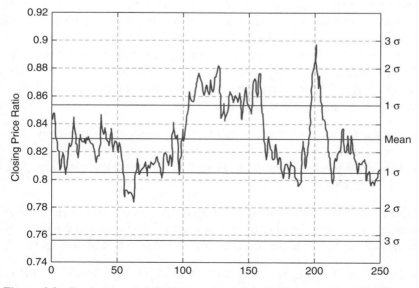

Figure 2.9   Previous year's historical closing price ratio for companies A and B

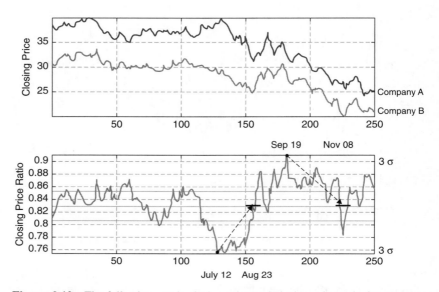

Figure 2.10 The following year's closing price and closing price ratio for company A and B

the 1σ and 2σ marker lines, suggesting the need to place lots of frequent trades if used as an entrance point for a trading strategy. A more suitable trading strategy would be to enter a pairs trade when the price ratio rises above the 3σ marker line, based on last year's historical data; this should reduce the number of trades and hopefully lead to a higher return.

As shown in Figure 2.10, the closing price ratio moved below the 3σ marker line on 12 July when company A was trading at \$38.98 and company B at \$29.46. Assuming an initial capital investment of \$1,000, the following pair trade is executed:

- sell \$500 worth of company A @ \$38.98 assuming company A is overvalued;
- buy \$500 worth of company B @ \$29.46 assuming company B is undervalued.

Figure 2.10 also shows that on 23 August the price ratio returned to the mean value and that company A was trading at \$31.79 and company B at \$26.42. In this case, the positions are exited so the fund manager will:

- buy shares in company A @ \$31.79, i.e. \$500 × (\$38.98/\$31.79) = \$613.09;

- sell shares in company B @ $26.42, i.e. $500 × ($26.42/$29.46) = $448.40.

The pair trade yields a profit of $61.49 or positive return of 6.149%.

Another trade possibility, as shown in Figure 2.10, arises on 19 September when the closing price ratio moved above the 3σ marker line and company A was trading at $33.02 and company B at $30.10. The following pair trade is executed:

- buy $500 worth of company A @ $33.02 assuming company A is undervalued;
- sell $500 worth of company B @ $30.10 assuming company B is overvalued.

Figure 2.10 also shows that on 8 November the price ratio returned to the mean value and that company A was trading at $27.78 and company B at $22.25. In this case, the positions are exited so the fund manager will:

- sell shares in company A @ $27.78 i.e. $500 * ($27.78/$33.02) = $420.65;
- buy shares in company B @ $22.25 i.e. $500 * ($30.10/$22.25) = $676.40.

The pair trade yields a profit of $97.05 or positive return of 9.705%.

The examples show that a pairs trading strategy, when correctly executed and exited at the appropriate points in time, leads to a positive return in both rising and declining markets. Pairs trading is not just restricted to the equity market but is a widely used strategy in many other markets, such as options, futures and interest rates. Indeed, the very nature of the quoting mechanism in the currency market is one large pair trade, e.g. buying £/$ is the same as buying sterling and selling US dollars.

In recent years pairs trading strategies have taken a great deal of advantage from the growth of financial technology and the advent of algorithmic trading systems and automated execution platforms. Such strategies are typically built around quantitative models that determine entry and exit criteria for the equity pairs based on historical data mining and in-depth technical analysis. While trading the strategy, the algorithms continually monitor for deviations in equity prices and automatically buy and sell to capitalise on any relevant pricing inefficiencies.

2.3.2   Event-Driven

2.3.2.1   *Distressed Securities*

Event-driven strategies (or special situations) rely solely on exploiting inefficiencies in the pricing of company shares before or after extraordinary corporate events, such as bankruptcies,[18] mergers and acquisitions (M&As), corporate restructurings or *spin-offs*.[19] In the case of an acquisition, a fund manager will analyse the reason for the acquisition, the terms involved and any legal issues related to the successful completion of the deal. If the manager is convinced the acquisition will go ahead, they will purchase the underpriced shares of the company being acquired and subsequently profit by selling the shares at a higher price after the acquisition goes ahead and the share price rises. However, many corporate events do not go ahead as planned and result in the decline of the company share price, causing the fund to lose a great deal of money. Managers will normally hedge against the continual decline of the share price by purchasing equity put options (see Box 2.3). Due to the high risks involved with event-driven strategies, they are typically employed only by large institutional investors who have the necessary skills and expertise to analyse the potential outcome of corporate events.

Box 2.3   Options

An *option* is a legally binding contract that gives the owner the right, but not the obligation, to buy (call) or sell (put) the underlying asset (e.g. stock) at a predetermined price (strike) at a predefined date (expiration) in the future. For example, an investor would purchase a call option on the anticipation that the stock price would rise and buy a put option on the expectation the stock price will decline.

In the case of event-driven strategies, fund managers often use put options to insure against a continual decline in the value of their stock portfolio. The figure below is the P&L profile for purchasing a put option and shows that whilst the share price declines below the

---

[18] In the US, when a company experiences bankruptcy it is normally delisted from the stock exchange since it no longer meets the necessary listing requirements. However, there is no law against such shares still being traded, despite being bankrupt stock, in the over-the-counter market or on pink sheets.

[19] A *spin-off* is a corporate transaction that involves forming a new company, subsidiary or entity.

strike price, the profit begins to rise with a boundary at a share price of zero. The downside to buying put options is that the share price does not fall enough to realise a profit exceeding the premium paid for the option. However, if the stock price does not continue to fall but rises, there will be a profit on the stock portfolio that the hedge was originally designed to protect. The worst case scenario is that the stock price remains unchanged and then the premium paid for the insurance will be lost.

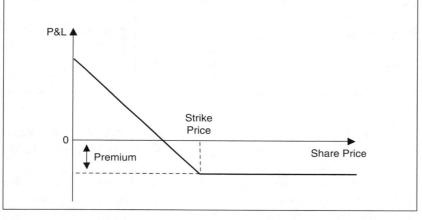

Event-driven investing is often used by hedge fund managers actively involved in the distressed securities market,[20] i.e. companies that are in some form of distress as a result of a corporate restructuring or bankruptcy.[21] Although there are many different opinions as to what constitutes a distressed security, they generally include corporate bonds, bank debt, trade claims,[22] common and preferred stock and warrants. Indeed, the distressed securities market itself is highly disorganised and an illiquid environment with no convincing price structure to debt

---

[20] Hedge funds involved in distressed securities are also known as *vulture funds* since they are likened to picking through the bones of a dying entity.

[21] In the U.S. a distressed opportunity arises when a company files for either Chapter 11, in order to continue trading but restructure the company and agree an acceptable payment plan for creditors, or Chapter 7, when the company is likely to be liquidated and any assets used to pay off creditors. Bankruptcy laws in Europe are very complex and vary from country to country, requiring specialist lawyers and experts acting in an advisory capacity. Indeed, the European distressed securities market lags behind that of the US in terms of maturity and size.

[22] Trade claims are claims held by suppliers who are owed for goods and services by the distressed company.

Table 2.3 Moody's and Standard & Poor's bond rating schemes

Bond Quality	Moody's	Standard & Poor's	
Highest	Aaa	AAA	Investment Grade
High	Aa	AA	
Upper Medium	A	A	
Medium	Baa	BBB	
Speculative	Ba	BB	
	B	B	Non-investment Grade
Highly Speculative	Caa	CCC	
	Ca	CC	
Default	C	C	Distressed Securities
		D	

securities. However, the very nature of the market is highly desirable to hedge fund managers who see such price inefficiencies as very profitable opportunities.

With corporate bonds, a manager has the advantage of using the detailed analysis undertaken by professional credit rating agencies to assess the creditworthiness of a bond and the quality of the issuer. Table 2.3 shows two of the major independent credit rating agencies that both use a specific indicator to depict the class of bond and their ranking in relation to other bonds. Typically a company in financial distress is likely to experience a downgrade, or, in the worst case scenario, a default in their bond rating. Bonds rated investment grade[23] are much less likely to be downgraded or default in relation to those in the lower rankings. Bonds that have been downgraded from investment grade to a lower grade are called *fallen angels* whereas those upgraded from a lower to higher investment grade are known as *rising stars*. In addition to analysing bond ratings, managers will also research the company and industry in order to ascertain if there has been any adverse market news or information that may negatively affect the bond or issuer. The most lucrative debt securities are those that have been heavily damaged by the markets but whose probability of survival are high.

The price of distressed securities generally falls when investors (and creditors) holding shares realise the company is in financial difficulty

---

[23] Investment grade is also known as *speculative grade*.

and rush to sell the shares. In many cases they have unknowingly overlooked the true value of the company by letting the emotional stigma associated with bankruptcy cloud their judgement. This is where hedge fund managers specialising in distressed debt pick up such stock at greatly discounted prices. These managers have the requisite knowledge and experience to accurately value the distressed company and potential outcome. They will thoroughly research why the company is in distress and what is forcing down the share price and ascertain the true value of the company. A company may have expanded too fast or diversified into an unknown market sector but may still have a strong core business and viable market that a company restructuring would address. In this case, after the successful restructuring, the original shares purchased at a discount will be worth a handsome profit once the share price begins rising again. Indeed, a manager may even try to purchase a substantial proportion of the outstanding distressed debt[24] in an attempt to influence the reorganisation process. Fund managers will also research the industry sector to determine if there is any negative news or information that will impact on the bond rating and subsequent share price. Apart from the amount of time spent on in-depth analysis and research of distressed securities, there is also a large element of risk involved with such strategies. The length of a corporate restructuring is often unknown and can vary considerably, depending on the existing debt structure, outstanding legal issues and other related variables that can slow down the deal process. It may even be that the restructuring attempt fails altogether and the company files for bankruptcy, in which case some securities may even become worthless. In order to mitigate against this possibility most fund managers will only invest in senior distressed debt, such as corporate bonds and bank debt which are likely to hold some value regardless of the outcome.

Over the past several years the distressed securities market has seen major growth due to the huge amount of company failures and restructures following the global financial crisis. As more and more companies face financial ruin, bankruptcy or reorganisation, and creditors sell off their discount shares, the distressed securities market will continue to grow. Figure 2.11 shows the shows the VAMI for the HFRI ED: Distressed/Restructuring Index performance against several major marker indices over the past five years.

---

[24] The securities of a distressed company emerging from a reorganisation are also known as *orphan shares*.

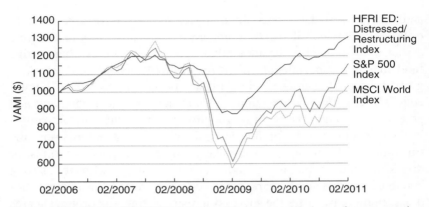

Figure 2.11   VAMI of HFRI ED: Distressed/Restructuring Index performance against major market indices over the past five years

Source: *Hedge Fund Research*

2.3.2.2   Merger Arbitrage

Merger arbitrage involves the investment in an event-driven situation, which is normally an M&A, but can also be leveraged and management buyouts[25] and hostile takeovers.[26] The fund manager will take advantage of the potential opportunities from such events by simultaneously buying and selling the stocks of the two companies involved. For example, consider a potential M&A in which company A (the *acquirer*) signals the intention to buy company B (the *target*). As a result of the market news generated by such an announcement, the stock price of company B will rise and that of company A fall. The stock price of company B, however, will usually be at a discount to the acquisition price in order to reflect the element of risk involved in the uncertainty over whether the corporate event will go ahead successfully. This provides an opportunity for arbitrage by taking a directional view on the *spread* between the values of the two companies. The fund manager will take a position on the spread with the hope that it narrows, i.e. the current market spread *converges* towards the offered one. If the deal fails the spread will widen due to the sharp fall in the share price of company B.[27]

---

[25] A leveraged buyout is the takeover of a company using borrowed funds. A management buyout is a leveraged buyout by the management of the company.

[26] A hostile takeover is one in which there is a strong resistance from the target company.

[27] In the case of hostile bids the spread can be much wider in the anticipation that the deal is more likely to fail.

Some fund managers refer to merger arbitrage as *risk arbitrage* since the arbitrage strategy relies solely on the risk associated with the outcome of the event-driven situation. Indeed, merger arbitrage is not simply a case of going long company B stock and short company A stock; there are many complications involved in extraordinary corporate deals and a successful fund manager must have strong skills and expertise to be active in such market environments.

Merger arbitrage can be divided into two main categories: cash mergers (or tender offers) and stock-for-stock mergers (or stock swap mergers), although other strategies exist that involve more complex deal structures, such as stock swap mergers with collars and multiple-bidder situations. With cash mergers, company A will simply buy the shares of company B for cash and then sell them after the acquisition has gone through and profit from the subsequent rise in the stock price. There are no short sales involved in cash merger arbitrage; rather it is more of a speculation on the M&A going through as planned. With a stock-for-stock merger, company A will *exchange*[28] its own stock for the stock of company B, i.e. the fund manager will buy the stock of company B and short sell the stock of company A. After the M&A is complete, the stock of company B is converted into the stock of company A and the converted stock used to cover the short position. In both the cash and stock swap merger strategies, the manager is taking a position on the spread (or merger arbitrage spread) between the prices of company A and company B stock with a view to the current market spread converging towards the final offered spread. The merger arbitrage spread is the percentage difference between the opening price of the offer and the closing price of the target company the day after the M&A announcement. Clearly the manager will make a profit if the spreads narrows, and will lose money if the spread widens. Many managers use leverage to enhance their returns since the spreads involved in such deals can be relatively small. Managers will also only focus on largely capitalised companies so that there is sufficient liquidity in the market to undertake the stock transactions in a timely and efficient manner. Figure 2.12 shows the VAMI for the HFRI ED: Merger Arbitrage Index performance against several major marker indices over the past five years.

As with managers who invest in distressed securities, those involved in merger arbitrage will try to accumulate a substantial holding in the

---

[28] The exchange is based on the *exchange ratio*, which in the case of a standard stock-for-stock merger is one-to-one.

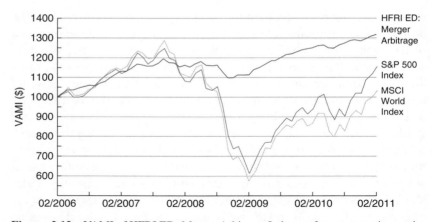

Figure 2.12   VAMI of HFRI ED: Merger Arbitrage Index performance against major market indices over the past five years

Source: *Hedge Fund Research*

shares of the target company in an attempt to influence the boardroom negotiations and the eventual outcome of the deal. Although the whole process seems simple enough there are many risks involved that may cause a planned M&A not to go ahead. For example, company A or B may not be able to meet all the requirements of a M&A, shareholder approval from either company may not be achieved, or legal and regulatory issues may prevent the merger from going ahead along with many other unforeseen factors. In order to hedge against the possibility of deal failure, the fund manager will diversify across many M&As in order to cushion the blow if one were to fail against all the other positive outcomes. As with distressed securities, managers will also hedge their positions by buying put options on the company stock when the spread is such that any profit will exceed the cost of buying the put insurance.

In a similar way to distressed securities, merger arbitrage requires the manager to have a sophisticated set of skills and experience in accurately assessing a potential M&A, the reasons for the corporate action, the length of time to a successful outcome and other possible risks involved. The fund manager will usually conduct a case study of the announced M&A and allocate a probability of success to the deal. In order to assess the probability of a positive outcome the fund manager will make use of many resources, such as company and analysts' reports, their network of contacts in the field, and the specific documents associated with the M&A (tender document, merger agreement, etc.). Historically, the vast majority of M&As are completed successfully after being announced, with only a small percentage (around 3–4%) failing.

2.3.3   Relative Value

2.3.3.1   Equity Market Neutral

In the equity market neutral strategy,[29] the manager takes matched long and short positions in stocks so that *market risk* can be reduced as much as possible. This is similar to the long/short strategy except that the net portfolio position is neutral, i.e. neither long nor short biased. The long and short positions are chosen with great care and attention so that a very high degree of hedging is achieved. Ideally a market neutral portfolio of stocks is constructed such that the portfolio is *beta* neutral. Beta is the measurement of the volatility of a stock in relation to a market index or benchmark (e.g. S&P 500). A stock with a beta of 1 tends to move in line with the market index, whereas a stock with a beta higher than 1 will generally be more volatile and a stock with beta less than 1 will be less volatile than the market index. Figure 2.13 shows the VAMI for the HFRI EH: Equity Market Neutral Index performance against several major marker indices over the past five years.

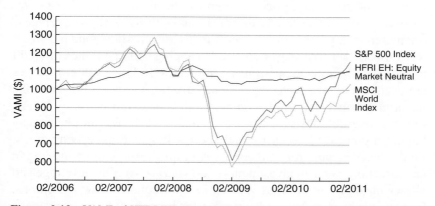

Figure 2.13   VAMI of HFRI EH: Equity Market Neutral Index performance against major market indices over the past five years

Source: *Hedge Fund Research*

---

[29] The equity market neutral strategy was employed by Alfred Winslow Jones who set up the first hedge fund in 1949.

The long/short equity market neutral strategy usually involves a large amount of buying and selling to maintain a neutral position, and therefore one of the major risks associated with this type of strategy is being able to get in and out of positions in the market with relative ease. This requires investments in only very liquid stocks with a high level of daily trading volume.[30] The major risk, however, is the fund manager's ability to select a set of long and short stocks that will produce an acceptable level of return. The returns achieved by this strategy rely on earning small, steady profits on the spreads between a range of different stocks. One of the main quantitative methods employed by managers to assist them in their stock selection is the *technical analysis* of historical stock prices. This generally involves simulating and analysing large amounts of data on the price history of stocks, to uncover trends and patterns, and to try and predict how they will perform in the future. Other fund managers may resort to *fundamental analysis* of stocks that involves the research of company reports and industry sectors.

2.3.3.2 Convertible Arbitrage

Arbitrage relies on capturing inefficiencies in the price spreads between related assets or those of similar characteristics and the ultimate convergence of the market price to a known, theoretical or equilibrium relationship. Typically spreads are narrow and returns small, so leverage is often used to improve returns to an attractive level. Many fund managers rely on borrowing, strong sources of financing and good lines of credit to successfully implement arbitrage strategies. Relative value strategies are designed to take advantage of such arbitrage opportunities and the mispricing between a single company's debt and equity, e.g. by investing in convertible instruments and common stock. By simultaneously buying a convertible security and short selling the underlying stock, fund managers can protect themselves against a stock price moving in any direction. Such an investment is known as convertible arbitrage and allows managers to generate a profit in a variety of market conditions. Fund managers can also use leverage to further enhance profits given the general low-risk investment that convertible arbitrage offers. When considering convertible securities the fund manager is usually considering

---

[30] Very liquid stocks with a high level of daily trading volume are usually those that have options written on them.

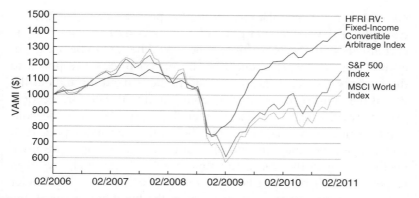

Figure 2.14   VAMI of HFRI RV: Fixed-Income-Convertible Arbitrage Index performance against major market indices over the past five years

Source: *Hedge Fund Research*

an investment in convertible bonds (see Box 2.4). The general idea behind the investment strategy is that the convertible bonds of a company
are priced inefficiently relative to the underlying stock and an arbitrage opportunity exists. Figure 2.14 shows the VAMI for the HFRI RV:
Fixed-Income-Convertible Arbitrage Index performance against several
major marker indices over the past five years.

Box 2.4   Convertible Bonds

A convertible bond is a fixed income security that gives the bond
holder the right to convert the par amount of the bond into a fixed
amount of common stock from the issuer under the terms of a bond
indenture. The bond indenture describes the specific contract details,
such as interest rate, maturity date, principal to be repaid, convert-
ibility and any other terms. There is an optionality component to the
convertible that allows the bond holder to convert debt into equity at
any time during the life of the bond. In this sense, a convertible bond
is a hybrid (or *mixed*) security consisting of a simple bond and an
embedded equity call option. The call option allows the bond holder
to take advantage of a rise in the underlying share price, while the
fixed income component provides capital protection against a decline
in share prices. However, for this added feature, bondholders receive
a lower yield than that of typical non-convertible securities.

   The conversion premium measures the spread between the price
paid per share to acquire the common stock of the issuer (i.e.

conversion price) and the current market price as a percentage. For example, if the conversion price of a stock is $70 and the stock is currently at $50, the convertible bond would be said to be trading at a 40% conversion premium. The conversion price corresponds to the *exchange price* of the shares and remains fixed throughout the life of the convertible bond. Any conversion will therefore become extremely attractive once the market share price exceeds the conversion price. If the share price falls below the conversion price then a conversion becomes increasingly unlikely and if the share price declines even further the convertible bond will settle at a level in respect to the share price (the *bond floor*). Of course, the bond holder will still receive interest payments from the bond and get back the principal when the bond matures, offering some capital protection.

A typical convertible bond payoff profile is shown in the diagram below:

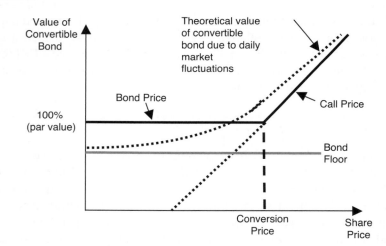

Convertible bonds offer a unique risk–return characteristic compared to that of pure bonds or equities, with the majority of risk being attributed to the failure of the issuer to repay the principal amount. Another downside to investing in convertible bonds is the fact that the issuer has the right to call the bonds, i.e. to forcibly convert them. This would usually happen when stock price is higher than it would be if the bond was redeemed. This provision places a *cap* on the potential profit to a convertible bond, unlike that with common stock in which there is no limit on the potential upside.

Table 2.4 A simplified example of a convertible arbitrage investment strategy

	Scenario 1	Scenario 2	Scenario 3
	No change in stock price	Stock price rises by 25%	Stock price falls by 25%
Stock price	$10	$12.50	$7.50
Interest on convertible bond @ 5% p.a.	$50	$50	$50
Gain/loss on convertible bond	—	$250	($80)
Interest on short sale @ 5% p.a.	$25	$25	$25
Gain/loss on short sale	—	($125)	$125
Fee paid to securities lender @ 0.25% p.a.	($1.50)	($1.50)	($1.50)
Net cash flow	$73.50	$73.50	$73.50
Annual return	**7.35%**	**19.85%**	**11.85%**

Consider a simplified convertible arbitrage example in which a 5% convertible bond maturing in one year at $1,000 is convertible into 100 shares of a non-dividend-paying common stock currently trading at $10 per share. The fund manager hedges against this long convertible bond position by short selling 50 shares of the underlying common stock at $10 per share with a 0.25% annual fee payable to the borrower of the securities. Pricing inefficiencies between these two investments allow for profitable annual returns when the stock price stays the same, rises or falls, as can be seen in Table 2.4.

The convertible arbitrage strategy is not completely without risks and a fund manager must carefully evaluate the company under consideration and its ability to meet its financial obligations over the life of the convertible bond. Since convertible bonds must be held for a specified amount of time before conversion is allowed, the fund manager must be able to determine in advance if market conditions will be favourable within the time before conversion is permitted. Another issue related to such arbitrage strategies is the variety of analytic and numerical valuation methods available to value convertible bonds. Such complex quantitative techniques require highly skilled mathematical modellers and computational systems in order to correctly assess the risk and potential rewards from investing in a particular convertible arbitrage strategy.

2.3.3.3 Fixed Income Arbitrage

Amongst the most widely used fixed income arbitrage strategies are capital structure arbitrage, swap-spread arbitrage, and yield curve arbitrage, all of which aim to exploit apparent mispricing among one or more fixed income instruments. Most of these strategies rely on detailed quantitative models of the term structure of interest rates to identify possible price discrepancies and manage interest rate risk. Most fund managers look for fixed income securities that are highly correlated and that, as a result of external market influences, are mispriced. At their most basic level, fixed income instruments are debt instruments, issued by private or public entities, which promise a fixed stream of income, e.g. Treasury and corporate bonds. There are, however, more sophisticated fixed income securities based on credit derivatives, such as credit default swaps (see Box 2.5). Fund managers who invest in fixed income arbitrage strategies have to be willing to accept the significant risks involved. Such strategies typically provide only relatively small returns, enhanced with leverage, but can potentially lead to huge losses. In fact, many hedge fund professionals refer to fixed income arbitrage as *'picking up nickels in front of a steamroller'*. Figure 2.15 shows the VAMI for the HFRI RV: Fixed-Income-Corporate Index performance against several major marker indices over the past five years.

Box 2.5   Credit Default Swap

Credit derivatives seek to transfer defined credit risks in a credit product to the counterparty of the derivative contract. The credit product might be the exposure associated with a credit asset (e.g. a loan) or a generic credit risk (e.g. company bankruptcy). As the risks, and any potential rewards, are transferred to the counterparty, they assume the position of a *synthetic* owner of the credit asset. The credit derivative allows trading in synthetic short and long positions in the credit risk of the entity, without having to explicitly trade in a credit asset, i.e. the loan or bond. Since the synthetic market does not have the same limitations and constraints of the bonds or loans market, credit derivatives have become an alternative investment product linked to the value of a company.

A very common credit derivative is the credit default swap (CDS), which is a contract between the buyer and seller of credit protection, i.e. an option purchased by the protection buyer and written by the protection seller. The strike price of the option is the par value of the reference asset, e.g. bond, and can only be exercised when there is a default. Whilst there is no default, the protection buyer makes quarterly payments (the *spread*) to the protection seller. If the counter-party defaults, the protection seller pays the buyer the par value of the bond in exchange for physical delivery of the bond. A default is known as a *credit event* and includes failure to pay debt obligations, a company restructuring or bankruptcy. The diagram below shows the structure of the CDS with and without default:

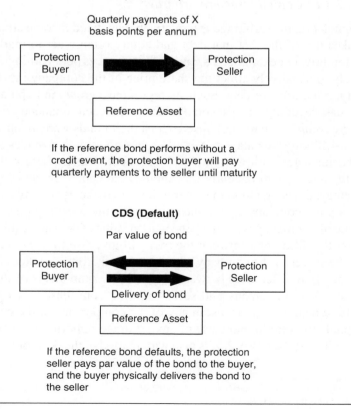

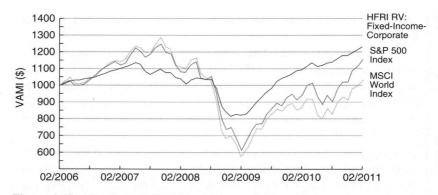

Figure 2.15 VAMI of HFRI RV: Fixed-Income-Corporate Index performance against major market indices over the past five years

Source: *Hedge Fund Research*

2.3.3.3.1 Capital Structure Arbitrage

Capital structure arbitrage is a relatively new fixed income strategy that makes use of the fact that debt and equity often react to market news differently. For example, if a company announces poor earnings it is very likely to negatively affect the share price of the company immediately, but not the price of debt. Such strategies have grown in popularity over the past several years, especially during the recent financial crisis when many company shares collapsed whilst their bonds were much slower to adjust. Taking advantage of this arbitrage opportunity provides the hedge fund manager with a profitable investment strategy before the credit rating agency subsequently downgrades the debt.[31] In devising such a strategy, the hedge fund manager will try to make use of any correlation between a company's debt and equity structure (see Figure 2.16). The value of a company is given by the market value of debt and equity; in this case, the difference between the two will give rise to a *spread* implied by the shares of the company's credit. Capital arbitrage takes advantage of the price differences between the various components of the capital structure of a company and seeks to profit from these misalignments. A fund manager can invest in any of the components of the company's capital structure to make use of any arbitrage opportunities. The credit default swap (see Box 2.5) is also widely used in the development of the

---

[31] There is a very fine line between the value of stocks of a fallen angel and those that are heading directly towards bankruptcy.

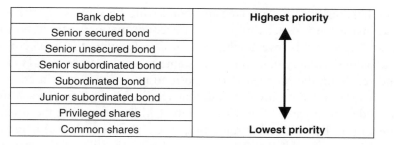

Bank debt	Highest priority
Senior secured bond	
Senior unsecured bond	
Senior subordinated bond	
Subordinated bond	
Junior subordinated bond	
Privileged shares	
Common shares	Lowest priority

Figure 2.16 Capital structure of a company and their order of priority in the case of bankruptcy

capital structure arbitrage strategy. A company's equity and associated CDS should be *negatively correlated* such that a rise in the stock price causes a tightening in the CDS spread since it is less likely to default. If the company's outlook worsens then the CDS spread will widen and the share price subsequently fall. A fund manager will attempt to exploit this variation in spread between a company's CDS and the share price.

As the global financial markets have slowly begun to rebound, fewer capital structure arbitrage opportunities have become available. However, other opportunities have arisen in the capital structuring arena. For example, on the back of strong dividend growth and payouts, borrowing such stock and purchasing the associated CDS, allows the fund manager to anticipate subsequent deterioration in the creditworthiness of the company. This is known as a *wings trade*; if dividend payouts do continue to grow, the long position in the equity can usually finance the investment strategy. In the event that credit does deteriorate, a profit will be achieved through the increased value of the CDS.

2.3.3.3.2 Swap-Spread Arbitrage

Another popular fixed income arbitrage strategy is swap-spread arbitrage. A swap-spread arbitrage is a bet on the relative levels of various swap rates, LIBOR, Treasury bonds, coupon rates and *repo rates*.[32] A common swap-spread arbitrage strategy involves entering into a par swap to receive a fixed coupon rate, i.e. the constant maturity swap (CMS) rate, and paying the floating LIBOR rate. The fund manager will

---

[32] The *repo rate* (or repurchase rate) is also known as the official bank rate. The repo rate is the discounted interest rate at which central banks repurchase government securities.

simultaneously sell a par Treasury bond with the same swap maturity and invest the proceeds in a margin account that earns the repo rate. Cash flows on this investment will consist of paying the fixed coupon rate on the Treasury bond, i.e. a constant maturity Treasury (CMT) rate, and receiving the proceeds from the repo rate on the margin account. The overall position involves the manager receiving a fixed cash flow from the swap spread (i.e. CMS minus CMT) and paying the floating spread (i.e. LIBOR minus repo rate). So, if the swap spread is greater than the average of the floating spread over the life of the strategy, a positive return will be achieved. Although the swap-spread strategy seems simple enough, one of the largest sources of loss for Long Term Capital Management (LTCM)[33] during the financial crisis of 1998 was attributable to massive swap-spread positions in European bonds. Despite the possibility of such huge losses, the swap-spread strategy has become one of the most popular fixed income strategies for relative value hedge funds.

2.3.3.3.3   Yield Curve Arbitrage

The yield curve (or term structure of interest rates) is a graphical representation of how the yields on bonds of equal credit quality but different maturities compare; a typical US Treasury yield curve is shown in Figure 2.17. The yield curve is often used as a benchmark for other debt within the markets, such as mortgage and bank lending rates. The curve is also a very useful indicator of future interest rate changes and economic conditions.

The shape and slope of the yield curve change as a result of the credit rating of the issuing government, the state of monetary and fiscal policy and other economic factors. A parallel shift[34] in the yield curve occurs when the yield on all maturities changes by the same amount. However, more likely scenarios are when changes in the spread between short and long maturities either increase (steepen) or decrease (flatten) the yield

---

[33] Long Term Capital Management (LTCM) used complex mathematical models to take advantage of fixed income arbitrage opportunities, amongst others, through U.S., Japanese and European government bonds, combined with extremely high leverage. The hedge fund failed spectacularly in 1998 after a major financial crisis, leading to a much publicised bailout by other major financial institutions.

[34] When discussing shifts in the yield it is often normal to talk of a certain basis point shift in the yield curve, e.g. a 100 basis point shift in the yield curve implies a 1% movement in the yields.

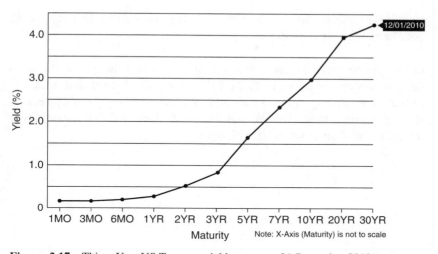

Figure 2.17   Thirty-Year US Treasury yield curve as of 1 December 2010
Source: www.treasury.gov

curve. Yield curve arbitrage seeks to profit from shifts in the yield curve by taking long and short positions in Treasury bonds across different maturities.[35] This could take the form of a spread trade, where the fund manager shorts the front end of the curve and goes long the back end of the curve. The idea is that the manager needs to identify points along the yield curve that are *rich* and *cheap*. Another very popular yield curve arbitrage strategy is the *butterfly trade* in which the hedge fund manager will buy the *dumbbells* (i.e. the *wings* of the butterfly) and sell the *bullets* (i.e. the *body* of the butterfly) to create a zero net *duration*[36] spread, e.g. going long the 3-year and 8-year maturities and shorting the 5-year maturity. In this case, large parallel moves in the yield curve in either direction will generate a positive return due to the positive *convexity*[37] created by the position. However, in practice, yield curves can tend

---

[35] Yield curve arbitrage can be further classified into *inter-curve* arbitrage in which the manager takes positions in securities of the same country, and *intra-curve* where positions are taken on securities across different countries using more than one yield curve of differing currencies.

[36] *Duration* measures the price sensitivity of a bond to the yield, the percentage change in price for a parallel shift in the yield, i.e. the change in the value of a bond from a 1% change in interest rates.

[37] *Convexity* is a measure of the sensitivity of the duration of a bond to changes in interest rates. The higher (lower) the convexity, the less (more) sensitive the bond to shifts in interest rates.

to move in many complex patterns and lead to a range of unexpected outcomes with such strategies.

In this chapter we have seen that the most common hedge fund classification system is by strategy and then by style within that strategy. In the many strategies covered, emphasis was placed on equity-related strategies since these will be the focus of more detailed quantitative modelling and analysis in later chapters.

3

Hedge Fund Data Sources

Obtaining accurate, reliable and timely data on hedge funds is of extreme importance to a manager or analyst wishing to measure monitor and assess the returns and performance of such investment opportunities. Consistent and robust hedge fund indices and trustworthy benchmarks are also necessary and valuable when trying to obtain a clear representation of a hedge fund's track record, and the current state of the industry.

This chapter reviews a range of prominent commercial hedge fund databases and the variety of indices and benchmarks they produce. In addition, the many pitfalls and problems that need to be understood when interpreting and using such summary statistics are discussed. In particular, the inherent heterogeneity and lack of representativeness within the hedge fund universe is highlighted as a major concern in the industry. Moreover, some of the most innovative products developed in order to overcome some such shortfalls are reviewed.

3.1 HEDGE FUND DATABASES

Many hedge fund managers voluntarily provide monthly hedge fund performance data to a variety of commercial databases. These hedge fund databases collect, assimilate and produce informative reports, indices and benchmarks based on this information for potential investors, consultants, analysts and academics involved in investment and research on hedge funds. Such data allow the construction and publication of numerous non-investable and investable indices that purport to give an indication of the state of the hedge fund industry and have an important benchmarking function. However, due to the voluntary nature of these monthly data submissions, the indices produced by these vendors can be misleading and contain several biases and anomalies. Moreover, a complete record of every single hedge fund in the industry is simply not available, relevant information comes only from samples of the hedge fund universe. The quality and quantity of such data varies between vendors, and an investor is left to their own judgement in accepting one set of hedge fund performance statistics over another. Table 3.1

Table 3.1 Summary of some of the major hedge fund databases as of September 2010

Company	Description	Established	No. of funds[*]	Graveyard[**]	UCITS III[†]
BarclayHedge (*www.barclayhedge.com*)	BarclayHedge is a privately owned, Iowa-based independent research and information provider to the alternative investment industry.	1985	16,228	10,279	No
Eurekahedge (*www.eurekahedge.com*)	Eurekahedge is the world's largest independent data provider and research house dedicated to the collation, development and continuous improvement of alternative investment data.	2002	22,781	4,727	Over 600
LipperTASS (*www.lipperweb.com*)	LipperTASS, a Thomson Reuters company, has been providing qualitative and quantitative hedge fund data for over 20 years with offices in Asia, Europe and the US.	1977	Over 6,300	Over 7,000	No
The Centre for International Securities and Derivatives Markets (CISDM) (*www.cisdm.org*)	Formerly the MAR database and subsequently Zurich Capital Markets, the CISDM database was donated to the University of Massachusetts in Amherst. CISDM is the longest-standing hedge fund and CTA database.	1979 (CTAs) 1994 (HFs)	4,500	Over 9,000	No
Morningstar (*www.morningstar.co.uk*)	Morningstar has grown its hedge fund database over the years through strategic acquisitions, including InvestorForce's Altvest database, S&P and MSCI hedge fund businesses.	2004	Over 9,000	Not known	No

Name (website)	Description				
HedgeFund.net (HFN) (*www.hedgefund.net*)	HFN, owned by Channel Capital Group Inc., is a leading source for hedge fund news and performance data.	1998	Over 7,250	9,000	Not known
FTSE Hedge (*www.ftse.com*)	FTSE is an independent company jointly owned by The Financial Times and London Stock Exchange.	—	8,000	Not known	No
Hedge Fund Research (HFR) (*www.hedgefundresearch.com*)	HFR, a Chicago-based firm, specialises in the areas of indexation and analysis of hedge funds and has also developed the industry's most detailed hedge fund classification system.	1994	6,500	8,000	350
Hedge Fund Intelligence (HFI) (*www.hedgefundintelligence.com*)	HFI is an independent publishing group, collator of hedge fund data and other activities. HFI is responsible for producing the InvestHedge, AsiaHedge, EuroHedge and Absolute Return + Alpha industry journals.	1998	Over 13,000	Not known	Over 200
Greenwich Alternative Investments (GAI) (*www.greenwichai.com*)	GAI, established as Van Hedge Fund Advisors in 1992 and rebranded in 2006, is the world's leading pioneer of hedge fund related investment products and services. GAI was one of the first to collect data and perform large-scale research on a broad universe of hedge funds.	1988	Over 9,000	Not known	Not known

* Includes hedge funds (HFs), FoHFs, CTAs and/or CPOs.

** Graveyard (or dead) funds are those that have stopped operating, merged, liquidated or ceased reporting for whatever reason.

†Indicates whether a UCITS III hedge fund database is available.

gives a summary of some of the major hedge fund databases currently available.

Since 2003, Pertrac Financial Solutions (PFS), a software solutions provider for the investment community, have been responsible for producing a regular report on the size and composition of the hedge fund industry. The study is carried out using data from a variety of well-known hedge fund databases, including BarclayHedge, Eurekahedge, HedgeFund.net, HFR, LipperTASS and Morningstar. The study identifies duplicate records of the combined database of records from single-manager hedge funds, CTAs and FoHFs using a set of statistical techniques, and subsequently analyses the remaining data to yield aggregate and concise information on the respective hedge fund universe.[1] In 2010, PFS published the annual Hedge Fund Database Study, which identified 16,328 single-manager hedge funds and 7,274 FoHFs across all databases after duplicate records were removed. Among all the distinct investments identified, approximately 1,997 represented CTAs. After taking into account those that actively submitted performance data to the databases,[2] a rise of approximately 9.0% was reported against 2009 figures. Indeed, total industry assets rose by 11% during the year to over $1.60 trillion, but still short of the 2007 peak of over $2 trillion in managed assets. This indicated that the hedge fund industry was starting to regain its presence after the recent market collapse and global financial crisis. Single-manager funds in the databases account for a large proportion of the AuM. Of these, 280 funds held assets in excess of $1 billion and about half of single-manager funds reported fund sizes of less than $25 million (see Figure 3.1). Around $518 billion was invested in hedge funds through FoHFs in 2010 and, like single-manager funds, a large percentage of FoHFs are relatively small, with approximately half of those reporting fund sizes less than $25 million (see Figure 3.2).

Approximately 48% of the funds in the study were present in only one of the list databases, with more than 70% of funds reporting to only three or fewer databases. Indeed, over the past several years hedge fund managers have chosen to be much more selective in the databases

---

[1] Some data vendors exclude particular investment styles, such as CTAs, since they consider them different from the structure of *normal* hedge funds or, in the case of FoHFs, they do not wish to double-count them, i.e. once in the fund and then again in the funds of hedge funds. However, this treatment is not true of all databases as some do include them.

[2] Non-reporting funds may have chosen to stop reporting for a variety of reasons, such as poor performance, strong performance, personnel changes or business failure.

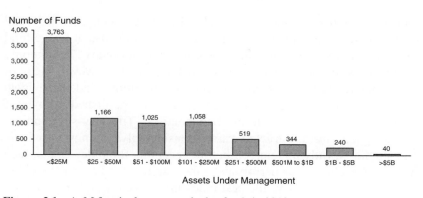

Figure 3.1 AuM for single-manager hedge funds in 2010

Source: PFS. Reproduced by permission of PerTrac, Inc.

to which they report. For this reason, it is important to note that any given database provides only a sample of the entire hedge fund universe, requiring investors to access multiple data sources to get a clearer understanding of the investment opportunities and the state of the hedge fund industry.

3.2 MAJOR HEDGE FUND INDICES

In traditional finance, the use of indices is a useful investment tool for managing the exposure of a portfolio of investments to *market risk*, i.e. a so-called *passively* managed investment style. In the hedge fund

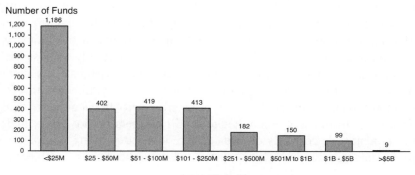

Figure 3.2 AuM for FoHFs in 2010

Source: PFS. Reproduced by permission of PerTrac, Inc.

world, where performance is generally driven by a manager's skill and expertise, reflecting an *active* management style, the use of hedge fund indices is more surprising, since the concept of an index is commonly associated with the notion of passive management. However, many of the commercial databases, and a selection of traditional index providers e.g. FTSE and Dow Jones, have developed and published a range of hedge fund indices and relevant benchmarks.[3] The way such indices are designed and constructed varies considerably amongst providers and should be fully understood before accepting the index as a valued industry benchmark or performance measurement. Many of the index providers purport to have the best index methodology and construction process with strict inclusion criteria and thorough due-diligence procedures. Nevertheless, many investors, as well as the industry itself, are wary of considering one index better than another and approach the hedge fund index and benchmark arena with caution.

3.2.1 Non-investable and Investable Indices

The hedge fund industry is highly heterogeneous, making the construction of a satisfactory performance index that comprises the available hedge fund universe extremely difficult. Non-investable hedge fund indices try, at best, to represent the performance of a sample of the hedge fund universe taken from a relevant database. However, such databases have diverse selection criteria and methods of index construction, leading to many differing published indices. Although aiming to be representative of the hedge fund universe, non-investable indices suffer from many unavoidable biases (see Section 3.3). A further difficulty associated with the heterogeneity of hedge funds is the classification of investment styles. With over 13,000 hedge funds in the industry, determining each manager's investment style is virtually impossible. Some index providers have developed their own classification system that attempts to capture a high level of homogeneity within each investment group and a subsequent level of heterogeneity between individual groups. Unfortunately, many hedge fund managers do not report their investment style correctly or often change it without giving prior notice to the database vendor. Clearly, then, hedge fund indices are subject to

---

[3] Over the past decade, many hedge fund databases and index providers have merged, been acquired by larger firms, or developed into *boutiques* offering specialist hedge fund services and consultancy.

a greater lack of representativeness as opposed to traditional indices. Such a problem goes beyond an insufficient classification of investment styles. Instead, it concerns the actual managers themselves who have a great deal of freedom and choice at their disposal.

By early 2000, many index providers had launched a series of investable indices offering a low-cost investment opportunity to gain exposure to the hedge fund industry. An index is investable when the investors are able to replicate the index by obtaining and maintaining a certain level of tracking error (see Section 3.4.1). Generally based on platforms of separate *managed accounts*,[4] this new generation of indices has been able to provide investors with improved liquidity and a low-cost method of gaining access to the hedge fund world. In addition, the composition, construction methodology and management principles are overseen by an independent committee and disclosed to the public, offering increased transparency.

To create an investable index, the index provider selects a range of hedge funds and develops a structured investment that delivers the performance of the investable index. To make them investable, each hedge fund agrees to accept investments on the terms given by the index provider. When investors buy an investable index the provider makes the investments in the underlying hedge funds, making such an index similar in many ways to a FoHFs investment. In fact, some refer to investable indices as merely FoHFs in disguise or with additional constraints. However, by their very construction, investable hedge fund indices are unable to represent the hedge funds universe. Such indices cannot represent the *open* funds universe, since they are not composed of funds belonging to this subset of the complete universe. They contain many *partially* closed hedge funds, i.e. funds that accept new investments only from investors who have reserved capacity. Hedge funds generally do have capacity issues as certain strategies only work well within certain limits of investment capital. Indeed, many hedge fund managers refuse further capital into a particular fund after they have reached a maximum level of AuM, assigning them thereafter as *closed* funds. As a result, it is very difficult for hedge fund indices to remain investable when the composite hedge funds have closed their doors to new

---

[4] *Managed accounts* are a rapidly growing, fee-based investment management product for individuals of high net worth. Such accounts allow access to professional money managers, high degrees of customisation and greater tax efficiencies. They are also said to provide the added benefits of greater transparency, liquidity and control.

investors. Most index providers argue that to be a truly representative index that acts as a gauge for hedge fund performance, both open and closed funds should be included in the hedge fund index. The trade-off, therefore, is between having as broad a representation as possible of hedge fund performance and having a smaller sample of hedge fund managers representing the performance accessible through investment.

By the end of 2006, hedge fund *replication* aimed to eliminate many of the problems associated with hedge fund indices. Instead of accessing the performance of hedge funds, a statistical approach is undertaken on the history of hedge fund returns, and this analysis used to construct a model of how hedge fund returns react to movements in a range of investable financial instruments. Such a model is then used to construct an investable portfolio of those assets. This makes the index investable, and in principle it can be as representative as the hedge fund database from which it is constructed. As the hedge fund industry becomes increasingly diversified, and offers greater opportunity for investors to gain exposure to hedge fund returns without direct involvement, the growth in such indices will surely increase.

3.2.2   Dow Jones Credit Suisse Hedge Fund Indexes

The Credit Suisse/Tremont Hedge Fund Indexes were rebranded in 2010 after Credit Suisse joined forces with Dow Jones Indexes to provide the Dow Jones Credit Suisse (DJCS) Hedge Fund Indexes (www.hedgeindex.com). Dow Jones is responsible for the calculation, distribution and marketing of the indices, whilst Credit Suisse affiliates manage the financial instruments associated with them.

The DJCS Hedge Fund (or *Broad*) Index is one of the industry's most respected indices tracking over 6,000 hedge funds from the proprietary Credit Suisse database and comprises 472 funds as of July 2010. The index includes only those hedge funds with a minimum of $50 million AuM[5] as well as audited accounts,[6] although hedge funds with an AuM of more than $500 million and a track record of less than a year may be considered under special circumstances. In terms of index participation, AuM does not include managed accounts and reflects only the assets of the hedge fund, not the AuM of the investment company. For index

---

[5] The amount of AuM can sometimes be difficult to determine, since hedge fund managers combine managed accounts and onshore/offshore vehicles, and also use different amounts of leverage, either through margining or by short selling.

[6] A hedge fund must have a minimum one-year track record to have audited financial accounts.

Table 3.2 Asset weights by investment strategy for the DJCS Hedge Fund Index

Investment style	Asset weight (%)
Convertible arbitrage	1.70
Dedicated short bias	0.30
Emerging markets	7.20
Equity market neutral	2.10
Event-driven	26.10
Fixed income arbitrage	4.50
Global macro	19.30
Long/short equity	20.80
Managed futures	4.50
Multi-strategy	13.50

Source: www.hedgeindex.com

inclusion, fund managers must report performance returns (or NAV) and AuM on a monthly basis. The index is asset-weighted (see Appendix A) and broadly diversified across ten style-based investment strategies (see Table 3.2) which seeks to be representative of the entire hedge fund universe. The DJCS Hedge Fund Index construction is based on a transparent and rule-based selection process. The methodology analyses the percentage of assets invested in each subcategory and selects funds for the index based on those percentages, matching the shape of the index to the shape of the universe. Fund *weight caps* can be applied to enhance diversification and limit concentration risk. The index is calculated and rebalanced monthly and funds are reselected on a quarterly basis as required. The index family currently consists of 17 indices, including a range of geographical and strategy-specific hedge fund indices. The current family includes the following indices:

- The *DJCS AllHedge Index*, formerly the CSFB/Tremont Sector Invest Indexes, is a diversified investable index comprised of an aggregate of all ten DJCS AllHedge Strategy Indexes and asset-weighted based on the sector weights of the Broad Index. The AllHedge Index was launched in October 2007, and any performance of the index predating October 2007 is simulated from returns on the underlying AllHedge Strategy Indexes as of October 2004. AllHedge seeks to represent the investable hedge fund universe and encompasses 83 funds as of July 2010.

- The *DJCS Blue Chip Hedge Fund Index*, formerly the CSFB/Tremont Investable Hedge Fund Index, is an investable index made up of the 60 largest hedge funds from the ten style-based sectors compromising the Broad Index.
- The *DJCS LEA Hedge Fund Index* is an emerging market asset-weighted composite[7] index covering the emerging economies of Latin America, Europe, Middle East, Africa and Asia. The index was launched in April 2008.

3.2.2.1 Liquid Alternative Betas

In addition to the above index family, Credit Suisse also publishes a series of liquid alternative beta (LAB) indices.[8] LAB indices aim to replicate (or *clone*) the aggregate return characteristics of alternative investment strategies using commonly traded instruments with high liquidity. LABs reflect the returns of a dynamic basket of investable market factors selected and weighted so as to approximate the aggregate returns of the universe of hedge funds represented by the family of DJCS hedge fund indexes. Such liquid replication strategies seek to provide hedge fund returns without direct hedge fund investment and thus enhance liquidity and eliminate hedge fund *headline*[9] risk (see Box 3.1). The range of LAB indices currently includes the CS Event Driven Liquid Index, CS Global Macro Liquid Index, CS Long/Short Equity Liquid Index and CS Merger Arbitrage Liquid Index.

Box 3.1   A LAB example

Problem. A pension plan with a traditional 60/40 (equity/fixed income) portfolio is planning a 5% hedge fund allocation. To implement the programme, the plan starts due-diligence on several hedge fund managers, a lengthy process that may delay capital deployment. If the funds remain in cash or short-maturity fixed income, expected returns could be negatively impacted.

---

[7] A composite index consists of individual hedge funds that cover a range of different investment strategies.

[8] Alternative beta refers to alternative systematic risks, i.e. those risks that cannot be diversified away and are compensated through risk premia or the expected rate of return above the risk-free interest rate.

[9] *Headline* risk is the impact that a negative news story could have on the value of an investment.

Solution. To better manage the transition and speed up the exposure of the plan to potential hedge-fund-like returns, the plan makes an allocation to a LAB strategy with daily liquidity.* The risk/return profile of this interim allocation is expected to provide a reasonably close match to that of the direct hedge funds in which it plans to invest. The plan can then draw down its replication exposure gradually to reallocate to the selected hedge funds as it completes the due-diligence process (see diagram below).

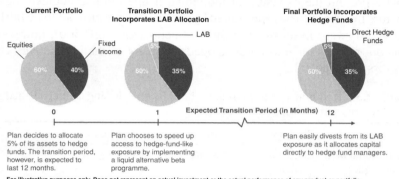

For illustrative purposes only. Does not represent an actual investment or the actual performance of any product or portfolio.

---

*The liquid alternative beta long/short equity data in this example is represented by the CS Long/Short Equity Liquid Index.

Source: Credit Suisse Asset Management, LLC. All data was obtained from publicly available information, internally developed data and other third party sources believed to be reliable. Credit Suisse has not sought to independently verify information obtained from public and third party sources and makes no representations or warranties as to accuracy, completeness or reliability of such information. Please refer to the legal information located at the back of this book for more information. Reproduced by permission of Credit Suisse Asset Management, LLC.

The three main components that drive hedge fund performance can be identified as:

- traditional beta,
- alternative beta, and
- alpha.

Traditional beta returns are based on long-only investment strategies that have exposure to traditional market factors, e.g. equity and credit risk, and act as a *proxy*[10] for well-known benchmark indices, such as the S&P 500 and Russell 2000 indices. Alternative beta involves other

---

[10] A *proxy* is an efficient approximation for another investment.

factors, for example currency carry and equity momentum, that can be captured using various investment strategies and proxied through *systematic* trading.[11] Alpha is attributable to the skill and expertise of the hedge fund manager and is often difficult to capture. Fung and Hsieh (2004), pioneers in the field of hedge fund replication, have shown traditional and alternative beta to be the largest contributors to aggregate hedge fund returns. For this reason, one of the first steps in hedge fund replication is to identify traditional and alternative beta factors that represent the exposure of individual hedge fund strategies. These factors then have to be represented by proxies. These turn out to be fairly straightforward in terms of traditional betas (e.g. S&P 500); however, custom proxies have to be developed for many of the alternative beta factors (see Table 3.3).

Table 3.3 Traditional and alternative beta factors driving aggregate hedge fund returns and their respective proxies

	Strategy	Factors	Proxies
Traditional beta examples	Long/short equity	US large cap	S&P 500 index
	Long/short equity	US small cap	Russell 2000 index
	Event-driven	High-yield fixed income	IBOX high yield liquid index
Alternative beta examples	Global macro	Currency carry	Custom currency carry proxy: long high-yielding currencies; short low-yielding currencies
	Long/short equity	Equity momentum	Custom trend-following proxy: long well-performing companies; short poorly performing companies
	Event-driven	Merger arbitrage	Custom M&A proxy: long companies being acquired; short companies that are acquirers

Source: Credit Suisse

---

[11] *Systematic* (or *rule-based*) trading involves using a automated system to trade on behalf of the trader. The system makes all trading decisions with respect to the rules set by the trader and the information available at the time. Another type of trading is *discretionary*; here the trader uses his intelligence and knowledge to make trading decisions with respect to the information available at the time.

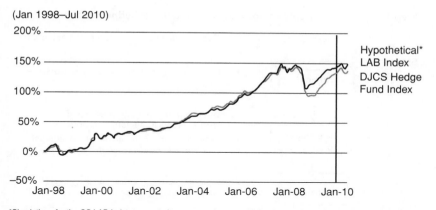

(Jan 1998–Jul 2010)

Hypothetical*
LAB Index
DJCS Hedge
Fund Index

*Simulations for the CS LAB Index were used to measure how a portfolio of securities and market indices designed to track hedge fund indices would have performed in the period beginning December 1997. The LAB Index was launched in January 2010 and is shown by the vertical black line.

Figure 3.3 Hypothetical performance of the CS LAB Index from January 1998 to December 2009 and actual historical performance from January 2010 to July 2010

Source: Reproduced by permission of Credit Suisse Asset Management, LLC

Once the factors and proxies have been determined it is necessary to ascertain the combination of exposure and weights that best replicates the hedge fund strategies. Investors can gain market exposure to the factors identified by the analysis using a variety of liquid commonly traded financial instruments, such as index funds, exchange traded funds,[12] swaps, listed futures and option contracts. Any factor exposures and their respective weights can be updated periodically based on ongoing quantitative analysis through factor modelling. Figures 3.3 and 3.4 show the hypothetical and actual performance of the CS LAB index and a schematic of the LAB index construction process, respectively.

3.2.3 Hedge Fund Research

Hedge Fund Research (HFR, www.hedgefundresearch.com) produces over 100 indices of hedge fund performance ranging from industry-aggregate levels down to specific, focused areas of sub-strategy and regional investment. The HFRI Fund Weighted Composite Index, created in 1994, is one of the most widely used standards of global hedge fund

---

[12] Exchange traded funds (or ETFs) are a security that tracks an index, a commodity or a basket of assets like an index fund, but can be traded like a stock on an exchange.

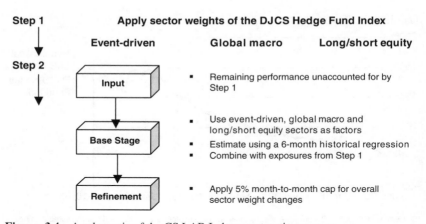

Figure 3.4 A schematic of the CS LAB Index construction process

Source: Reproduced by permission of Credit Suisse Asset Management, LLC

performance. The HFRI index is constructed using equally weighted composites of over 2,000 single-manager hedge funds reporting to the HFR database. The HFRI FoHF Index is another equally weighted index composite from the HFR database of over 800 FoHFs. Figure 3.5 shows the growth of $1,000 since the inception of the HFRI Fund Weighted Composite Index against several global industry indices.

Figure 3.5 The growth of $1,000 since inception of HFRI Fund Weighted Composite Index

Source: HFR

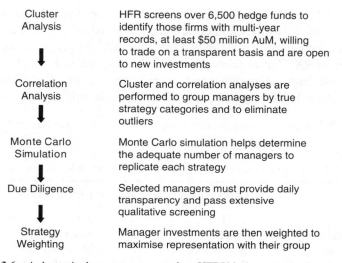

Cluster Analysis	HFR screens over 6,500 hedge funds to identify those firms with multi-year records, at least $50 million AuM, willing to trade on a transparent basis and are open to new investments
Correlation Analysis	Cluster and correlation analyses are performed to group managers by true strategy categories and to eliminate outliers
Monte Carlo Simulation	Monte Carlo simulation helps determine the adequate number of managers to replicate each strategy
Due Diligence	Selected managers must provide daily transparency and pass extensive qualitative screening
Strategy Weighting	Manager investments are then weighted to maximise representation with their group

Figure 3.6 A dynamic, bottom-up approach to HFRX index construction

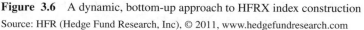

Source: HFR (Hedge Fund Research, Inc), © 2011, www.hedgefundresearch.com

Since 2003, HFR has also produced a range of investable HFRX indices constructed from a variety of quantitative methods, including multi-level screening, cluster analysis, Monte Carlo simulation and optimisation techniques to ensure each index is a unique representation of its investment criteria (see Figure 3.6). HFRX Indices are designed to offer full transparency, daily pricing and consistent fund selection, as well as stringent risk management and strict reporting standards.

HFRX indices use four constituent weighting methodologies and each strategy, sub-strategy and regional investment focus has a corresponding index. The four constituent weighting methodologies are defined as follows:

1. The *HFRX Global Hedge Fund Index* represents the overall composition of the hedge fund universe comprised of a range of hedge fund strategies, including but not limited to convertible arbitrage, distressed securities, equity hedge, equity market neutral, event-driven, macro, merger and relative value arbitrage. The underlying constituents and indices are asset weighted based on the distribution of assets in the hedge fund universe.
2. The *HFRX Equally Weighted Index* applies an equal weight to all selected constituents.

3. The *HFRX Absolute Return Index* incorporates hedge funds that exhibit low volatilities and correlations to standard directional benchmarks of equity market and hedge fund industry performance.
4. The *HFRX Market Directional Index* incorporates hedge funds that exhibit high volatilities and correlations to standard directional benchmarks of equity market and hedge fund industry performance.

Table 3.4 shows a summary comparison of the HFRI and HFRX indices.

Table 3.4 Summary comparison of the HFRI and HFRX indices

Category	HFRI monthly indices	HFRX indices
Created	1994	2003
Weighting	Equally	Index-specific
Reporting style	Net of all fees	Net of all fees
Index calculated	Three times a month: flash update (5th business day of the month), mid update (15th of the month) and an end update (1st business day of following month)	Monthly or daily
Index rebalanced	Monthly	Quarterly
Criteria for inclusion	Listing in HFR database; reports monthly net of all fees monthly performance and assets in US dollars	In addition to meeting HFRI criteria, funds must be open to new investment
Minimum asset size and/or track record for fund inclusion	$50 million or greater than a 12-month track record	$50 million and 24-month track record
Investable index	No	HFR Asset Management, LLC constructs investable products that track HFRX
Number of funds	Over 2000 in HFRI Fund Weighted Composite Over 800 in HFRI FoHFs Composite	Over 250 in total constituent universe

Source: HFR

Table 3.5   The family of HFN Indices

HFN index name	No. of indices
HFN Aggregate Indices	4
HFN UCITS III Indices	2
HFN Regional Indices	6
HFN Country Specific Indices	7
HFN Fund of Fund Indices	3
HFN Single Strategy Indices	26
Total	**48**

Source: HFN

3.2.4   HedgeFund.net

Hedge Fund.net (HFN) produces a series of equally weighted average performance indices for all those hedge funds that comprise a given strategy or grouping. HFN estimates are updated on a daily basis for the first 45 days after the end of the month as fund performance is reported throughout the month, after which the numbers become final. Currently HFN publish a total of 48 indices (see Table 3.5). HFN uses the 20 largest hedge funds that account for over 70% of hedge fund capital, and most of these 20 funds do not report returns to any other database other than HFN.

3.2.5   FTSE Hedge

Since December 1997, FTSE Hedge (www.ftse.com) has provided a series of global indices based on a detailed quantitative and qualitative screening process of over 8,000 hedge funds taken from the FTSE database. The indices give a daily measure of the aggregate risk and return characteristics of a broadly based global universe of investable hedge funds that allow a sound basis for the creation of liquid and structured investments within a high degree of transparency. For index inclusion, hedge funds must have a minimum of $50 million AuM along with audited accounts for the past 24 months. FTSE Hedge currently includes the FTSE Hedge Index, eight trading strategy indices (equity hedge, CTA, global macro, merger arbitrage, distressed securities, convertible arbitrage, equity arbitrage and fixed income relative value) and three management style indices (directional, event-driven and non-directional).

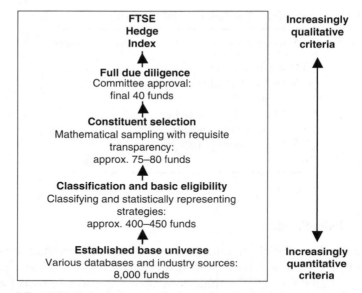

Figure 3.7 FTSE Hedge Index quantitative and qualitative index construction
Source: HFR (Hedge Fund Research, Inc), © 2011, www.hedgefundresearch.com

The construction methodology follows four main stages, namely a classification process, quantitative screening, statistical sampling and a due-diligence stage, as shown in Figure 3.7. In essence, the funds are classified into strategic categories within the FTSE Hedge Index, which results in around 400 funds remaining. These funds are then further screened by mathematical sampling, to ensure transparency, down to 80 funds. Finally, 40 hedge funds are selected, by an independent committee of leading market professionals, to make up the actual index.

3.2.5.1   FTSE Hedge Momentum Index

Since January 2000, FTSE Hedge has also produced the FTSE Hedge Momentum Index, an investment strategy index designed to outperform the underlying FTSE Hedge Index. All constituents of the FTSE Hedge Momentum Index are selected from the FTSE Hedge Index based on a strictly defined quality, liquidity and capacity criteria. By under- or overweighting the constituent funds in terms of whether they show persistent positive return (i.e. momentum), the index can be shown to outperform the FTSE Hedge Index. Indeed, over an eight-year period

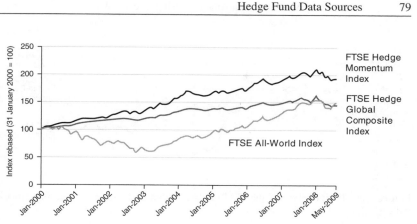

Figure 3.8   Performance of the FTSE Hedge Momentum Index (net asset value)
Source: HFR (Hedge Fund Research, Inc), © 2011, www.hedgefundresearch.com

the FTSE Hedge Momentum Index has returned a 9.4% annualised performance, representing a 2.1% outperformance over and above the FTSE Hedge Index (see Figure 3.8).

3.2.6   Greenwich Alternative Investments

First published in 1995, the Greenwich Alternative Investments (GAI, www.greenwichai.com) global hedge fund indices provide more than 22 years of risk and return history that represents both the overall hedge fund universe as well as various constituent groups of funds as defined by their investment strategies. The flagship index, the GAI Global Hedge Fund Index, is designed to reflect the dynamic nature of the hedge fund universe and does not have a fixed set of constituent funds. Instead, GAI attempts to include as many funds as possible, excluding all FoHFs, based on monthly returns data. Funds are not excluded on the basis of size, location, or other factors but must have a minimum track record of 3 months. Currently around 1,000 hedge funds are used to calculate the GAI Global Hedge Fund Index at month end. Figure 3.9 shows the monthly performance of the GAI Global over the past several years against several industry benchmarks.

Each hedge fund is categorised by investment strategy based on the information supplied by the fund manager and according to the GAI hedge fund strategy definitions. In 2004, four broad strategy groups were introduced in the GAI Global Hedge Fund Index, namely Market Neutral Group, Long/Short Equity Group, Directional Trading Group

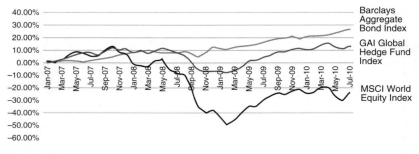

Figure 3.9 Performance of the GAI Global Hedge Fund Index versus benchmark indices

Source: HFR (Hedge Fund Research, Inc), © 2011, www.hedgefundresearch.com

and Specialty Strategies Group. In January 2010, ten regional indices were introduced as a result of an increasing number of funds focused exclusively on specific geographic regions. The indices were created in two sets, i.e. Developed Markets and Emerging Markets, with each set containing five indices, namely Composite, Global, Asia, Europe and Americas.

3.2.6.1   GAI Investable Indices

The GAI investable hedge fund indices are an additional series of hedge fund benchmarks designed to represent the expected performance of these investable hedge funds that are open and considered suitable for institutional investment. The GAI investable indices are designed to replicate the performance of the unique strategies of the hedge fund universe (see Figure 3.10).

The GAI global hedge fund indices form the basis for the construction of the GAI investable indices. Asset weights follow those of the GAI global hedge fund indices in order to most accurately represent the current asset allocation within the hedge fund index. The GAI investable indices provide sophisticated investors with an investable benchmark for the hedge fund industry designed to track the various strategies of the GAI Global Hedge Fund Indices. Table 3.6 shows the family of GAI investable indices along with their respective replicating performance index.

The hedge fund selection process begins with a quantitative review of the performance of all the funds in the GAI Global Hedge Fund Index.

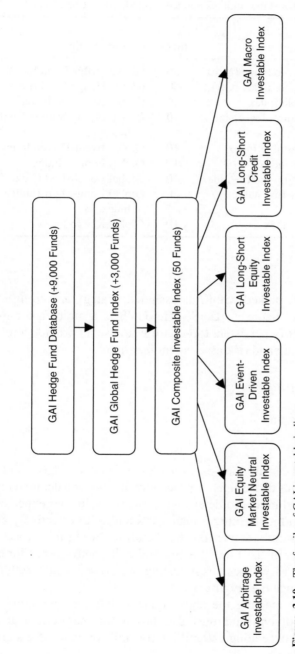

Figure 3.10 The family of GAI investable indices

Source: GAI

Table 3.6 GAI investable indices and associated replicating index

GAI investable index name	No. of funds	GAI replicating index
Composite Investable Index (Mth)	50	Global Hedge Fund Index
Composite Investable Index (Qtr)	50	Global Hedge Fund Index
Arbitrage Investable Index	10	Global Arbitrage Index
Equity Market Neutral Investable Index	10	Global Equity Market Neutral Index
Event-Driven Investable Index	10	Global Event-Driven Index
Futures Investable Index	10	Global Futures Index
Long-Short Credit Investable Index	10	Global Long-Short Credit Index
Long-Short Equity Investable Index	20	Global Long-Short Equity Index
Macro Investable Index	10	Global Macro Index

Source: GAI

Each one is then ranked within its assigned strategy according to the Greenwich Value Score™ (GVS). The GVS is a multi-factor model designed to identify persistent top-quartile funds and provide a relative performance rating and risk assessment based on:

- risk adjusted performance,
- volatility,
- downside risk, and
- correlations.

Potential candidates are then examined on a qualitative basis and subjected to a rigorous due-diligence procedure, including a detailed review of the hedge fund model to determine strategy, style, and expected returns whilst also highlighting a manager's ability to effectively create alpha and consistently deliver positive returns. During this process, an in-depth analysis of the fund strategy and risk control procedures are also undertaken as well as stress testing at various points within the fund's performance (see Figure 3.11).

In addition to meeting the above quantitative and qualitative processes, the constituent fund must also have a minimum one-year track record and AuM exceeding $50 million (overall company assets greater than $100 million).

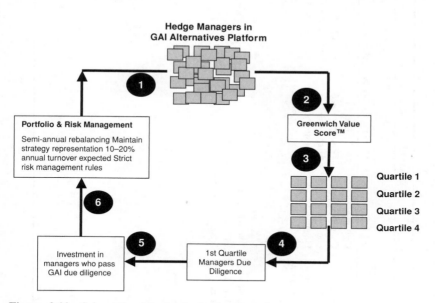

Figure 3.11   Schematic of the fund selection process
Source: GAI

3.2.7   Morningstar Alternative Investment Center

(*http://alternativeinvestments.morningstar.com*)

In September 2008, Morningstar acquired the Morgan Stanley Capital International (MSCI) Hedge Fund Index family and agreed to use their industry-leading categorisation and index construction methodology. The Morningstar MSCI Hedge Fund Indexes currently consist of over 190 indices.

3.2.7.1   MSCI Hedge Fund Classification Standard

In July 2002, MSCI launched the MSCI Hedge Fund Classification Standard (HFCS), one of the most comprehensive hedge fund classification models to date. The HFCS uses three primary characteristics, namely the hedge fund investment style, asset class and geography, in order to classify funds and define hedge fund strategies. In addition, secondary characteristics are defined through the Global Industry Classification Standard (GICS), and cover capitalisation size for equity-oriented strategies, and fixed income focus for credit-oriented strategies (see Table 3.7). The investment process determines the approach

Table 3.7 MSCI primary and secondary characteristics breakdown

Primary characteristics					Secondary characteristics		
Investment process		Asset class	Geography		GICS sector	Fixed income sector	Market cap
Process group	Process		Area	Region			
Directional Trading	Discretionary	Commodities	**Developed Markets**	Europe	Consumer Discr.	Asset-Backed	Small
	Tactical	Convertibles		Japan	Consumer Staples	Gov. Sponsored	Small & Mid Cap
	Systematic	Currencies		North America	Energy	High Yield	Mid & Large Cap
	Multi-Process	Equity		Pacific ex Japan	Financial	Investment Grade	No Size Focus
		Fixed Income		Diversified	Health Care	Mortgage-Backed	
		Diversified			Industrials	Sovereign	
Relative Value	Arbitrage		**Emerging Markets**	EMEA	IT	No Sector Focus	
	Merger Arb.			Asia Pacific	Materials		
	Statistical Arb.			Latin America	Telecom Services		
	Multi-Process			Diversified	Utilities		
Security Selection	Long Bias		**Global Markets**	Europe	No Industry Focus		
	No Bias			Asia ex Japan			
	Short Bias			Asia			
	Variable Bias			Diversified			
Specialist Credit	Credit Trading						
	Distressed						
	Private						
	Multi-Process						
Multi-Process Group	Event Driven						
	Multi-Process						

Source: MSCI

Hedge Fund Composite Indices					Weighting
					Asset & Equal
Process Group	**Process Group**	**Process Group**	**Process Group**	**Process Group**	Asset & Equal
Directional Trading	Relative Value	Security Selection	Specialist Credit	Multi-Process	
Investment Process	**Investment Process**	**Investment Process**	**Investment Process**	**Investment Process**	Equal
Discretionary Trading Tactical Allocation Systematic Trading Multi-Process	Arbitrage Merger Arbitrage Statistical Arbitrage Multi-Process	Long Bias No Bias Short Bias Variable Bias	Distressed Securities Long-Short Credit Private Placements Multi-Process	Event Driven Multi-Process	
Strategy Indices	**Strategy Indices**	**Strategy Indices**	**Strategy Indices**	**Strategy Indices**	Equal

Figure 3.12 The MSCI Hedge Fund Index classification structure
Source: MSCI

fund managers use to select investments in order to generate returns and manage risk. They are grouped into five broad categories, or investment process groups i.e. Directional Trading, Relative Value, Security Selection, Specialist Credit and Multi-Process. The indices are equal weighted at all four levels of aggregation and asset weighted at the two highest levels as can be seen in Figure 3.12.

Classification schemes attempt to group hedge funds based on their strategy and characteristics; however, such meaningful groupings are challenging due to the inherent heterogeneity of hedge fund investing. Such diversification does not allow the development of a simple group-based system and any classification is likely to be subject to a large degree of subjectivity. The MSCI HFCS attempts to overcome this problem by attempting to capture the multi-dimensional nature of hedge fund investing through the use of primary and secondary characteristics, as described above, to more accurately and effectively identify and define hedge fund strategies. The MSCI HFCS strives to offer a balance between a suitable level of detail which permits an accurate classification of a large number of strategies whilst also allowing an intuitive understanding of its interpretation and implementation.

3.2.7.2 MSCI Investable Indices

In addition to the family of MSCI hedge fund indices, MSCI developed an index construction methodology aimed at building a range of MSCI investable hedge fund indices. The idea was to develop a set of replicable and tradable hedge fund indices reflecting the aggregate performance of a diversified range of hedge fund strategies. Such objectives require that the investable hedge fund indices are based on well-diversified managed platforms offering more frequent pricing and liquidity than otherwise possible.

An investable hedge fund reference framework (HFRF) is designed to establish which hedge fund investment processes and strategies will be represented in the investable index. The HFRF is further supplemented by a series of index calculation, maintenance rules and guidelines relating to segment diversification, fund eligibility, concentration, investment capacity and fund and segment weight allocation. The MSCI Hedge Fund Composite Index (HFCI) is used as a proxy for the hedge fund universe. The HFCI is an equally weighted index that measures the performance of a diverse portfolio of hedge funds (AuM greater than $15 million) across the range of available investment strategies. Figure 3.13 shows a schematic of the MSCI investable index construction methodology.

A review of the investable hedge fund index is conducted on a quarterly basis where funds are added or deleted and adjustments made to the constituent weights for available investment capacity. Segment weights are also realigned to the HFRF and checked to ensure that they still adhere to the general index construction and maintenance principles.

3.2.8   EDHEC Risk and Asset Management Research Centre (*www.edhec-risk.com*)

As detailed above, the different hedge fund indices available in the market conform to a range of selection criteria and are developed through a variety of construction methodologies attached to various commercial databases. With such inherent heterogeneity in the hedge fund industry, investors cannot rely on competing hedge fund indices to obtain a *true and fair* representation of hedge fund performance. As a response to this lack of representativeness and *purity* in the hedge fund industry, EDHEC Risk and Asset Management Research Centre (EDHEC) introduced a novel *index of indexes* idea to overcome the problem. Such *alternative indices* were first discussed in an EDHEC working paper by Amenc and Martellini (2003) who argued that, due to the impossibility of ascertaining the *best* index available on the market, a better construction method would be to use a combination of competing indices to determine a more robust and representative industry benchmark. Since competing indices are based on different sets of hedge funds in their

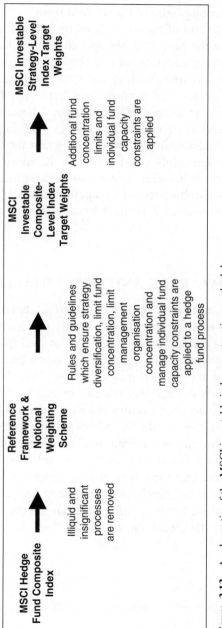

Figure 3.13 A schematic of the MSCI investable index construction methodology

Source: MSCI

composition, the resulting portfolio of indices must be more exhaustive than any of the competing indices it is derived from.

EDHEC uses a method of factor analysis to develop a set of hedge fund indices that are the best possible one-dimensional summaries of information within the competing indices for a given investment style. Mathematically, this involves finding the first component[13] of competing indices using historical performance data. The first principal component has a built-in element of *optimality*,[14] because there is no other linear combination of competing indices that implies a lower information loss. Indeed, information is lost when the heterogeneity in the competing hedge funds construction is the most severe. Since such indices are affected in different ways by measurement biases, determining the linear combination of competing indices that implies a maximisation of the variance explained leads implicitly to a minimisation of the bias.

3.3   DATABASE AND INDEX BIASES

Hedge funds report monthly returns to commercial databases on a voluntary basis. Such participation means that only a portion of the hedge fund universe is observable and represented. For example, hedge fund managers will tend to report to databases only when their performance is good and may stop reporting if it deteriorates. This effect ultimately creates a variety of bias in databases which can lead to vendors publishing misleading and incomplete return statistics. Such a problem does not occur in the mutual fund industry, where public disclosure of NAVs is enforceable by law, causing a natural convergence of the universe and database of mutual funds. However, it is well known that hedge fund performance data and their benchmarks inherit measurement biases from the databases on which they are based. As a consequence, it is particularly important to be completely aware of the origin and the consequence of potential measurement biases.

---

[13] Such an analysis usually involves applying the method of principal component analysis (PCA).

[14] The term *optimal* as used here means stable, more representative, easy to replicate, non-commercial and with fewer biases.

3.3.1 Survivorship Bias

If a database contains only information on funds that are active and report regularly to a database (i.e. *live* funds), then a *survivorship bias* can be introduced into calculated performance measures and indices constructed from such data. It is, however, important to distinguish between funds that have simply exited a database (i.e. *defunct* funds) and those that have ceased operation altogether due to bankruptcy or liquidation (i.e. *dead* funds). A defunct fund is a fund that was in a database but ceases to report information to the vendor for whatever reason (e.g. merger); a dead fund is one that is known to have terminated operations and closed down completely. Clearly, a dead fund must also be a defunct fund, but a defunct fund need not necessarily be a dead fund. Other funds that are defunct but not dead are those that have reached their capacity and no longer require additional capital or need to attract new investors. Moreover, a fund manager may believe their performance is so good that their investment style must remain private and no longer wish to provide sensitive information to a database that may be publicly available.

The effect of survivorship bias has been well known in the mutual fund industry for some time and is fairly straightforward to determine. The standard method of determining survivorship bias, first proposed by Malkiel (1995), is to obtain the universe of all mutual funds that are active during a given time period. The average return of all funds is compared with that of the surviving funds at the end of the period. The return difference is *survivorship bias*. However, survivorship bias in hedge funds cannot be measured directly because the universe of hedge funds is not readily observable. Survivorship bias can only be estimated using a sample of hedge funds in a database. Technically, over any sample period, if a complete record of defunct funds is available, survivorship bias can be estimated through tedious data manipulation. The problem lies in verifying the completeness of historical records on defunct hedge funds. The magnitude of the survivorship bias generally depends on two parameters, namely

- the attrition rate[15] and
- the average returns difference between surviving and dead funds.

---

[15] The *attrition rate* is the percentage of hedge funds that fail over a given time period, e.g. a year.

The hedge fund industry is all too aware that the exclusion of a fund from a database can lead to an upward bias in hedge fund returns and an understated historical risk. Xu *et al.* (2009) studied a major commercial database of hedge funds from January 1994 to March 2009 and found that hedge fund returns were generally much worse than the industry would have us believe since many failing funds stopped reporting their performance. The gap in returns between these failing funds and others averaged 0.54% a month, or about 6% per annum. This is an extremely high figure and suggests that average reported hedge fund returns set an unrealistic expectation for hedge fund investors.

When considering defunct funds, there exists another type of bias, namely *liquidation bias*. This is a result of the fund ceasing to report hedge fund performance to the database several months prior to the final liquidation value of the fund whilst they concentrate on winding down their operations. This generally causes an upward bias in the returns of defunct funds. The opposite of liquidation bias is *participation bias*. This bias can occur when a successful hedge fund manager closes the fund and stops reporting results because they no longer need to attract new capital.

Another related concept to survivorship bias, and again a result of voluntary reporting, is *self-selection bias*. Funds not performing well can hide bad results in order to avoid investors withdrawing their money, whereas funds performing well may wish to protect their investment strategies and stop the inflow of capital by ceasing to report and closing the fund. In fact, some hedge fund managers choose to be included in a database, period by period, depending on the fund's performance.[16] The fact that hedge fund managers can choose when to participate in the database leads to a self-selection bias. Such a bias is almost impossible to determine, let alone measure.

3.3.2   Instant History Bias

For many databases, there is often a sizeable lag between a fund's inception date and the date at which the fund returns are submitted to a particular database. This time lag typically corresponds to the hedge fund incubation period (12–18 months) where the performance of the fund is evaluated using *seed* investment before being publicly offered

---

[16] Many hedge fund index compilers prohibit this practice and insist that managers regularly and punctually submit performance data in order to be considered for inclusion in an index.

to investors in order to attract further capital. Once a manager is in a position to submit attractive performance data to a database, they naturally choose the start date that shows the hedge fund in the most positive light. The database vendor introduces an *instant history bias* into the data when they decide to *backfill* data to show the historic performance of the hedge fund even though such data was not available when the database was established. Clearly, such funds are likely to be those that offer higher returns and therefore backfilled data will invariably inflate the performance of the fund in the earlier days. Different databases handle the issue of backfilling data differently, and as a result, the impact of this bias varies between vendors. To reduce or avoid this bias some databases do not backfill returns at all. Others backfill only a few months, in any event, performance returns obtained from databases should be handled with care.

3.4 BENCHMARKING

The development of traditional indices rests on the assumptions that the underlying instruments are homogeneous, and that an investor follows a simple *buy and hold* strategy. Traditional indices are constructed to represent the return of the *market portfolio*, an asset-weighted combination of all investable instruments in that asset class or a suitably equivalent proxy. These indices are designed to directly define the risk premium available to investors willing to expose themselves to the systematic risk of the asset class. For example, an investor buying the Dow Jones will be exposed to a broad range of market risks based on 30 US large cap equities, i.e. there exists a general equilibrium model. However, such a model is still absent from the hedge fund world. In the early years of hedge funds, investment committees established a type of hedge fund performance indicator based on the idea of an *absolute return*, loosely defined as a flat rate of return obtainable under any market condition (i.e. 14% per annum) with no reference to a market average or *peer* group measure. As the market became more complex and competitive for hedge fund managers, benchmarking to an absolute return in its purest sense has become practically impossible. Hedge fund managers naturally focus their efforts on liquid markets, where trading opportunities and leverage are readily available. Thus, as the dynamics in the global markets change, the nature of hedge funds in the market also changes. Benchmarking such a dynamic industry in itself is an arduous task, and the difficulty is further exemplified by the fact that the hedge funds that constitute the benchmarks are drawn from a sample of funds managed by managers with diverse investment styles. For this reason, investors are increasingly relying on a range of hedge fund indices, as discussed above, along with their inadequacies, as their primary method of benchmarking. Benchmarking with an index only makes sense if the index is representative, rule-based, fully investable, transparent, diversified, reported in a timely manner, and liquid.

Having a reliable benchmarking system is one of the biggest challenges that institutional investors face when selecting and evaluating hedge fund managers and their returns. Most institutional investors are interested in analysing how hedge fund strategies correlate with and compare to broad market indices for portfolio construction, optimisation and asset allocation purposes. As the hedge fund industry matures and becomes ever more driven by large institutional investment, benchmarking will surely be an ever-increasing active process.

3.4.1 Tracking Error

The *tracking error* is a measure of how closely a portfolio follows the index to which it is benchmarked. The lower the tracking error, the more the fund resembles its benchmark's risk and return characteristics. In all cases, the benchmark is the measured position of *neutrality* for the hedge fund manager. If a manager were to simply follow the benchmark, the expectation would be that their performance should equal the performance of the benchmark, and their tracking error should be zero. The most common measure of tracking error is the difference in the return earned by a portfolio and the return earned by the benchmark against which the portfolio is constructed. For example, if a particular hedge fund earns a return of 9.15% during a period when the particular benchmark produces a return of 9.07%, the tracking error is 0.08%, or 8 basis points.

Tracking error may be calculated from historical performance data or estimated based on future returns. The former is called *ex-post* and the latter *ex-ante* tracking error. Mathematically, tracking error (TE) can be defined in terms of the standard deviation (SD), such that

$$TE = \sqrt{\frac{1}{N-1} \sum_{i=1}^{N} \left(r_{N-1,N} - r_{N-1,N}^{bm} \right)^2}. \qquad (3.1)$$

where N is the total number of sample data points, $r_{N-1,N}$ is the hedge fund return and $r_{N-1,N}^{bm}$ is the benchmark return. Many practitioners have

Table 3.8 Calculating of the tracking error using both the quadratic and linear methods

	A	B	C	D	E	F	G
		Hedge Fund	**Benchmark**				
1							
2	**Date**	**RoR (%)**	**RoR (%)**	**Tracking Error**			
3	Jul-09			Quadratic (SD)	12.58	=fncTESD(B4:B65,C4:C65)	
4	Aug-09	18.15	0.94	Linear (MAD)	8.67	=fncTEMAD(B4:B65,C4:C65)	
5	Sep-09	6.50	1.40				
6	Oct-09	11.22	3.86				
7	Nov-09	8.95	3.25				
8	Dec-09	10.60	-2.53				
9	Jan-10	-2.10	1.89				
10	Feb-10	-0.73	-1.91				
60	Apr-09	-14.32	5.31				
61	May-09	9.27	0.02				
62	Jun-10	-4.85	7.41				
63	Jul-10	-5.35	3.36				
64	Aug-10	-1.08	3.57				
65	Sep-10	9.08	2.30				

argued that the quadratic form of the *TE* is difficult to interpret, and that hedge fund managers generally think in terms of linear and not quadratic deviations from a benchmark. In this case, *TE* in terms of mean absolute deviations (*MAD*) can be used which is written as

$$MAD = \frac{1}{N-1} \sum_{i=1}^{N} \left| r_{N-1,N} - r_{N-1,N}^{bm} \right|. \quad (3.2)$$

Table 3.8 shows an example of calculating the tracking error using both the quadratic (*SD*) and linear (*MAD*) methods for a time series of monthly hedge fund and benchmark returns. Source 3.1 shows the user-defined VBA functions for both tracking error models.

Source 3.1   User-defined VBA functions to calculate the two tracking errors against a benchmark

'function to calculate TRACKING ERROR using STANDARD DEVIATION (SD)
Function fncTESD(RoR As Range, BMR As Range) As Double

```
'initialise n, sum to zero
N = 0
sum = 0
```

```vba
'count returns in arrays
N = RoR.Count
M = BMR.Count

'check for N = M i.e. same number of
returns in both arrays
If N <> M Then
   MsgBox "Invalid returns array",
vbExclamation, "Error Message"
End If

For i = 1 To N
  sum = sum + (RoR(i) - BMR(i)) ^ 2
Next

fncTESD = Sqr((1 / (N - 1)) * sum)

End Function

'function to calculate TRACKING ERROR
using MEAN ABSOLUTE DEVIATION (MAD)
Function fncTEMAD(RoR As Range, BMR As Range) As
 Double

'initialise n, sum to zero
N = 0
sum = 0

'count returns in arrays
N = RoR.Count
M = BMR.Count

'check for N = M i.e. same number of returns
 in both arrays
If N <> M Then
   MsgBox "Invalid returns array",
vbExclamation, "Error Message"
End If
```

```
For i = 1 To N
  sum = sum + Abs(RoR(i) - BMR(i))
Next

fncTEMAD = (1 / (N - 1)) * sum

End Function
```

In this chapter we have discussed the major hedge fund databases available in the market and the range of products they offer. We have highlighted the fact that the hedge fund universe is highly heterogeneous, which makes the construction of a useful market index that comprises the available hedge fund universe extremely difficult. Moreover, the issues relating to the variety of ways in which hedge funds report to commercial databases create a range of data biases which can lead to vendors publishing misleading and incomplete performance measures. Non-investable hedge fund indices try to represent the performance of a sample of the hedge fund universe taken from a particular database; however, such vendors have diverse selection criteria and methods of index construction, leading to many differently published indices. More recently, many index providers have developed investable indices that offer a low-cost investment and exposure to the hedge fund industry. Nevertheless, one should be fully aware of the limitations and constraints before accepting a particular index has a valued industry benchmark.

Over the past three chapters we have covered the fundamentals and key issues related to the hedge fund industry. In the following chapters we will build and develop a quantitative and theoretical approach to modelling and analysing hedge funds. Chapter 4 begins this process by introducing the main statistical methods and techniques available to hedge fund managers.

APPENDIX A: WEIGHTING SCHEMES

When measuring the performance of a portfolio of hedge funds or an average of a group of funds, it is necessary to assign a particular weight to each of the individual funds. There are three major weighting schemes used in the industry, namely *equal*, *asset* and *arbitrary* weightings. Table A.1 gives an illustration of how the use of different weighting schemes

Table A.1 The performance of a hedge fund group based on different weighting schemes

	A	B	C	D	E	F	G	H	I
1					Weighting				
2	Fund	Monthly Return	Monthly NAV ($m)	Equal	Arbitrary	Asset			
3	A	5.19%	2150	1/4	30%	66.01%	=C3/C7		
4	B	12.65%	750	1/4	30%	23.03%			
5	C	-11.32%	245	1/4	28%	7.52%			
6	D	-1.02%	112	1/4	12%	3.44%			
7			3257	100%	100%	100%	=SUM(F3:F6)		
8									
9			Group Performance	1.38%	2.06%	5.45%	=SUMPRODUCT(F3:F6,B3:B6)		
10									

can give rise to varying values for the performance of a group of hedge funds.

A.1 EQUAL

If there are N hedge funds in the group of funds, then each fund return has an equal weight, w_i, in the average that is given by

$$w_i = \frac{1}{N}. \qquad (A.1)$$

The average is a measure of the average behaviour of the fund returns irrespective of the amount of AuM (or *market capitalisation*) of each hedge fund.

A.2 ASSET

Each hedge fund return is weighted with respect to the amount of AuM in proportion to the total assets managed within the group of funds, i.e. dollar-weighted averages. If a particular fund i has AuM denoted by A_i, then the weight of fund i in the average is given by

$$w_i = \frac{A_i}{\sum_{i=1}^{N} A_i}. \qquad (A.2)$$

A.3 ARBITRARY

Each hedge fund return is given an arbitrary weight w_i within the average which can be changed over time. However, the total of all the arbitrary weights must always sum to 100%. For example, suppose we have N

hedge funds in a group where the return on fund i is denoted by r_i and respective weight w_i. Then a performance measurement (or index) for the group can be determined as the weighted average of the individual hedge fund returns, such that:

$$r_{\text{index}} = \sum_{i=1}^{N} w_i r_i. \qquad (A.3)$$

4

Statistical Analysis

In order for hedge fund managers (and investors) to make informed investment decisions it is essential that a range of statistical analyses and investigations are performed. This will usually involve analysing a time series of monthly returns (or NAVs) to ascertain relevant properties of the data in order to make critical inference about the characteristics and performance of the hedge fund. Many visual and mathematical methods are available that allow hedge fund managers to understand the underlying data structure and identify potential anomalies that may need further investigation whilst also allowing them to make better informed decisions. It is also important for a serious investor or hedge fund manager to have a working knowledge of many of the probability and statistical concepts encountered in the industry so as to be confident and knowledgeable when explaining their investment strategies to potential investors.

This chapter covers the main concepts, principles and techniques employed in the statistical analysis of hedge fund returns. Both visual and theoretical methods are presented which show how to extract and interpret the informational content and underlying characteristics within a time series of hedge fund returns.

4.1 BASIC PERFORMANCE PLOTS

4.1.1 Value Added Monthly Index

Table 4.1 shows a time series of hypothetical monthly[1] returns for a CTA index between 2005 and 2010, i.e. a total of 72 individual positive and negative monthly returns. Extracting any valuable information from the table is practically impossible with such a relatively large time series. However, a simple plot of the monthly returns gives an instant snapshot of the historical performance of the CTA index, as shown in Figure 4.1.

---

[1] Some hedge funds provide weekly returns, but monthly returns are the most common and have been adopted throughout this book.

Table 4.1   Monthly returns (%) for a hypothetical CTA index, 2005–2010

	Jan	Feb	Mar	Apr	May	June	July	Aug	Sept	Oct	Nov	Dec
2005	-0.74	1.45	0.74	1.29	0.24	-0.51	1.57	2.01	0.33	-0.42	-0.29	3.00
2006	-0.87	0.81	1.83	2.17	1.18	-1.94	3.10	0.80	2.24	0.03	-3.40	1.84
2007	1.27	4.20	2.41	-0.20	-0.63	0.29	2.49	3.47	1.00	1.45	-2.10	0.37
2008	1.63	-0.36	-0.44	4.44	0.70	1.73	1.47	1.66	-0.42	-1.03	1.66	1.07
2009	2.50	0.26	2.45	2.23	-0.03	1.60	0.78	2.43	2.37	-0.70	-1.34	2.02
2010	1.89	-0.25	0.13	0.75	0.15	0.53	1.87	-1.43	1.35	0.57	-1.67	0.46

The value-added monthly index (VAMI) is an index that shows the monthly performance of a hypothetical $100 investment[2] based on the monthly returns of a hedge fund. The current month's VAMI is given by:

$$\text{Current VAMI} = (1 + \text{Current Monthly Return}) \times \text{Previous VAMI}.$$
$$(4.1)$$

Table 4.2 shows the calculation of the VAMI for a $100 initial investment for the hypothetical CTA index between 2005 and 2010. The subsequent VAMI plot is shown in Figure 4.2. It is straightforward to read off the final value of the $100 investment in the CTA index over the five year period i.e. $183.03, however, it does not tell us much about the performance of the index since 2005.

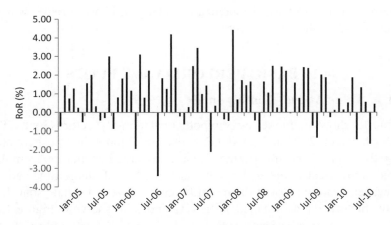

Figure 4.1   Monthly returns for a hypothetical CTA index, 2005–2010

---

[2] Some hedge fund managers prefer to use $1,000 instead of $100 for the initial value.

Table 4.2 VAMI for a hypothetical CTA index of monthly returns, 2005–2010

	A	B	C	D	E	F
1		**CTA Index**				
2	**Date**	**RoR (%)**	**VAMI ($)**			
3			100			
4	Jan-05	-0.74	99.26	=(1+(B4/100))*C3		
5	Feb-05	1.45	100.70			
6	Mar-05	0.74	101.45			
7	Apr-05	1.29	102.76			
8	May-05	0.24	103.00			
9	Jun-05	-0.51	102.47			
10	Jul-05	1.57	104.08			
11	Aug-05	2.01	106.18			
70	Jul-10	1.87	184.44			
71	Aug-10	-1.43	181.79			
72	Sep-10	1.35	184.25			
73	Oct-10	0.57	185.29			
74	Nov-10	-1.67	182.20			
75	Dec-10	0.46	183.03			

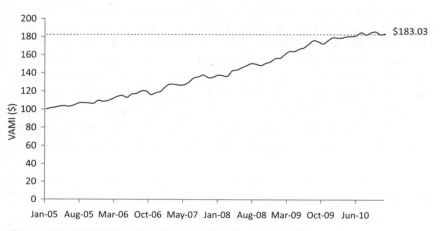

Figure 4.2 VAMI for a hypothetical CTA index, 2005–2010

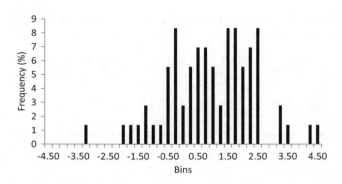

Figure 4.3   Histogram of a hypothetical CTA index of monthly returns, 2005–2010

4.1.2   Histograms

A histogram is a graphical summary of the frequency distribution of a set of *empirical data*,[3] for example as a time series of monthly hedge fund returns (or NAVs).[4] The frequency is an absolute value in which each value represents the actual count of the number of occurrences of a particular value in a group of data. Relative frequencies involve *normalising* the frequencies through division of the absolute frequency by the total number of observations in the group of data. A typical histogram for a time series of monthly hedge fund returns is shown in Figure 4.3. Table 4.3 shows the calculations required in order to transform the series of monthly hedge fund returns into a set of values that can be represented by a histogram. Using two user-defined VBA functions (fncMAXIMUM() and fncMINIMUM() as shown in Source 4.1), the maximum and minimum values of the monthly returns can be determined: 4.44% and –3.40%, respectively. Using these values, it is possible to set a range that encompasses all the monthly returns in the data set. This range is then divided into equal intervals (or *bins*) and an absolute frequency determined for each number of values that fall within each bin using the FREQUENCY()[5] function. Once the absolute values have been determined, a relative frequency can be calculated using the

---

[3] *Empirical data* are data gained by means of a series of observations or by experiment. Empirical measures are those determined from observed values, as opposed to those calculated using theoretical models.

[4] A set of NAV figures can easily be converted into a series of returns using $r_{t_1,t_2} = (NAV_{t_2} - NAV_{t_1})/NAV_{t_1}$, where r_{t_1,t_2} is the return on the fund between any time t_1 and t_2 ($t_2 > t_1$).

[5] The FREQUENCY() function calculates how often values occur within a range of values, and then returns a vertical array of numbers. Note that FREQUENCY() is an array-based formula,

Table 4.3 Calculations for the histogram of a hypothetical CTA index of monthly returns, 2005–2010

	A	B	C	D	E	F
1			Max.	4.44	=fncMAXIMUM(B5:B76)	
2			Min.	-3.40	=fncMINIMUM(B5:B76)	
3		CTA Index		Absolute	Relative	
4	Date	RoR (%)	Bins	Frequency	Frequency (%)	
5	Jan-05	-0.74	-4.50	0	0	
6	Feb-05	1.45	-4.25	0	=(D5/$D$42)*100	
7	Mar-05	0.74	=C5+0.25	0	0	
8	Apr-05	1.29	-3.75	0	0	
9	May-05	0.24	-3.50	{=FREQUENCY(B5:B76,C5:C41)}		
10	Jun-05	-0.51	-3.25			
11	Jul-05	1.57	-3.00	0	0	
39	Nov-07	-2.10	4.00	0	0	
40	Dec-07	0.37	4.25	1	1	
41	Jan-08	1.63	4.50	1	1	
42	Feb-08	-0.36	Sum	72	100	=SUM(E5:E41)
43	Mar-08	-0.44		=SUM(D5:D41)		
44	Apr-08	4.44				
75	Nov-10	-1.67				
76	Dec-10	0.46				

total number of data points (i.e. 72) and a subsequent histogram of the frequency distribution plotted.

The histogram is a very useful representation of the complete set of monthly returns over the five-year period; it gives a good indication of the shape of the distribution and highlights areas of high negative and positive returns.

Source 4.1 User-defined VBA functions to calculate the minimum and maximum values of a returns array

```
'function to calculate the MINIMUM value of a
returns array
Function fncMINIMUM(RoR As Range) As Double

'initialise n, min to zero
   n = 0
   Min = 0
```

meaning that the combination keystroke CTRL + SHIFT + ENTER must be used to fill the vertical array with numbers.

```
 'count returns array
 n = RoR.Count

 'determine maximum return in array
 For i = 1 To n
  If RoR(i) < Min Then
     Min = RoR(i)
  End If
 Next

 fncMINIMUM = Min

End Function

'function to calculate the MAXIMUM value of a
returns array
Function fncMAXIMUM(RoR As Range) As Double

 'initialise max to zero
 Max = 0

 'count returns array
 n = RoR.Count

 'determine maximum return in array
 For i = 1 To n
   If RoR(i) > Max Then
     Max = RoR(i)
   End If
 Next

 fncMAXIMUM = Max

End Function
```

Table 4.4   The discrete probability distribution for the random variable X

Number of heads	Probability
0	$^1/_4$
1	$^1/_2$
2	$^1/_4$
Total probability	**1**

4.2   PROBABILITY DISTRIBUTIONS

In order to understand probability distributions, it is important to understand what is meant by a *random variable*. When a numerical value of a variable is determined by an unknown (or *chance*) event, that variable is said to be *random*. Random variables can be either *discrete* or *continuous*. For example, suppose an experiment consists of flipping a coin six times and recording the number of heads that appear after each toss. The number of heads results from a *random process* (i.e. flipping the coin) and the actual number recorded is a value between 0 and 6, i.e. a *finite* integer value. Therefore, the number of heads is said to be a *discrete* random variable. Now suppose the same experiment is performed, but the *average* number of heads after flipping the coin an *infinite* number of times is recorded. The average number of heads again results from a random process; however, the actual number recorded can now be any value between 0 and 1, i.e. an infinite number of values. In this case, the average number of heads after a given number of coin flips is said to be a *continuous* random variable.

A *probability distribution* describes all the possible values that a random variable can take within a given range. Probability distributions can also be discrete or continuous. For example, consider an experiment in which a coin is flipped twice and let a random variable[6] X represent the number of heads (H) that occur. The four possible outcomes to this experiment are HH, HT, TH and TT so the discrete random variable X can only have values 0, 1 or 2. That is, the experiment can be described by a discrete probability distribution as shown in Table 4.4.

---

[6] Generally a random variable is denoted by an uppercase letter, e.g. X, and the possible values of the random variable denoted by lowercase letters, e.g. $\{x_1, x_2, x_3\}$.

A continuous probability distribution differs from a discrete probability distribution in that the probability that a continuous random variable will equal a certain value is always zero. That is, the continuous random variable can take on an infinite number values. As a result, continuous probability distributions cannot be expressed in tabular form (as in Table 4.4) but have to be described in terms of a mathematical function known as a probability density function (PDF). However, before looking at such density functions, it is worth taking the time to understand the difference between populations and samples when discussing probability distributions and associated statistical measures.

4.2.1   Populations and Samples

A *population* includes every element from a set of possible observations (i.e. the entire data set), whereas a *sample* consists only of those elements drawn from the population. Depending on the sampling method, it is possible to derive any number of samples from a population (see Figure 4.4). Furthermore, a statistical measure associated with a population, such as mean or standard deviation, is known as a *parameter*; but a statistical measure associated with a particular sample of the population is called a *statistic*. However, most statistical measures in the finance world, although determined from samples of data, are often referred to as parameters.

A sampling method is the process of selecting a sample from the population. When considering random sampling, several properties must hold, for example:

- the population consists of N elements;
- the random sample consists of n elements; and
- all random samples of n elements are equally likely to occur.

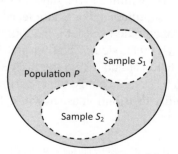

Figure 4.4   Several samples can be taken from the population of the data set

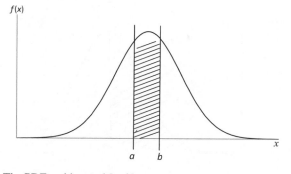

Figure 4.5 The PDF and interval $[a, b]$

Adhering to the above properties ensures that the chosen random sample is representative of the total population and that any statistical assumptions made about the random sample will be valid.[7]

4.3 PROBABILITY DENSITY FUNCTION

Given a continuous random variable, X, the PDF[8] of X is a function $f(x)$ such that for two numbers, a and b with $a \le b$, we have:

$$P(a \le X \le b) = \int_a^b f(x)dx. \qquad (4.2)$$

Where $f(x) \ge 0$ for all x. Thus, the PDF of a continuous random variable is a function which when integrated over the limits a to b, gives the probability that the random variable will have a value within that given interval (or *domain*). More formally, the probability that X is a value within the interval $[a, b]$ equals the area under the PDF from a to b (see Figure 4.5).

As with discrete probability distributions, the total probability for a continuous probability distribution must also be one. Also, the total area

---

[7] Although the sample may be subject to a *bias* compared with the population.

[8] The probability density function is also known as the probability distribution function, the probability mass function or density function.

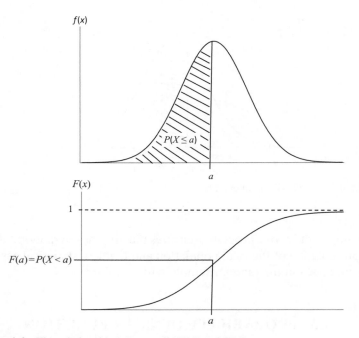

Figure 4.6   The relationship between the PDF and CDF

under the PDF is always equal to one:

$$\int_{-\infty}^{\infty} f(x)dx = 1. \tag{4.3}$$

4.4   CUMULATIVE DISTRIBUTION FUNCTION

The cumulative distribution function (CDF) describes the probability that a random variable X with a given probability distribution will be found at a value less than or equal to x. The CDF is a function $F(x)$ of a random variable, X, for a number x, such that

$$F(x) = P(X \leq x) = \int_{-\infty}^{x} f(s)ds. \tag{4.4}$$

That is, for a given value x, $F(x)$ is the probability that the observed value of X will be at most x. Figure 4.6 shows the relationship between a typical PDF and CDF.

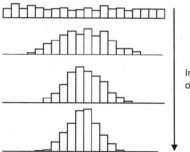

Figure 4.7   The central limit theorem

4.5 THE NORMAL DISTRIBUTION

A very popular probability distribution is the *normal* (or *Gaussian*[9]) distribution which has the following PDF:

$$f(x) = \frac{1}{\sigma\sqrt{2\pi}} \exp\left(-\frac{(x-\mu)^2}{2\sigma^2}\right). \tag{4.5}$$

Where μ and σ are the *mean* and *standard deviation* of the probability distribution. The normal distribution is considered the most prominent in probability and statistical theory (and in finance), and, in many real-life studies, probability distributions tend towards the normal distribution provided they involve a sufficient number of random variables. Indeed, the *central limit theorem* (also known as the *law of large numbers*) states that the sum of a large number of *independent* and *identically distributed* (iid) random variables have an approximate normal distribution. The approximation improves as the number of random variables increases as illustrated in Figure 4.7.

In fact, the normal distribution is often used as a first approximation to a random variable that tends to *cluster* around a single mean value, μ. The graph of the normal distribution is symmetric about the mean and usually referred to as the *bell*-shaped curve, as shown in Figure 4.8. The normal distribution can be fully described by two statistical parameters, the mean and standard deviation. When a random variable

---

[9] The *Gaussian* distribution is named after Carl Friedrich Gauss (1777–1885), a German mathematician and scientist who made major contributions in the fields of number theory, statistics, differential geometry, astronomy and optics.

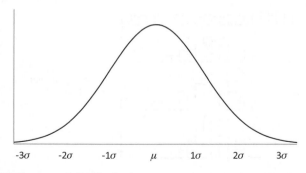

Figure 4.8 The normal distribution

X is distributed with a mean μ and standard deviation σ, the normal distribution can be denoted in the following compact notation:

$$X \sim N(\mu, \sigma^2). \qquad (4.6)$$

The normal distribution is assumed to approximate the model for many financial time series, including the distribution of monthly hedge fund returns, although these can often deviate from normality and this must be taken into account when making inferences from such data.

4.5.1 Standard Normal Distribution

If $\mu = 0$ and $\sigma = 1$, the distribution is said to be a *standard* normal distribution (or z-distribution), denoted by

$$X \sim N(0, 1). \qquad (4.7)$$

With the following PDF:

$$f(x) = \frac{1}{\sqrt{2\pi}} \exp\left(-\frac{x^2}{2}\right). \qquad (4.8)$$

The normal random variable of a standard normal distribution is known as a z-score (or *standard* score). Every normal random variable X can be converted into a z-score using the transformation

$$z = \frac{X - \mu}{\sigma}. \qquad (4.9)$$

Where X, μ and σ are the random variable, mean and standard deviation from the original normal distribution, respectively. The z-score indicates the number of standard deviations above or below the mean. For example, if the z-score is 2, then the original random variable X is 2 standard deviations above the mean. A negative z-score means that X is below the standard deviation by a certain amount.

4.6 VISUAL TESTS FOR NORMALITY

4.6.1 Inspection

A quick and simple visual test for a series of data being normally distributed is to plot the histogram of the empirical distribution against the fitted normal distribution. Table 4.5 shows the calculations required to perform a visual inspection of the monthly returns for the hypothetical CTA index. After determining the mean and standard deviation of the returns, the z-score can be found for each monthly return in the empirical data set. Using bin intervals of width 0.25, the absolute frequencies can be determined within each interval (as in Table 4.3). The bins are used to calculate each normal value across the bin range using equation (4.9). So that the empirical values can be plotted against the normal values, it is necessary to *unitise* each value with respect to the total so that each complete set forms a unit area. Figure 4.9 shows the plot of the empirical distribution against a normal distribution for the hypothetical CTA index.

Table 4.5 Calculations for a visual inspection of the monthly returns distribution for a hypothetical CTA index, 2005–2010

	A	B	C	D	E	F	G	H	I	J
1			Mean	0.85	=AVERAGE(B4:B75)					
2			St. Dev.	1.48	=STDEV(B4:B75)		Empirical		Normal	
3	Date	RoR (%)	z-score		z Bins	Frequency	Unit Area	Normal	Unit Area	
4	Jan-05	-0.74	1.0788		-4.00	0	0.0000	0.0001	0.0000	
5	Feb-05	1.45	=(B4-$D$1)/$D$2		-3.75	0	=F4/$F$37	0.0004	=H4/$H$37	
6	Mar-05	0.74			-3.50	0	0.0000	0.0009	0.0002	
7	Apr-05	1.29	0.2934		-3.25	{=FREQUENCY(C4:C75,E4:E36)}	020	0.0005	
8	May-05	0.24	-0.4156		-3.00	0	0.0000	0.0044	0.0011	
9	Jun-05	-0.51	-0.9271		-2.75	1	0.0139	=(1/SQRT(2*PI()))*EXP(-0.5*E8^2)		
10	Jul-05	1.57	0.4859		-2.50	0	0.0000			
11	Aug-05	2.01	0.7840		-2.25	0	0.0000	0.0317	0.0079	
12	Sep-05	0.33	-0.3548		-2.00	1	0.0139	0.0540	0.0135	
35	Aug-07	3.47	1.7707		3.75	0	0.0000	0.0004	0.0001	
36	Sep-07	1.00	0.0980		4.00	0	0.0000	0.0001	0.0000	
37	Oct-07	1.45	0.4032		Sum	72	1.0000	3.9999	1	
38	Nov-07	-2.10	-2.0043			=SUM(F4:F36)		=SUM(H4:FH36)		
39	Dec-07	0.37	-0.3312							
73	Oct-10	0.57	-0.1951							
74	Nov-10	-1.67	-1.7096							
75	Dec-10	0.46	-0.2676							

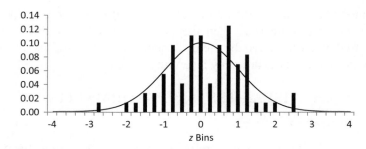

Figure 4.9 Empirical versus normal distribution for a hypothetical CTA index, 2005–2010

Figure 4.9 shows that the distribution of monthly returns has a reasonable bell-shaped curve which approximates the normal distribution. However, there seem to be several spikes that fall outside the normal which would need to be investigated further by considering higher moments, for example the skewness and kurtosis measures.

4.6.2 Normal Q-Q Plot

Another very useful data visualisation technique and test for normality is the normal Q-Q plot (or *normal probability plot*). Table 4.6 outlines a method for obtaining the normal Q-Q plot for the hypothetical CTA index.

Table 4.6 Calculations for the normal Q-Q plot

	A	B	C	D	E	F	G
1	Date	RoR (%)	Count	Percentiles	z-Score	RoR (%) (Ordered)	
2	Jan-05	-0.74	1	0.01370	-2.2058	-3.40	
3	Feb-05	1.45	2	=C2/($C$74+1)	-1.9205	=SMALL($B$2:$B$73,C2)	
4	Mar-05	0.74	3	0.04110	-1.7381	-1.94	
5	Apr-05	1.29	4	0.05479	=NORMSINV(D4)	-1.67	
6	May-05	0.24	5	0.06849	-1.4871	-1.43	
7	Jun-05	-0.51	6	0.08219	-1.3905	-1.34	
8	Jul-05	1.57	7	0.09589	-1.3053	-1.03	
9	Aug-05	2.01	8	0.10959	-1.2287	-0.87	
10	Sep-05	0.33	9	0.12329	-1.1587	-0.74	
70	Sep-10	1.35	69	0.94521	1.6000	3.10	
71	Oct-10	0.57	70	0.95890	1.7381	3.47	
72	Nov-10	-1.67	71	0.97260	1.9205	4.20	
73	Dec-10	0.46	72	0.98630	2.2058	4.44	
74		# Data Points	72				
75				=COUNT(B2:B73)			
76							

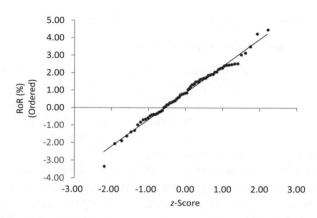

Figure 4.10   Normal Q-Q plot

Once the monthly returns have been counted they need to be transformed into q-quantiles. *Quantiles* are points taken at regular intervals
from the CDF of a random variable. Dividing ordered data into q equal-
sized data subsets leads to the required q-quantile; e.g. the 100-quantiles
are called *percentiles*. More formally, given a sample size n, each quantile can be determined by $k / (n+1)$ for $k = 1, \ldots, n$. Each percentile is
then transformed into the equivalent z-score using the NORMSINV()[10]
function. Once the monthly returns have been ordered in ascending order (lowest to highest) using the SMALL()[11] function, they are plotted against the z-scores to give the normal Q-Q plot, as shown in
Figure 4.10. If the data are normal, the plot should fall more or less
on a straight line between the data points. The hypothetical CTA index
shows a very good fit to normality except around the tails of the distribution, which can be seen from the departure of the data around the top
and bottom of the straight line. Indeed, Q-Q plots are often *S*-shaped,
indicating that the sample data are skewed or have heavier tails in relation to the normal distribution. A statistical measure of the *goodness
of fit* is the correlation between the ordered data and z-scores. If the
data are approximately normally distributed then the correlation should
be a high positive value. Normal probability plots are easy to construct
and interpret, with the added advantage that outliers within the data are
easily identified.

---

[10] The NORMSINV() function returns the inverse of the standard normal cumulative distribution,
i.e. a distribution with a mean of zero and a standard deviation of one.

[11] The SMALL() function returns the kth smallest value in a data set.

4.7 MOMENTS OF A DISTRIBUTION

4.7.1 Mean and Standard Deviation

The *mean* and *standard deviation* are the first and second moments of a probability distribution and without doubt the two most quoted statistical measures in finance.[12] The mean measures the average value of the distribution of a random variable, and the standard deviation is the dispersion (or spread) of these values around the mean. Indeed, the dispersion of returns around the mean is generally considered the amount of *risk* associated with a hedge fund. That is, the larger the standard deviation, the greater the potential hedge fund risk. For this reason, market practitioners often refer to the standard deviation as the *volatility* of the hedge fund.

For both the mean and standard deviation it is important to distinguish between individual population and sample measures. The mean for the population is denoted by μ, and for the sample by $\bar{x}$. Similarly, the number of independent observations in a population is defined by N and for a sample taken from the population by n (where $n < N$). Mathematically, the mean for a population and for a sample is given by:

$$\mu = \frac{\sum_{i=1}^{N} x_i}{N}. \tag{4.10}$$

$$\bar{x} = \frac{\sum_{i=1}^{N} x_i}{n}. \tag{4.11}$$

The standard deviation for the population is denoted by σ, and for a sample by s. Mathematically, the standard deviation[13] for a population and for a sample is given by:

$$\sigma = \sqrt{\frac{\sum_{i=1}^{N} (x_i - \mu)^2}{N}}. \tag{4.12}$$

$$s = \sqrt{\frac{\sum_{i=1}^{N} (x_i - \mu)^2}{n - 1}}. \tag{4.13}$$

[12] Such statistical measures are generally known as *point estimates* since they use a sample data set to determine a single value (or statistic) which is a *best guess* for an unknown population parameter. Point estimates can be contrasted with *interval estimates*, e.g. confidence intervals.

[13] The standard deviation squared is known as the *variance*. However, the resulting formula gives a value in terms of squared units, e.g. returns squared (%^{2}). Taking the square root of the variance gives the standard deviation and the correct units for returns (i.e. %).

Box 4.1   Square root rule

If a series of returns are quoted in monthly or quarterly figures then they can be transformed into an equivalent annualised series using the so-called *square root rule*. To get the annualised figure, the original standard deviation is multiplied by the square root of the frequency representing the original time period, i.e. 12 for monthly and 4 for quarterly. More formally:

$$\sigma_{annual} = \sigma_{monthly} \times \sqrt{12}.$$
$$\sigma_{annual} = \sigma_{quarterly} \times \sqrt{4}.$$

Table 4.7 shows the calculation of the annualised mean and standard deviation of monthly returns for the hypothetical CTA index using two user-defined VBA functions as shown in Source 4.2. In this case, the annual mean and standard deviation for the CTA index and volatility are 10.25% and 5.11%, respectively.

Table 4.7   Annualised mean and standard deviation of the CTA index, 2005–2010

	A	B	C	D	E
1	**CTA Index**				
2	**Date**	**RoR (%)**	**Moments**		
3	Jan-05	-0.74	**Mean**	10.25	=fncMEAN(B3:B74)
4	Feb-05	1.45	**St. Dev.**	5.11	
5	Mar-05	0.74		=fncSTDEV(B3:B74)	
6	Apr-05	1.29			
7	May-05	0.24			
8	Jun-05	-0.51			
9	Jul-05	1.57			
10	Aug-05	2.01			
11	Sep-05	0.33			
70	Aug-10	-1.43			
71	Sep-10	1.35			
72	Oct-10	0.57			
73	Nov-10	-1.67			
74	Dec-10	0.46			

Source 4.2   User-defined VBA functions to calculate the mean and standard deviation of a returns array

```
'function to calculate the MEAN of a returns array
Function fncMEAN(RoR As Range) As Double

  'initialise sum to zero
  sum = 0

  'count number in returns array
  n = RoR.Count

  For i = 1 To n
     sum = sum + RoR(i)
  Next

  fncMEAN = (sum / n) * 12 'annualised

End Function

'function to calculate the STANDARD DEVIATION
of a returns array
Function fncSTDEV(RoR As Range) As Double

 'count number in returns array
 n = RoR.Count

 'the mean of returns array
 avg = (fncMEAN(RoR) / 12)

 'initialise sum to zero
 sum = 0

  For i = 1 To n
     sum = sum + (RoR(i) - avg) ^ 2
  Next

 fncSTDEV = Sqr(sum/(n - 1))*Sqr(12) 'annualised

End Function
```

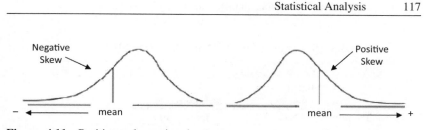

Figure 4.11 Positive and negative skew

One of the major advantages of using standard deviation, apart from the ease of calculation, is that it gives a direct measure of the riskiness of the distribution of returns for a hedge fund. However, most hedge fund returns do not exhibit a normal distribution, i.e. the familiar bell-shaped curve, but can be skewed or stretched in some way. In order to fully define a probability distribution it is necessary to investigate higher moments of the distribution, such as skewness and kurtosis.

4.7.2 Skewness

Skewness is the third moment of a probability distribution and measures the degree of *asymmetry* (or skew) of a distribution. Skew can be either zero, positive or negative. Positive (or right) skew indicates a distribution with an asymmetric tail extending towards more positive values, whereas with negative (or left) skew the tail extends toward more negative values (see Figure 4.11). The skew of a normal distribution is zero. Hedge fund returns are generally assumed to have either positive or negative skew; knowing the direction of the skew can help fund managers estimate whether a given (or future) return will be larger or smaller than the mean value. If a particular return distribution is skewed, which is generally the case, there is a greater probability that the returns will be either higher or lower than that of a normal distribution. Unlike mean and standard deviation, skewness has no units like a z-score.

Mathematically, the sample skewness, S, is given by:

$$S = \frac{n}{(n-1)(n-2)} \sum_{i=1}^{n} \left(\frac{x_i - \bar{x}}{s} \right)^3. \tag{4.14}$$

Table 4.8 shows the calculation of the skewness of the distribution of monthly returns for the hypothetical CTA index using the user-defined

Table 4.8 Skewness of the CTA index, 2005–2010

	A	B	C	D	E
1	**CTA Index**				
2	**Date**	**RoR (%)**	**Moments**		
3	Jan-05	-0.74	Mean	10.25	
4	Feb-05	1.45	St. Dev.	5.11	
5	Mar-05	0.74	**Skewness**	**-0.1723**	
6	Apr-05	1.29		=fncSKEWNESS(B3:B74)	
7	May-05	0.24			
8	Jun-05	-0.51			
9	Jul-05	1.57			
10	Aug-05	2.01			
11	Sep-05	0.33			
70	Aug-10	-1.43			
71	Sep-10	1.35			
72	Oct-10	0.57			
73	Nov-10	-1.67			
74	Dec-10	0.46			

VBA function shown in Source 4.3. It shows that the skewness value is −0.1723, which can be considered relatively low in comparison to the normal distribution value of zero but indicating a definite skew towards more negative returns.

Source 4.3 User-defined VBA function to calculate the skewness of a returns array

```
'function to calculate the SKEWNESS of a
returns array
Function fncSKEWNESS(RoR As Range) As Double

  'count number in returns array
  n = RoR.Count

  'the mean of returns array
  avg = (fncMEAN(RoR) / 12) 'monthly
  'the standard deviation of returns array
  std = (fncSTDEV(RoR) / Sqr(12)) 'monthly
```

```
'initialise sum to zero
sum = 0

For i = 1 To n
   sum = sum + ((RoR(i) - avg) / std) ^ 3
Next

fncSKEWNESS = (n / ((n - 1) * (n - 2))) * sum

End Function
```

4.7.3   Excess Kurtosis

Excess kurtosis,[14] the fourth moment of a probability distribution, measures the degree of peakedness or flatness of a distribution compared to the normal distribution. Positive kurtosis (or leptokurtosis) indicates a relatively peaked distribution and heavy tails with more extreme values, whilst negative kurtosis (platykurtosis) refers to a flatter distribution with thinner tails and relatively fewer extreme values. A distribution with an excess kurtosis of zero is known as a mesokurtic distribution – for example, the normal distribution (see Figure 4.12). A higher kurtosis usually indicates that the variability in the data is due to a few extreme variations from the mean, rather than many relatively small differences. As with skewness, kurtosis also has no units.

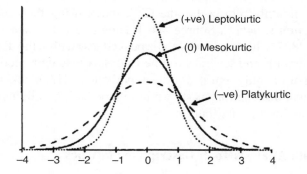

Figure 4.12   Positive, negative and zero kurtosis

---

[14] Note thatexcess kurtosis = kurtosis – 3.

Table 4.9 Excess kurtosis for the CTA index, 2005–2010

	A	B	C	D	E
1	**CTA Index**				
2	**Date**	**RoR (%)**	**Moments**		
3	Jan-05	-0.74	Mean	10.25	
4	Feb-05	1.45	St. Dev.	5.11	
5	Mar-05	0.74	Skewness	-0.1723	
6	Apr-05	1.29	**Excess Kurtosis**	**0.2827**	
7	May-05	0.24		=fncXSKURTOSIS(B3:B74)	
8	Jun-05	-0.51			
9	Jul-05	1.57			
10	Aug-05	2.01			
11	Sep-05	0.33			
70	Aug-10	-1.43			
71	Sep-10	1.35			
72	Oct-10	0.57			
73	Nov-10	-1.67			
74	Dec-10	0.46			

Mathematically, the sample excess kurtosis, K, is given by

$$K = \left[\frac{n(n+1)}{(n-1)(n-2)(n-3)} \sum_{i=1}^{n} \left(\frac{x_i - \bar{x}}{s} \right)^4 \right] - \frac{3(n-1)^2}{(n-2)(n-3)}.$$

(4.15)

Table 4.9 shows the calculation of the excess kurtosis of the distribution of monthly returns for the CTA index using the user-defined VBA function shown in Source 4.4. It shows that the excess kurtosis value is 0.2827, which indicates some peakedness within the distribution with heavier tails and several extreme values. A visual inspection of the histogram of monthly returns for the hypothetical CTA index in relation to the normal distribution, as shown in Figure 4.13, highlights the skew and kurtosis for this distribution.

4.7.4 Data Analysis Tool: Descriptive Statistics

A summary statistics report for a set of data can easily be generated using the **Descriptive Statistics** Data Analysis Tool available in Excel as part of the **Analysis ToolPak** add-in (see Figures 4.14 and 4.15 and Table 4.10).

Source 4.4 User-defined VBA function to calculate the excess kurtosis of a returns array

```
'function to calculate the EXCESS KURTOSIS of a
returns array
Function fncXSKURTOSIS(RoR As Range) As Double

  'count number in returns array
  n = RoR.Count

  'the mean of returns array
  avg = (fncMEAN(RoR) / 12) 'monthly
  'the standard deviation of returns array
  std = (fncSTDEV(RoR) / Sqr(12)) 'monthly

  'initialise sum to zero
  sum = 0

  For i = 1 To n
    sum = sum + ((RoR(i) - avg) / std) ^ 4
  Next

  fncXSKURTOSIS = sum * (n * (n + 1) / ((n - 1) *
  (n - 2) * (n - 3))) - (3 * (n - 1) ^ 2 /
  ((n - 2) * (n - 3)))

End Function
```

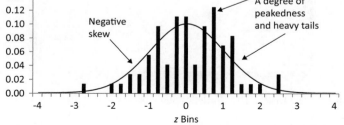

Figure 4.13 Skewness and kurtosis for the hypothetical CTA index, 2005–2010

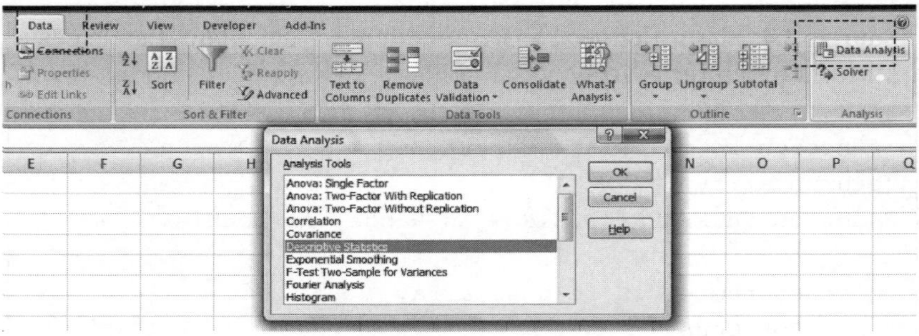

Figure 4.14   Locating the **Descriptive Statistics** Analysis Tool

Note that the mean and standard deviation values have been calculated in monthly figures and would need to be converted to annualised values (see Box 4.1) to be consistent with those determined in the examples above.

4.8   GEOMETRIC BROWNIAN MOTION

A stochastic differential equation (or SDE) is an equation for a *stochastic process*[15] that describes the time evolution of a probability distribution.

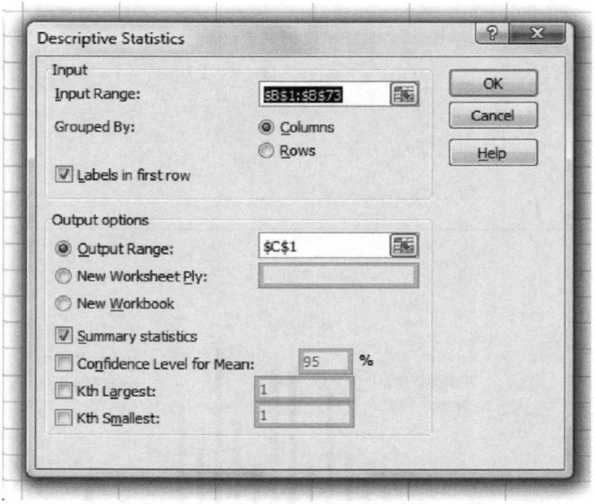

Figure 4.15   The **Descriptive Statistics** dialogue box

---

[15] In a *stochastic* (or *random*) *process* there is some level of indeterminacy in the future evolution of a variable described by a probability distribution. If the initial value is known with certainty, there will still be a variety of possibilities that the process will undertake in the future.

Table 4.10 Summary statistics report for the CTA index, 2005 and 2010

	A	B	C	D	E
1	Date	CTA Index (RoR%)		*Summary Statistics*	
2	Jan-05	-0.74			
3	Feb-05	1.45		Mean	0.8537709
4	Mar-05	0.74		Standard Error	0.173889
5	Apr-05	1.29		Median	0.8055468
6	May-05	0.24		Mode	#N/A
7	Jun-05	-0.51		Standard Deviation	1.475497
8	Jul-05	1.57		Sample Variance	2.1770915
9	Aug-05	2.01		Kurtosis	0.2826616
10	Sep-05	0.33		Skewness	-0.172318
11	Oct-05	-0.42		Range	7.8304782
12	Nov-05	-0.29		Minimum	-3.395043
13	Dec-05	3.00		Maximum	4.435435
14	Jan-06	-0.87		Sum	61.471501
15	Feb-06	0.81		Count	72
16	Mar-06	1.83			
17	Apr-06	2.17			
70	Sep-10	1.35			
71	Oct-10	0.57			
72	Nov-10	-1.67			
73	Dec-10	0.46			

Such equations are used often in quantitative finance, for example to model the fluctuation in equity prices over time (see Figure 4.16). A widely used SDE for stock price behaviour can be written as[16]

$$\frac{dS_t}{S_t} = \mu dt + \sigma dB_t. \tag{4.16}$$

Where S_t is a stochastic (or diffuse) process, μ is the drift coefficient, σ is the diffusion (or volatility) coefficient and B_t is a geometric Brownian[17] motion (or GBM, also called a Wiener[18] process). If we consider

[16] This SDE is the model that describes the stock price process used in the Black–Scholes analysis.

[17] Robert Brown (1773–1858) was a Scottish botanist who made important contributions to the field through his pioneering work on the microscope.

[18] Norbert Wiener (1894–1964) was an American mathematician.

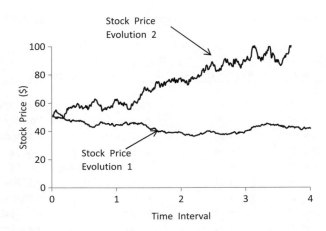

Figure 4.16 Two sample paths of a stock price process using a GBM with two different sets of μ and σ

a small interval of time Δt, the stochastic process S_t can be thought of as changing its value, in the interval Δt, by an amount that is normally distributed with mean $\mu \Delta t$ and variance $\sigma^2 \Delta t$. The change in value during the interval Δt is *independent* of the past behaviour of the stochastic process since the increments of a GBM are independent (as well as normally distributed).

GBM is not a completely realistic model. For example the diffusion coefficient that represents the volatility of the stock price process is assumed to be constant,[19] but volatility clearly changes over time. In addition, the changes in the stochastic process are expected to be normally distributed, but we have already shown that certain processes can possess a degree of skewness and kurtosis, such as a series of hedge fund returns.[20] In an attempt to make GBM more realistic, it is possible to relax the assumption that the volatility is constant and assume that it is itself random and introduce a *stochastic volatility* into the price process. This often involves modelling a different SDE driven by an alternative GBM which can soon become mathematically complex.

---

[19] A volatility that is assumed to be a deterministic function of the stock price and time is said to be a local volatility.

[20] Indeed, it is generally assumed that most hedge fund returns are not adequately described by GBM due to the effect of skewness and kurtosis. However, the model serves well as a building block for more advanced SDEs.

4.8.1   Uniform Random Numbers

It is possible to define the GBM dB_t in equation (4.16) as follows:

$$dB_t = dz = \varepsilon\sqrt{dt}. \qquad (4.17)$$

Where ε is a random drawing from a standardised normal distribution $N(0, 1)$. If a random variable U has a uniform distribution on the interval $[0, 1]$ then its mean and variance are $1/2$ and $1/12$, respectively. Applying the central limit theorem, the sum of 12 observations of U can be shown to have a distribution that is approximately normal with a mean of $6 (= 12 \times 1/2)$ and variance of $1 (= 12 \times 1/12)$. Therefore, the sum of 12 independent uniform random numbers minus 6 gives an approximate standard normal random variable (RV) with $\mu = 0$ and $\sigma = 1$. That is:

$$RV = \left(\sum_{i=1}^{12} \varepsilon_i\right) - 6. \qquad (4.18)$$

Where ε_i represents a different independent random number drawn from a uniform distribution on the interval $[0, 1]$. Table 4.11 shows an

Table 4.11   Calculation of a series of independent standard normal random variables and subsequent distribution

	A	B	C	D	E	F	G	H
1				Absolute	*RV*		Normal	
2	#	*RV*	z-Bins	Frequency	Unit Area	Normal	Unit Area	
3	1	0.0245	-4.00	0	0.00000	0.00013	0.00003	
4	2	=RAND()+RAND()+RAND()+			=D3/$D$36	0.00035	=F3/$F$36	
5	3	RAND()+RAND()+RAND()+				0.00087	0.00022	
6	4	RAND()+RAND()+RAND()+			0.00100	=(1/SQRT(2*PI()))*EXP(-0.5*C3^2)		
7	5	RAND()+RAND()+RAND()-6			0.00200			
8	6	0.4168	-2.75	2	0.00200	0.00909	0.00227	
9	7	1.1852	-2.50	4	0.00400	0.01753	0.00438	
10	8	0.9443	-2.25	{=FREQUENCY(B3:B1002,C3:C35)}			0.00794	
33	31	-0.9640	3.50	0	0.00000	0.00087	0.00022	
34	32	-0.4076	3.75	0	0.00000	0.00035	0.00009	
35	33	0.1666	4.00	0	0.00000	0.00013	0.00003	
36	34	-1.2270	Sum	1000	1	3.9999	1	
37	35	1.0213		=SUM(D3:D35)		=SUM(F3:F35)		
1000	998	0.6635						
1001	999	-0.6211						
1002	1000	1.2372						

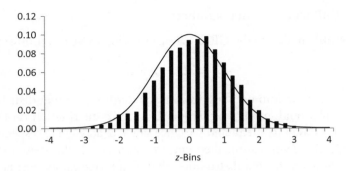

Figure 4.17 A series of simulated standard normal random variables against the normal

implementation of equation (4.18) using the RAND()[21] function, and Figure 4.17 shows the comparison to the normal distribution. Again, in order to compare the randomly generated standard normal variables with the normal distribution, a *unitisation* of the area under each curve is performed. As can be seen from Figure 4.17, equation (4.18) is a quick and accurate method of obtaining a series of normally distributed independent random variables suitable for modelling a GBM.

4.9 COVARIANCE AND CORRELATION

Both *covariance* and *correlation* are related measures that indicate the degree of variation between two sets of random variables, for example a set hedge fund returns and the market benchmark (say, S&P 500). More formally, given any pair of random variables, X_i and X_j, their covariance is denoted by $\mathrm{cov}(X_i, X_j)$ or, in matrix form, by Σ_{ij}. By definition, the covariance is a symmetric matrix,[22] i.e. $\Sigma_{ij} = \Sigma_{ji}$. Note that the covariance of any element X_i with itself is the variance, that is,

$$\mathrm{cov}(X_i, X_i) = \mathrm{var}(X_i). \qquad (4.19)$$

---

[21] The RAND() function returns an evenly distributed independent random real number greater than or equal to 0 and no more than 1, i.e. uniformly distributed on the interval [0, 1]. It is also possible to generate a random number from a standard normal distribution using the function NORMSINV(RAND()).

[22] The covariance matrix must also be *positive definite*, i.e. a matrix that is analogous to a positive real number.

The covariance matrix, Σ, can be written in matrix form as

$$
\Sigma = \begin{pmatrix}
\Sigma_{11} & \Sigma_{12} & \Sigma_{13} & \cdots & \Sigma_{1n} \\
\Sigma_{21} & \Sigma_{22} & \Sigma_{23} & \cdots & \Sigma_{2n} \\
\Sigma_{31} & \Sigma_{32} & \Sigma_{33} & \cdots & \Sigma_{3n} \\
\vdots & \vdots & \vdots & \vdots & \vdots \\
\Sigma_{n1} & \Sigma_{n2} & \Sigma_{n3} & \cdots & \Sigma_{nn}
\end{pmatrix}. \tag{4.20}
$$

To obtain a more direct indication of how two random variables co-vary, a correlation measure can be used. The correlation is simply a scaled version of the covariance with relation to the standard deviations of the two sets of random variables. There are several measures for the correlation, often denoted ρ (for a population) or r (for a sample), that indicate the degree of variation between two random sets of variables. The most common of these is the Pearson[23] product-moment correlation coefficient, which is relevant only to *linear* relationships between two sets of random variables. The correlation is $+1.0$ in the case of a perfectly positive (increasing) linear relationship, -1.0 for a perfectly negative linear relationship, and a value between -1.0 and 1.0 in all other cases (see Figure 4.18). Note that if the elements of X and Y are independent then the correlation is zero, however, this does not indicate a lack of variation between X and Y, only that there is no linear relationship between them. Although, there may be some other form of relationship between X and Y, such as a curvilinear[24] one.

Given any pair of random variables, X_i and X_j, the correlation ρ_{ij} is defined as

$$
\rho_{ij} = \frac{\text{cov}\left(X_i, X_j\right)}{\sigma_i \sigma_j}. \tag{4.21}
$$

Where σ_i and σ_j are the standard deviations of X_i and X_j, respectively. The correlation is defined only if σ_i and σ_j are finite and non-zero.

---

[23] Karl Pearson (1857–1936) was an extremely influential English mathematician who has been most cited for the establishment of the field of mathematical statistics.

[24] A *curvilinear* relationship indicates that the relationship between the two sets of random variables may be curved.

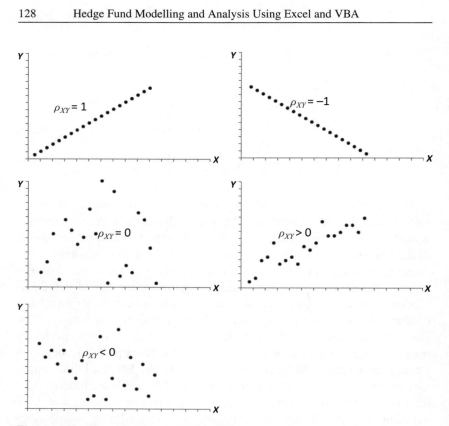

Figure 4.18 Some typical correlation plots

As with covariance, ρ_{ij} is more often seen in the form of a correlation matrix[25] ρ, that is,

$$\rho = \begin{pmatrix} 1 & \rho_{12} & \rho_{13} & \cdots & \rho_{1n} \\ \rho_{21} & 1 & \rho_{23} & & \\ \rho_{31} & \rho_{32} & 1 & & \\ \vdots & \vdots & & \ddots & \\ \rho_{n1} & & & & 1 \end{pmatrix}. \qquad (4.22)$$

Clearly, correlation inherits the symmetric property of covariance, i.e. $\rho_{ij} = \rho_{ji}$. Note that $\rho_{ii} = 1.0$ for $i = j$. The correlation can also be

---

[25] As with covariance matrices, correlation matrices must also be positive definite.

determined from the following:

$$\rho_{XY} = \frac{\sum_{i=1}^{n}(x_i - \bar{x})(y_i - \bar{y})}{\sqrt{\sum_{i=1}^{n}(x_i - \bar{x})^2 \sum_{i=1}^{n}(y_i - \bar{y})^2}}. \qquad (4.23)$$

Where $\bar{x}$ and $\bar{y}$ are the mean values of X and Y. Source 4.5 shows an implementation of equation (4.23) using a user-defined VBA function.

Source 4.5 User-defined VBA function to calculate the correlation coefficient for two returns arrays

```
'function to calculate the CORRELATION
COEFFICIENT for two returns arrays
Function fncCORR(RoRX As Range, RoRY As Range) As
Double

   'initialise n, m, sum1, sum2, sum3 to zero
   n = 0
   m = 0
   sum1 = 0
   sum2 = 0
   sum3 = 0

'count returns in arrays
n = RoRX.Count
m = RoRY.Count

'check for n = m i.e. same number of returns
in both arrays
If n <> m Then
   MsgBox ''Invalid returns array'',
   vbExclamation, ''Error Message''
End If

'the mean of returns for X and Y
avgX = (fncMEAN(RoRX) / 12)
avgY = (fncMEAN(RoRY) / 12)
```

```
'the mean of returns for X and Y
stdX = fncSTDEV(RoRX)
stdY - fncSTDEV(RoRY)

'determine maximum return in array
For i = 1 To n
  sum1 = sum1 + (RoRX(i) - avgX) * (RoRY(i) - avgY)
  sum2 = sum2 + (RoRX(i) - avgX) ^ 2
  sum3 = sum3 + (RoRY(i) - avgY) ^ 2
Next

fncCORR = sum1 / Sqr((sum2 * sum3))

End Function
```

Since correlation measures the relative strength of variability between two sets of random numbers it is a very useful tool for determining the degree of diversification within a portfolio of hedge funds or FoHFs. That is, a correlation matrix representing a portfolio of hedge funds should ideally have relatively low values, indicating a well-diversified portfolio. Table 4.12 shows the individual correlations using the CORREL()[26] function for 10 hypothetical hedge fund returns. The correlation values range between –0.30 and 0.27, with the majority close to zero, indicating a small degree of positive and negative variability between the set of hedge funds.

Investing in hedge funds and hedge fund strategies that have low correlations with each other is an ideal way for a fund manager to maximise the potential returns of an investment under a wide range of economic and market conditions.[27] Clearly, creating a well-diversified portfolio of low-correlated hedge funds is an extremely valuable process for constructing a profitable FOHFs strategy.

[26] The CORREL() function returns the value of the correlation coefficient between two sets of variables.

[27] Assuming that correlations remain *stable* over time, which is not always the case, especially in times of market turmoil and stress.

Table 4.12 Ten hypothetical hedge fund returns and their correlation matrix, 2005 and 2010

	A	B	C	D	E	F	G	H	I	J	K
1						RoR (%)					
2	Date	CTA1	CTA2	CTA3	GM1	GM2	LS1	LS2	LS3	MN1	MN2
3	Jan-05	4.68	0.10	-2.69	0.89	-6.66	0.37	5.80	2.36	-3.09	2.81
4	Feb-05	-0.18	1.79	3.61	-0.90	2.93	-1.06	4.27	0.32	-0.87	-3.51
5	Mar-05	0.66	2.04	-0.28	-5.38	6.68	0.62	-3.11	-0.44	0.19	-1.56
6	Apr-05	-1.45	1.34	2.95	1.33	2.26		-4.67	4.89	0.56	-0.07
7	May-05	3.11	-0.16	-4.83	0.88	2.21	-1.40	4.12	-1.54	-0.82	0.38
8	Jun-05	1.10	-1.40	5.01	-1.02	-6.26	1.36	-0.31	1.02	0.97	-0.07
9	Jul-05	-5.11	1.15	8.03	-2.88	6.66	2.02	6.87	1.12	1.50	-2.85
10	Aug-05	4.91	-1.20	3.25	3.81	-0.72	0.74	0.31	4.32	2.41	0.62
11	Sep-05	-0.70	-1.99	-1.96	5.93	0.38	0.54	-6.94	-0.10	2.23	-0.46
12	Oct-05	1.33	2.20	-0.75	-6.20	1.30	1.77	1.97	-6.56	0.51	-0.33
73	Nov-10	-0.85	1.27	1.42	-4.46	-5.71	0.78	7.45	-0.01	-0.74	-0.14
74	Dec-10	0.45	0.10	-1.33	0.59	2.48	0.10	-0.54	1.27	-0.75	0.50
75						Correlation Matrix					
76		CTA1	CTA2	CTA3	GM1	GM2	LS1	LS2	LS3	MN1	MN2
77	CTA1	1	-0.07	0.02	-0.01	-0.16	-0.04	0.04	0.14	0.11	0.27
78	CTA2	=CORREL($B$3:$B$74,B3:B74)				0.03	-0.07	0.10	0.01	-0.07	-0.30
79	CTA3	0.02	-0.25	1	0.04	-0.00	=CORREL($C$3:$C$74,G3:G74)				0.09
80	GM1	-0.01	0.05	0.04	1	0.01	0.04	-0.11	-0.08	0.20	-0.06
81	GM2	-0.16	=CORREL($E$3:$E$74,C3:C74)			1	-0.07	0.02	-0.13	-0.01	-0.23
82	LS1	-0.04	-0.07	-0.06	0.04	-0.07	1	0.19	-0.09	0.03	-0.01
83	LS2	0.04	0.10	-0.10	-0.11	0.02	0.19	1	0.09	-0.09	0.08
84	LS3	0.14	0.01	0.06	-0.08	-0.13	-0.09	0.09	1	0.14	0.15
85	MN1	0.11	-0.07	=CORREL($I$3:$I$74,D3:D74)			3	-0.09	0.14	1	-0.05
86	MN2	0.27	-0.30	0.09	-0.06	-0.23	-0.01	0.08	0.15	-0.05	1

4.10 REGRESSION ANALYSIS

4.10.1 Ordinary Least Squares

Since the majority of hedge fund strategies involve investments in financial instruments, a hedge fund manager is heavily exposed to the risks involved in using such instruments, or to so-called *market risk factors*. Many hedge fund managers invest in a whole range of different financial instruments in order to effectively implement a particular strategy and incorporate a degree of diversification into their portfolios. In order to help with this process, fund managers can identify the risk exposure of a given strategy by employing a combination of *correlation* and *regression* techniques. That is, for a certain hedge fund strategy or index, a set of correlated market factors can be identified and the strength of their relationship quantified through *regression analysis*. In this way, a relationship can be determined

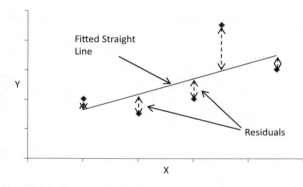

Figure 4.19   Simple linear regression

between a *dependent* variable (e.g. hedge fund strategy or index) and a set of *independent* variables (i.e. correlated market factors). Since many fund managers rely on the use of derivative instruments and varying degrees of leverage,[28] correlation and regression analysis can only explain part of the risk exposures faced by hedge funds. In these cases, a thorough knowledge of the particular strategy and market environment allows managers to supplement these *quantitative* measures with *qualitative* estimates.

Linear regression is a parametric method, i.e. the regression model is defined in terms of a finite number of unknown parameters estimated from a set of data. Linear regression involves using the method of ordinary least squares (OLS) to relate a dependent variable Y to an independent variable X.[29] More technically, simple linear regression fits a straight line through a set of n data points such that the sum of squared errors, i.e. the vertical distances between the data points and fitted straight line, are as small as possible (see Figure 4.19).

The standard linear regression model is given by

$$Y_i = a + bX_i + e_i. \qquad (4.24)$$

Where the X_i are the independent[30] variables, Y_i are the dependent[31] variables, b is the *slope* (or *gradient*) of the straight line, a the intercept and the e_i are the error terms.[32] The e_i capture all of the other factors that

---

[28] The use of derivatives and leverage introduces an element of *non-linearity* into the analysis.

[29] For each data point both X and Y are known.

[30] The X_i are also known as the regressor, exogenous, explanatory, input, or predictor variables.

[31] The Y_i are also known as the regressand, endogenous, response, or measured variables.

[32] The e_i are also known as the residual, disturbance or noise term.

influence the dependent variables Y_i other than the independent variable X_i. It is a necessary condition that the independent variables X_i are *linearly independent*, i.e. it is not possible to express any independent variable as a linear combination of the others. This can also be expressed in terms of the regression model having no *multicollinearity*, i.e. there is no strong correlation between two or more independent variables. The dependent variables Y_i should also be approximately normally distributed.

4.10.1.1   Coefficient of Determination

The strength of the relationship between the dependent and independent variables can be determined by calculating the *coefficient of determination* (denoted by R^2). R^2 can be interpreted as the proportion of the variance in the dependent variable that is *predicted* (or *explained*) by the independent variable. R^2 ranges between zero and one, zero indicating that the dependent variable cannot be predicted from the independent variable and one indicating that there is no error in the relationship between the dependent and independent variable. An R^2 of 0.40 means that 40% of the variance in the dependent variable Y is predicted or explained by the independent variable X. Mathematically, R^2 is the square of the correlation, as can be seen in Source 4.6 which shows an implementation of R^2 using a user-defined VBA function.

Source 4.6   User-defined VBA function to calculate the coefficient of determination for two returns arrays

```
'function to calculate the COEFFICIENT OF
DETERMINATION for two returns arrays
Function fncCOD(RoRX As Range, RoRY As Range) As
Double

  'the correlation of returns for X and Y
  corrXY = fncCORR(RoRX, RoRY)

  fncCOD = corrXY ^ 2

End Function
```

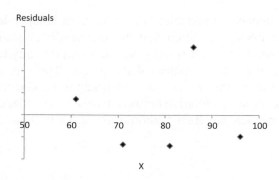

Figure 4.20   A residual plot

A measure related to the coefficient of determination is the *standard error* (SE) in the regression line. Standard error is the average amount by which the regression model over- or underpredicts, i.e. the higher the value of R^2, the lower the standard error, and the more accurate any predictions based on the regression model will be.

4.10.1.2   Residual Plots

The error term in the linear regression model must possess the following properties:

1. The errors in the regression model must be random variables and have a mean of zero.
2. The variance of the errors must be constant, i.e. *homoscedastic*.[33]

Once a regression model has been fitted to a set of data, a further investigation of the error terms allows the validity of the assumption that the model is a linear relationship can be tested. The difference between the observed values and those predicted from the linear regression model is given by

$$e = Y - \hat{Y}. \tag{4.25}$$

Where $\hat{Y} = a + bX$. A residual plot, as shown in Figure 4.20, can reveal the possibility of any non-linear relationship between the variables as well as the presence of *outliers*. Such outliers may represent erroneous data, or indicate a poorly fitting regression model. If the residual plot shows a random scatter of data points, as in Figure 4.20, then this is consistent with the model being linear.

---

[33] If this condition is violated the errors are said to *heteroscedastic*.

4.10.1.3 Jarque–Bera Normality Test

We have already looked at several visual methods for testing for normality of a distribution of monthly hedge fund returns, namely inspection and the Q-Q normal plot. Jarque and Bera (1987) developed a numerical test for normality[34] based on the sample skewness and kurtosis known as the Jarque–Bera (JB) test. The JB test relies on a chi-square distribution (see Box 4.2) with two degrees of freedom (one for the skewness and one for the kurtosis) and tests the validity that a distribution of hedge fund

---

Box 4.2   Chi-squared distribution

The chi-square (or χ^2) distribution is the sum of the squared values of the number of independent random variables with finite mean and variance drawn from a standard normal distribution. The χ^2 distribution is dependent on the number of degrees of freedom. As the number of degrees of freedom increases the χ^2 distribution approaches the normal distribution, as shown below. As a result of the central limit theorem, the χ^2 distribution converges to a normal distribution only for large values of n, i.e. it is an *asymptotic distribution*.

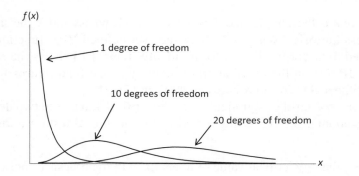

The χ^2 distribution is used most commonly in χ^2 tests for the goodness of fit of an observed probability distribution to a theoretical one, and in confidence interval estimation for a population standard deviation.

---

[34] There are several other statistical tests for normality, i.e. Kolmogorov–Smirnov, Anderson–Darling and Shapiro–Wilk. All of these tests have their advantages and disadvantages.

Table 4.13 Jarque–Bera test for normality

	A	B	C	D	E	F	G
1		CTA Index					
2	Date	RoR (%)	Normality Test				
3	Jan-05	-0.74	Jarque-Bera Value	0.5960	=fncJBVALUE(B3:B74)		
4	Feb-05	1.45	Level of Significance	5%			
5	Mar-05	0.74	Degrees of Freedom	2			
6	Apr-05	1.29	Critical Value	5.9915	=fncJBCRITICAL(D4,D5)		
7	May-05	0.24	p-Value	0.7423	=fncJBpVALUE(D3,D5)		
8	Jun-05	-0.51					
9	Jul-05	1.57		Critical Test	p Test		
10	Aug-05	2.01	Normality	YES	YES	=IF(D7<D4,"NO","YES")	
11	Sep-05	0.33		=IF(D3>=D6,"NO","YES")			
71	Sep-10	1.35					
72	Oct-10	0.57					
73	Nov-10	-1.67					
74	Dec-10	0.46					

returns are normal. More formally, the *null* hypothesis[35] is a joint hypothesis that the skewness is zero and kurtosis is 3 (or excess kurtosis is zero), which are consistent with a normal distribution.

The JB test statistic is given by

$$JB = \frac{n}{6}\left(S^2 + \frac{1}{4}K^2\right). \qquad (4.26)$$

Where n is the sample size, S is the sample skewness and K the sample excess kurtosis. Source 4.7 shows the user-defined VBA functions required to perform a JB test for normality. Table 4.13 shows the results of a JB test on the distribution of monthly hedge fund returns for the hypothetical CTA index between 2005 and 2010.

For a 5% level of significance, the χ^2 critical value with two degrees of freedom is 5.9915. Using the critical value, the JB test for normality states:

if JB value $\geq \chi^2$ critical value $\rightarrow$ reject the null hypothesis of normality.

Using the p-value, for the same level of significance, the JB test for normality states:

if p-value $< 0.05 \rightarrow$ reject the null hypothesis of normality.

---

[35] The *null* hypothesis attempts to show that no variation exists between the variables, or that a single variable is no different from zero. It is presumed to be true until statistical tests nullify it in favour of an *alternative* hypothesis. The null hypothesis assumes that any kind of difference/or *significance* you see in a set of data is due only to chance. If a null hypothesis is proven true, a p-value gives the probability that a random sample of data would deviate from the normal distribution as much as the test data.

Source 4.7 User-defined VBA functions to test for normality using the Jarque–Bera test

```
'function to calculate JARQUE-BERA value
Function fncJBVALUE(RoR As Range) As Double

  'count number in returns array
  n = RoR.Count

  'sample skewness and kurtosis of returns array
  Skew = fncSKEWNESS(RoR)
  Kurt = fncKURTOSIS(RoR)

  fncJBVALUE = (n / 6) * ((Skew^2) + ((Kurt^2) / 4))

End Function

'function to calculate critical value at a given
level of significance and degrees of freedom
Function fncJBCRITICAL(Significance As Double,
Degrees As Integer) As Double

  'using Excel built-in function ChiInv()
  fncJBCRITICAL = WorksheetFunction.ChiInv
  (Significance, Degrees)

End Function

'function to calculate p-value for a number
of degrees of freedom
Function fncJBpVALUE(JBvalue As Double, Degrees
As Integer) As Double

  'using Excel built-in function ChiDist()
  fncJBpVALUE = WorksheetFunction.ChiDist
  (JBvalue, Degrees)

End Function
```

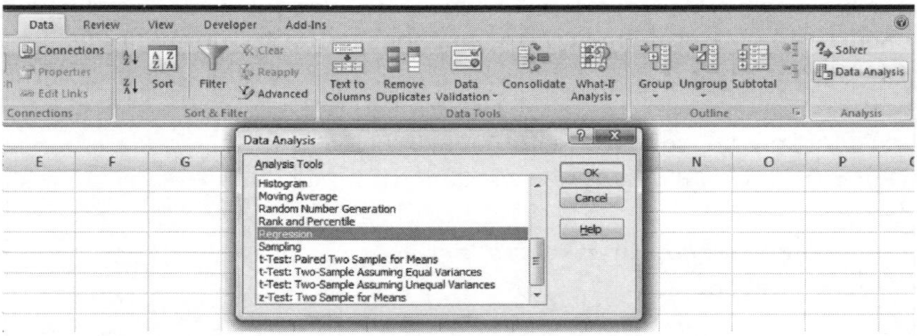

Figure 4.21   Locating the **Regression** Data Analysis Tool in Excel

Table 4.13 shows that the null hypothesis of normality cannot be rejected at the 5% level of significance with both the critical and p-value tests, i.e. the distribution of monthly returns for the CTA index between 2005 and 2010 are assumed to be normal.[36] Note that the JB test is only assumed valid for large sample sizes ($n \geq 50$), and can produce misleading results for smaller samples due to the asymptotic nature of the χ^2 distribution and related critical values. The D'Agostino–Pearson test for normality, which is also based on the calculations of skewness and kurtosis, usually gives more accurate results for smaller sample sizes.

4.10.1.4   Data Analysis Tool: Regression

A regression report for a set of data can be generated using the **Regression** Data Analysis Tool available in Excel has part of the **Analysis ToolPak** add-in (see Figures 4.21 and 4.22 and Table 4.14).

The S&P index was used to compare the returns for a long/short (LS) hedge fund index to that of the equity market. The analysis involved regressing monthly returns for the LS index (dependent variable) against those of the benchmark S&P index (independent variable). The regression was run over the period 2005–2010. In Table 4.14 those statistics that are of interest to this analysis have been highlighted in bold. **Multiple R** is the correlation coefficient and **R Square** is just the correlation coefficient squared, i.e. coefficient of determination. The Adjusted **R Square** is a version of **R Square** that has been adjusted to take into account the number of independent variables in the regression model. **R Square** tends to overestimate the strength of the relationship between

---

[36] A Type I error occurs when a null hypothesis is rejected when it is in fact true.

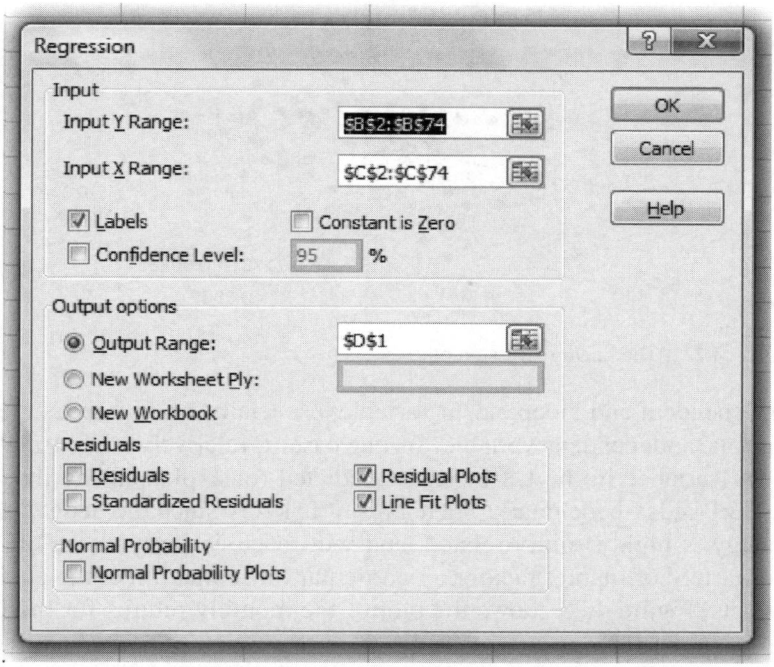

Figure 4.22 The **Regression** dialogue box

Table 4.14 Summary regression report

	A	B	C	D	E	F	G	H	I	J	K
1		LS Index (Y)	S&P Index (X)								
2	Date	RoR%	RoR%		**Regression Statistics**						
3	Jan-05	1.83	2.33		**Multiple R**	0.40117					
4	Feb-05	0.20	-0.57		**R Square**	0.16094					
5	Mar-05	0.03	0.63		**Adjusted R Square**	0.14895					
6	Apr-05	0.83	0.53		Standard Error	1.66881					
7	May-05	0.97	-0.24		Observations	72					
8	Jun-05	-0.05	3.30								
9	Jul-05	1.68	-3.41			*df*	*SS*	*MS*	*F*	*Significance F*	
10	Aug-05	1.28	5.07		Regression	1	37.3916	37.3916	13.4264	0.0005	
11	Sep-05	0.20	2.32		Residual	70	194.9454	2.7849			
12	Oct-05	-0.45	-2.85		Total	71	232.3369				
13	Nov-05	1.15	-0.44								
14	Dec-05	1.87	4.25			*Coefficients*	*Standard Error*	*t-statistic*	*p-Value*	*Lower 95%*	*Upper 95%*
15	Jan-06	-0.66	-2.73		Intercept (*a*)	0.6086	0.2027	3.0025	0.0037	0.2043	1.0129
16	Feb-06	1.51	2.40		Slope: S&P Index (*b*)	**0.2178**	**0.0594**	**3.6642**	**0.0005**	0.0993	0.3364
17	Mar-06	2.25	-0.18					=F16/G16	=TDIST(H16,F7-2,2)		
18	Apr-06	0.88	-1.57								
19	May-06	1.03	0.45								
20	Jun-06	2.05	0.60								
72	Oct-10	0.48	-0.60								
73	Nov-10	2.47	2.95								
74	Dec-10	2.25	1.53								

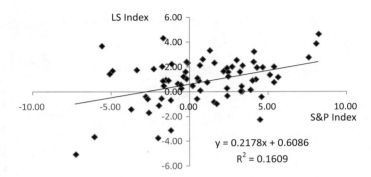

Figure 4.23 The linear regression plot

the dependent and independent variable, especially when there is more than one independent variable. In our case, a relatively high 16.09% of the variance in the LS index is predicted (or explained) by that in the S&P index benchmark. Such a result is likely since the hedge fund strategy is highly equity-related, and will react similarly to the effect of a variety of market factors, in particular those that affect the equity markets. Figure 4.23 shows the plot of the monthly returns for the LS index and S&P index as well as the fitted regression line and R^2 value.

In order to be confident of the validity of such a regression model it is necessary to investigate the statistical significance of the estimated coefficients in the regression model, especially the slope, i.e. $b = 0.2178$ (see Box 4.3).

Box 4.3   Statistical significance

The standard error (SE) about the regression line is a measure of the average amount by which the regression equation over- or under-predicts the model. The SE is a measure of the standard deviation of the coefficient in the regression model. The SE is used for calculating the t-statistics used in statistical tests of significance. The t-statistic (t) is given by

$$t = \frac{b}{SE}.$$

Where b is a coefficient calculated from the regression analysis, e.g. the slope. The t-statistic is compared with the value from the Student's t distribution so as to determine a p-value.

The Student's t distribution is generally defined as the probability distribution of a set of random variables that best fit the data without knowing the population standard deviation. The particular form of the t distribution depends on the number of degrees of freedom, i.e. the number of independent observations in a set of data. The higher the degrees of freedom, the closer the t distribution to the standard normal distribution. The t distribution is very similar in shape to the normal distribution but has fatter tails, resulting in more values being further away from the mean value as shown below.

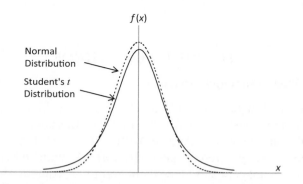

The t distribution plays a central role in the associated t-test for assessing the statistical significance of the difference between two sample means, the development of confidence intervals to determine the difference between two population means, and in linear regression analysis.

The p-value is the probability of obtaining a test statistic (e.g. t-statistic) at least as extreme as the one that was actually observed, assuming that the null hypothesis is true. It is often necessary to reject the null hypothesis when the p-value is less than 0.05, i.e. a 5% chance of rejecting the null hypothesis when it is true. When the null hypothesis is rejected, the result is said to be *statistically significant*. That is, if 95% of the t distribution is closer to the mean than the t-statistic for the coefficient of the regression, this relates to a p-value of 5%. With such a value there is only a 5% chance that the results of the regression analysis would have occurred in a random distribution, or there is a 95% probability that the coefficient is having some effect on the regression model. It is important to note that the size of the p-value for a coefficient indicates nothing about the effect the coefficient is having on the regression model, i.e. it is possible to have a coefficient with a very low p-value which has only a minimal effect on the model.

If there is a significant relationship between the dependent and independent variable (i.e. LS and S&P index), the slope (b) will not equal zero. In this case, the null hypothesis states that the slope is equal to zero. From Figure 4.23 the t-statistic[37] for the slope is 3.6642, which gives a p-value of 0.0005. The p-value is the probability that a t-statistic having 70 degrees of freedom is more extreme than 3.6642. Since the p-value is less than the significance level of 5% (0.05) the null hypothesis must be rejected.

4.11 PORTFOLIO THEORY

4.11.1 Mean–Variance Analysis

All hedge fund managers would like to achieve the highest possible return from their investment portfolios; however, this has to be weighed up against the amount of risk they are willing to accept. It is not unknown that assets with higher returns generally correlate with higher risk. However, a fund manager can reduce their overall exposure to the risk from individual assets by investing in a well-diversified portfolio of uncorrelated assets. For example, it is generally accepted that equity markets move *independently* of the bond market, and so a combination of both assets in a portfolio can lead to an overall lower level of risk. Indeed, diversification can lead to a reduction in risk even if asset returns are not negatively correlated. By holding a combination of assets that are not perfectly correlated (i.e. $-1 < \rho_{ij} < 1$) one can effectively achieve the same expected portfolio return but with a much lower level of portfolio risk (as measured by the portfolio variance). H.M. Markowitz[38] (1952) was one of the first to look at the correlation between various assets in order to obtain a mean portfolio return and subsequent reduction in the overall risk through diversification.[39] More technically, for a portfolio

---

[37] The TDIST() function returns the probability for the Student's t distribution where a numeric value (x) is a calculated value of t for which the probability is to be determined. For our case, the number of degrees of freedom is $n - 2$.

[38] Harry Markowitz (1927–) is an American economist and best known for his pioneering work in modern portfolio theory, studying the effects of asset risk, return, correlation and diversification on portfolio returns.

[39] Under the assumption that asset returns are normally distributed, investors are rational and markets are efficient.

made up of N risky assets, $i = 1, \ldots, N$, the expected portfolio return r_p is given by

$$r_p = \sum_{i=1}^{N} w_i \bar{r}_i. \qquad (4.27)$$

Where $\bar{r}_i$ is the mean return associated with each risky asset i and w_i are the individual holdings (or *weights*) invested in each risky asset i. It is assumed that the portfolio is *fully invested* so that the total holdings in each asset always add up to 100%, i.e. the following condition on the weights must hold:

$$\sum_{i=1}^{N} w_i = 1. \qquad (4.28)$$

The portfolio variance σ_p^2 is given by

$$\sigma_p^2 = \sum_{i=1}^{N} \sum_{j=1}^{N} w_i w_j \sigma_i \sigma_j \rho_{ij}, \qquad (4.29)$$

where ρ_{ij} is the correlation between the returns of assets i and j. Using equation (4.21) for the correlation, portfolio variance can also be written as

$$\sigma_p^2 = \sum_{i=1}^{N} \sum_{j=1}^{N} w_i w_j \sigma_{ij}. \qquad (4.30)$$

Where $\sigma_{ij} = \text{cov}\left(\bar{r}_i, \bar{r}_j\right)$, the covariance between the mean returns associated with assets i and j, and $\sigma_i^2 = \text{cov}\left(\bar{r}_i, \bar{r}_i\right)$. Both the mean portfolio return and variance can also be transformed into a compact matrix notation. That is, for the mean portfolio return we have

$$r_p = \sum_{i=1}^{N} w_i \bar{r}_i = W^T \times R. \qquad (4.31)$$

Where W^T is the matrix transpose of W which contains all the individual asset weights, w_i, and R is the matrix of mean returns for all assets i. W,

W^T and R are given by:

$$W = \begin{pmatrix} w_1 \\ w_2 \\ w_3 \\ \vdots \\ w_N \end{pmatrix}. \tag{4.32}$$

$$W^T = \begin{pmatrix} w_1 & w_2 & w_3 & \ldots & w_N \end{pmatrix}. \tag{4.33}$$

$$R = \begin{pmatrix} \bar{r}_1 \\ \bar{r}_2 \\ \bar{r}_3 \\ \vdots \\ \bar{r}_N \end{pmatrix}. \tag{4.34}$$

For the portfolio variance we have

$$\sigma_p^2 = \sum_{i=1}^{N} \sum_{j=1}^{N} w_i w_j \sigma_{ij} = W^T \Sigma W. \tag{4.35}$$

Where Σ is the variance–covariance matrix[40] for the individual assets i and j given by[41]

$$\Sigma = \begin{pmatrix} \sigma_1^2 & \text{cov}_{12} & \text{cov}_{13} & \ldots & \text{cov}_{1n} \\ \text{cov}_{21} & \sigma_2^2 & \text{cov}_{23} & \ldots & \text{cov}_{2n} \\ \text{cov}_{31} & \text{cov}_{32} & \sigma_3^2 & & \\ \vdots & \vdots & & \ddots & \\ \text{cov}_{n1} & \text{cov}_{n2} & & & \sigma_N^2 \end{pmatrix}. \tag{4.36}$$

Markowitz's work ultimately led to the development of *mean–variance portfolio optimisation*[42] as a method of achieving a desired level of portfolio expected return for a degree of portfolio risk. Given

---

[40] This is also known as the **VCV** matrix.

[41] As with all covariance matrices, Σ must be positive definite.

[42] Such a technique is known as *quadratic programming* and involves the optimisation (either *minimisation* or *maximisation*) of a quadratic function of several variables subject to a set of linear constraints on these variables. In this case, portfolio variance is a quadratic function of the weights w_i.

a target expected return of r^*, the mean–variance optimisation problem can be stated as follows:

$$\min W^T \Sigma W.$$

Subject to the constraints

$$W^T \times R = r^*, \qquad \sum_{i=1}^{N} w_i = 1.$$

The above optimisation problem assumes that *short selling* is allowed, i.e. the weights can be negative. If no short selling is allowed, the optimisation problem can be modified in the following way:

$$\min W^T \Sigma W,$$

subject to the constraints

$$W^T \times R = r^*, \qquad \sum_{i=1}^{N} w_i = 1, \quad w_i \geq 0.$$

It is also possible to impose a constraint on the maximum allowable investment (or limit) on one or more of the assets in the portfolio, i.e. $w_i \leq b$, where b is a real number.

4.11.2   Solver: Portfolio Optimisation

A mean–variance portfolio optimisation problem can be solved using the **Solver** tool available in Excel as part of the **Solver** add-in. Table 4.15 shows the necessary calculation for a 10-fund optimisation using the monthly returns for the hedge funds used in Section 4.9. In Table 4.15 rows 1 –74 have been hidden and contain the monthly returns for the 10 hedge funds.

Table 4.15 shows the calculation of the Σ and R matrices required to determine the portfolio expected return and variance using an initial equal weighting of 0.10 for each of the 10 hedge funds.[43] The expected portfolio return and variance for the 10 hedge fund portfolio is 8.55%

---

[43] The VAR() function returns the variance of a sample of data, the COVAR() function returns the covariance of two samples of data, the MMULT() function returns the matrix product of two arrays, and the TRANSPOSE() function returns the matrix transpose of an array. Note that MMULT() is an array-based formula, meaning that the combination keystroke CTRL + SHIFT + ENTER must be used in the relevant cell range.

Table 4.15   Ten-fund optimisation with all weights initially set to 0.10

	A	B	C	D	E	F	G	H	I	J	K	L	M	N	O
75					Covariance Matrix (Σ)										
76		CTA1	CTA2	CTA3	GM1	GM2	LS1	LS2	LS3	MN1	MN2				
77	CTA1	77.41	-0.27	0.16	-0.08	-1.81	-0.24	0.37	1.06	0.45	1.14				
78	CTA2	=VAR($B$3:$B$74)*12		0.33	0.17	-0.22	0.51	0.03	-0.18	-0.78					
79	CTA3	0.16	-1.37	163.26	0.64	-0.08	=COVAR($C$3:$C$74,G3:G74)				0.55				
80	GM1	-0.08	0.33	0.64	202.70	0.19	0.38	-1.47	-1.03	1.33	-0.45				
81	GM2	-1.81	=COVAR($E$3:$E$74,C3:C74)			233.16	-0.66	0.30	-1.77	-0.09	-1.72				
82	LS1	-0.24	-0.22	-0.45	0.38	-0.66	53.85	1.35	-0.59	0.11	-0.04				
83	LS2	0.37	0.51	-1.20	-1.47	0.30	1.35	134.24	0.95	-0.48	0.47				
84	LS3	1.06	0.03	0.65	-1.03	-1.77	-0.59	=VAR($H$3:$H$74)*12			0.76				
85	MN1	0.45	-0.18	1.53	1.33	-0.09	0.11	-0.48	0.67	31.82	-0.14				
86	MN2	1.14	-0.78	0.55	-0.45	-1.72	-0.04	0.47	0.76	-0.14	34.79				
87															
88	Return Matrix (R)				Weight Matrix (W)										
89	Fund	Return (%)			Fund	Weight									
90	1	12.82			CTA1	0.10									
91	2	6.86			CTA2	0.10									
92	3	14.21	=fncMEAN(D3:D74)			0.10									
93	4	11.81			GM1	0.10									
94	5	5.52			GM2	0.10									
95	6	9.84			LS1	0.10									
96	7	9.57			LS2	0.10									
97	8	6.91	=fncMEAN(B:I74)			0.10			Portfolio						
98	9	4.65			MN1	0.10			Return	8.55	={MMULT(TRANSPOSE(E90:E99),B90:B99)}				
99	10	3.32			MN2	0.10			Variance	10.72					
100						1					={MMULT(MMULT(TRANSPOSE(E90:E99),B77:K86),E90:E99)}				
101															

and 10.72 (i.e. $\sigma = 3.27\%$), respectively. Figures 4.24 and 4.25 show how to access the **Solver** tool and set the necessary parameters to find a solution to the 10-hedge fund optimisation problem.

For this problem, the target expected return[44] was set to 9.00% and no short sales are allowed. Table 4.16 shows that the optimised set of

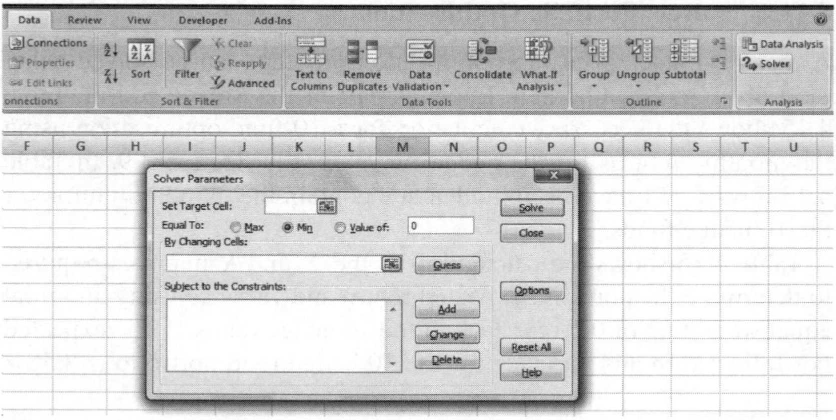

Figure 4.24   Locating the **Solver** tool in Excel

---

[44] Clearly, the targeted expected return cannot be more than the highest return for each asset unless negative holdings are possible, i.e. short sales are allowed.

	A	B	C	D	E
88	Return Matrix (R)		Weight Matrix (W)		
89	Fund	Return (%)	Fund	Weight	Limit
90	1	12.82	1	0.10	0.50
91	2	6.86	2	0.10	0.50
92	3	14.21	3	0.10	0.50
93	4	11.81	4	0.10	0.50
94	5	5.52	5	0.10	0.50
95	6	9.84	6	0.10	0.50
96	7	9.57	7	0.10	0.50
97	8	6.91	8	0.10	0.50
98	9	4.65	9	0.10	0.50
99	10	3.32	10	0.10	0.50
100			TOTAL	1	
101					
102			Target Return (%)	9.00	
103					
104			Portfolio		
105			Return (%)	8.55	
106			Min. Variance	10.72	

Solver Parameters

Set Target Cell: $E$106

Equal To: ○ Max ● Min ○ Value of: 0

By Changing Cells:
$D$90:$D$99

Guess

Subject to the Constraints:
$D$100 = 1
$D$90 <= $E$90
$D$90:$D$99 >= 0
$D$91 <= $E$91
$D$92 <= $E$92
$D$93 <= $E$93

Add   Change   Delete

Solve   Close   Options   Reset All   Help

Figure 4.25   Setting the parameters for the **Solver** tool

weights gives a minimum portfolio variance of 8.40 (i.e. $\sigma = 2.90\%$), which is less than the original value ($\sigma = 3.27\%$). That is, the portfolio of weighted assets has been optimised to give the minimum variance (or risk) for a higher expected portfolio return. Clearly, as markets conditions and risk preferences change, the portfolio must be rebalanced and a new set of optimised weights determined. In the original work by Markowitz, the costs of the transactions associated with buying and selling assets were not included. However, such transaction costs could represent a significant amount to the hedge fund manager and need to be taken into account when considering the results from mean–variance optimisations.

Table 4.16   Set of optimised weights for the minimum variance portfolio

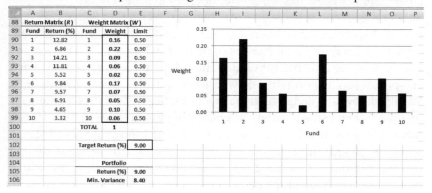

	A	B	C	D	E
88	Return Matrix (R)		Weight Matrix (W)		
89	Fund	Return (%)	Fund	Weight	Limit
90	1	12.82	1	0.16	0.50
91	2	6.86	2	0.22	0.50
92	3	14.21	3	0.09	0.50
93	4	11.81	4	0.06	0.50
94	5	5.52	5	0.02	0.50
95	6	9.84	6	0.17	0.50
96	7	9.57	7	0.07	0.50
97	8	6.91	8	0.05	0.50
98	9	4.65	9	0.10	0.50
99	10	3.32	10	0.06	0.50
100			TOTAL	1	
101					
102			Target Return (%)	9.00	
103					
104			Portfolio		
105			Return (%)	9.00	
106			Min. Variance	8.40	

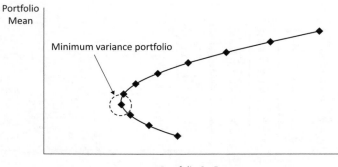

Figure 4.26   The efficient frontier and minimum variance portfolio

4.11.3   Efficient Portfolios

Markowitz reduced the mean–variance optimisation problem to that of finding the locus of *efficient portfolios*, where 'efficient' means having the highest expected portfolio return for a given level of portfolio variance (or risk). Portfolios with the best combinations of weights lie on the *efficient frontier*, where a target expected return is achieved with minimum risk. The efficient frontier contains a unique minimum variance, and overall there will be a minimum variance portfolio. Figure 4.26 shows the efficient frontier for a set of risky assets. As shown in Figure 4.26, all possible combinations of the risky assets can be plotted in so-called risk–expected return space, and the collection of all such possible portfolios defines a region in this space. The left boundary of this region is a hyperbola with the upper edge being the efficient frontier (also known as the *Markowitz bullet*). For combinations along this upper edge there is lowest risk for a given level of expected return.

In this chapter we have covered the main visual and mathematical techniques for analysing a time series of hedge fund returns. We have noted that such hedge fund returns tend to show departures from degree of and can possess some normality skewness and kurtosis in their distribution. We also know that hedge fund managers are heavily exposed to the risks involved when using a variety of underlying instruments in their investment strategies. In this case, for a certain hedge fund strategy or index, a set of correlated market factors can be identified and the strength of their relationship quantified using regression analysis. Indeed, along with a thorough knowledge of the particular strategy and market environment, hedge fund managers can further supplement these quantitative measures with qualitative estimates. Moreover, a fund manager can reduce their overall exposure to the risk from individual assets by investing in a well-diversified portfolio of uncorrelated assets. With this in mind, we finally looked at mean–variance portfolio optimisation and showed how this technique can effectively achieve the same expected return but with a much lower level of risk for a portfolio of hedge funds.

In Chapters 5 and 6 many of the statistical methods developed in this chapter are used in analysing risk-adjusted return metrics and other more advanced hedge fund models.

5
Risk-Adjusted Return Metrics

Since hedge funds use mainly derivatives (e.g. futures, forwards and options) and collateralised over-the-counter (OTC) instruments (e.g. interbank foreign exchange, contracts for difference, credit and correlation products) for investment and trading purposes, the degree of exposure to each underlying instrument may vary from low to high and is not necessarily a function of the AuM available for investment as in the world of traditional investing. In other words, in the world of hedge funds, leverage is a variable controlled directly by the fund manager and can typically vary dynamically from zero to 20 times or even higher. Leverage is typically accomplished using real-time margining and collateralisation facilities through prime brokers or banks for OTC instruments and via futures contracts which are traded through futures commission merchants (FCMs). It is therefore not good enough to use historical returns only (as in traditional investments) to measure the performance of a hedge fund manager since they could be an average performer who simply use excessive leverage to produce high returns.

The essence of modern-day hedge fund appraisal therefore lies in the ability to measure *risk-adjusted* returns which show how well each hedge fund manager performs on a net basis per unit risk. As we progress through this chapter and into Chapter 6, other methods will be introduced to show that it is not just how well a manager performs in a risk-adjusted way that matters, but rather how difficult the fund is to replicate. This is because, regardless of the manager's claims of being absolute, hedge funds typically have dynamic exposures to other asset classes (and so could be partially replicated at lower cost), as demonstrated by Fung and Hsieh (2000a, 2004). Thus, for the sophisticated investor, what at first sight seems like a great hedge fund in the risk-adjusted sense could turn out to be easily replicable once some in-depth analysis has been performed using asset pricing models (see Chapter 6). The hedge fund investment process is therefore quite akin to that of the detective process where each clue is painstakingly examined and every lead is followed up in order to establish a realistic picture of the scene despite the opacity of the situation. In this way the managers who provide genuine exotic alpha (and so have real measurable skill and deserve to be paid typical hedge fund fees) can be separated from those who are producing sophisticated alternative beta (which is available at lower cost), unsophisticated alternative beta (which can usually be cheaply replicated) and those who are managing traditional beta (which should be virtually free). This chapter uses hypothetical hedge fund data to demonstrate the selection and filtering process typically applied today by sophisticated hedge fund investors in the risk-adjusted world.

5.1   THE INTUITION BEHIND RISK-ADJUSTED RETURNS

Consider two CTAs – manager A and manager B – and assume both managers are operating in the same style (e.g. diversified managed futures) and use similar underlying instruments for investment and trading purposes. Also assume that *notional funding*[1] is available for an investor who has $5 million to collateralise a managed account through their FCM of choice and is hoping one CTA will manage all or part of their capital through a *power of attorney*[2] at 2% management fee and 20% incentive fee.[3] Neglecting higher moments, the annualised first two moments (M1 = return and M2 = volatility[4]) and the risk-adjusted return ratio = M1/M2 are shown in Table 5.1.

Figure 5.1 shows the VAMI for managers A and B. At first glance, an unsophisticated investor who had to choose between managers A and B (an *all-or-nothing* investment choice) would choose manager B, since manager B obviously has a historical record of providing higher returns over time for their investors. However, due to the possibility of notional

---

[1] *Notional funding* can be used to maximise investment capital efficiency since, with a margined account, only a certain amount of collateral is required for the margin (M). Usually the investor adds a cushion (C) of capital for future potential drawdowns. If the managed account has a minimum value of P, then actual funds committed are $A = M + C$, and the notional funding amount is $N = P - A$. It follows that the leverage L obtained by the investment as a function of notional funding for a fixed minimum account size is given by $L(N) = [1 - N/P]^{-1}$.

[2] The *power of attorney* is an official document signed by the CTA, the investor and the FCM that legally authorises the CTA to manage the client's account (i.e. investor) at the FCM and receive payment for their management services.

[3] 2% of AuM and 20% of net new profits is the industry standard fee structure for CTAs.

[4] Strictly speaking, the second central moment of a normal distribution is the *variance*.

Table 5.1 Two CTAs – managers A and B

	A	B	C	D	E	F	G	H	I
1	**Month**	**Mgr A**	**Mgr B**						
2	Jan-05	0.10	0.89		**Mgr A**	**Mgr B**			
3	Feb-05	1.79	-0.90	**M1**	6.86	11.81	=AVERAGE(C2:C73)*12		
4	Mar-05	2.04	-5.38	**M2**	5.27	14.14	=STDEVP(C2:C73)*SQRT(12)		
5	Apr-05	1.34	1.33	**M1/M2**	1.30	0.84	=F3/F4		
6	May-05	-0.16	0.88						
7	Jun-05	-1.40	-1.02						
8	Jul-05	1.15	-2.88						
9	Aug-05	-1.20	3.81						
10	Sep-05	-1.99	5.93						
70	Sep-10	1.06	5.06						
71	Oct-10	-0.69	6.19						
72	Nov-10	1.27	-4.46						
73	Dec-10	0.10	0.59						

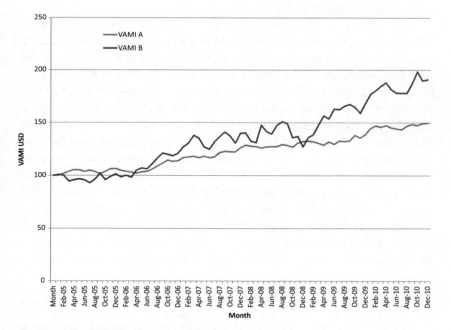

Figure 5.1   VAMI for two CTAs – managers A and B

funding commonly found in the world of managed account investing[5] with CTAs, a sophisticated investor would notice that they could fund each account at a range of funding levels and up to the CTA to decide at what actual level of funds they would set their limits for trading and investing. Notional funding can be used to set an investment return target, regardless of the CTA's historical annualised returns (see Example 5.1).

5.1.1 Risk-Adjusted Returns

Assuming the first two moments of the hedge fund return distribution are the only important estimates for investment appraisal, the logical way to proceed for investment analysis would be to create a Cartesian[6] diagram in these two dimensions. The concept of investment analysis in *risk-adjusted return*, *mu–sigma* or *mean–variance* space was pioneered by Harry Markowitz (1952).[7] The two-dimensional Cartesian points for each CTA are shown in Figure 5.2.

This method of looking at unique points per manager in two-dimensional space is one way to allow the investor to visualise their investment. The major drawback is of course that it assumes only the first two moments of the return distribution are important. However, hedge funds also exhibit higher moments, as discussed in Chapter 4 as well as by Favre and Ranaldo (2005). For now, though, we assume that the investor is only interested in the returns and the riskiness of those returns as measured by volatility. Assuming the investor faces an all-or-nothing choice, which manager would be preferable? Since we know due to notional funding that an investor can in theory leverage their investment, the objective function for the investor is simply that of a rational one. For a certain return expectation, they want to arrive at their target wealth expectation with the *minimum of risk*. Since we are measuring risk at this stage solely by volatility, it therefore follows that if we were to draw two straight lines from the origin of Figure 5.2

---

[5] Note that notional funding is usually associated with investing in managed accounts, as opposed to hedge funds which usually have a predefined and fixed risk and return profile.

[6] Descartes (1596–1650) was a French mathematician and philosopher who developed the Cartesian coordinate system.

[7] Milton Friedman, Markowitz's external examiner, was so shocked to read Markowitz's pioneering work on risk reduction that he did not think the thesis could even be considered part of the then nascent field of financial economics. Nowadays, Markowitz's work is considered to be the foundation of modern portfolio theory.

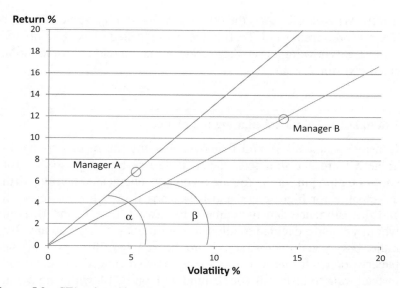

Figure 5.2   CTAs plotted in mu–sigma space

through the unique location point of each manager, and measure the angle of each line from the x-axis, i.e. the angles α and β, the manager of preference in the risk-adjusted sense would be the manager who has the largest angle. In this case, it is clear that $\alpha > \beta$, so A is preferred over B in the risk-adjusted sense. As can be seen from Figure 5.2, each angle is directly proportional to the *gradient*[8] and it therefore follows that

$$\frac{R_A}{\sigma_A} > \frac{R_B}{\sigma_B}. \tag{5.1}$$

The investor's risk-adjusted investment objective is therefore to maximise their risk-adjusted returns, i.e.

$$\theta = \left[\frac{E(R_P)}{\sigma_P}\right]_{\max}. \tag{5.2}$$

Where $E(R_p)$ is the expected future returns of the investment and σ_p the expected volatility of returns. As can be seen from Table 5.1, for

---

[8] A *gradient* is measured as the ratio of vertical distance to the origin over the horizontal distance to the origin for a point in two-dimensional space.

the ratio M1/M2, CTA A is the obvious winner with a value of 1.30, so CTA A is preferred over CTA B in the risk-adjusted sense. Example 5.1 demonstrates how important these concepts are in reality for the sophisticated investor.

Example 5.1   Notional funding in practice

Consider managers A and B above. Assume the results shown in Table 5.1 are net after fees and that the risk-free rate is 0.0% for simplification purposes. You are a young sophisticated investor with an appetite for high return and have carried out all your research and due diligence and particularly like two CTAs, A and B, with whom you have decided to allocate your money. Since you are also rather busy you do not want to go to the trouble of filling out all the paperwork and forms necessary to set up two managed accounts, and instead want to invest all your capital with one CTA with whom you wish to develop a long-term relationship. In particular, you want to earn around 30.0% per annum on your capital of $5 million (each manager accepts minimum account sizes of $1 million). Since CTA A has the highest risk-adjusted return ratio you have decided to choose them as your only manager. From their track record, you know that on average you have an expectation that they can produce annualised net returns of 6.86% with an estimated volatility of 5.27% on the minimum account sizes of $1 million. Considering you want to earn around 30.0% per annum and not just 6.86%, this means you need the manager to leverage by a factor $L = 30.0/6.86 = 4.37$ times, i.e. the CTA should set up an account that is leveraged 4.37 times. From footnote 2, $L(N) = \left[1 - \frac{N}{P}\right]^{-1}$ and $N = P - A$. Since $L = 4.37$ and $A = 5$, $P = N + 5$. Solving for N gives $N = \$16.85$ million and, since the fully funded account size is $P = N + 5$, then $P = \$21.85$ million. Therefore, you set up an account with CTA A for the value of $21.85 million, of which $5 million are the actual funds and the rest notional funds of $16.85 million. Thus, you will expect a net return per annum of 30.0% on your $5 million through this CTA. You will, however, also expect an associated volatility of L times the CTA volatility, i.e. $4.37 \times 5.27\% = 23.0\%$. Since the risk-adjusted ratio of the CTA remains constant, the returns (numerator) are increased by a factor L; the volatility (denominator) must also be increased by a factor L for the risk-adjusted return ratio to remain constant.

Since you are risk-averse and $5 million represents a fraction of your net worth, you are happy to accept such a level of volatility for an expected annual return of 30.0%. You are also happy with the decision to accept margin funding since the manager has an average *margin-to-equity* (M/E)[9] of only 5.0% (in reality this can range up to 30% and higher for highly leveraged managers). With an account of $21.85 million, this will translate into an operational daily requirement of margin equal to 5.0% of $21.85 million i.e. $1.09 million ($M$). Since you are investing $5 million in actual funds (A), the cushion is $C = A - M = 5.0 - 1.09 = $3.91 million. Again you are happy with this since this cushion should buffer you from future margin calls with a low probability of having to inject further collateral into the account in the event of a margin call. The notional funding level is defined as $NF = (N \times 100)/P = (16.85 \times 100)/21.85 \approx 77\%$.

Note the situation if you had been naïve and uninformed as to the virtues of risk-adjusted investing through CTAs. If you had erroneously chosen CTA B (perhaps because at first glance CTA B had higher returns) and assumed notional funding, whilst you could have engineered an account to return 30.0% net per annum, your volatility expectation would have been 35.9% for CTA B (i.e. $30.0/11.81 \times 14.14$). This shows that by using risk-adjusted returns to measure the manager's relative performance and by correctly choosing CTA A to invest in, your expected volatility for reaching an annual return of 30.0% would be around 23.0% for CTA A versus 35.9% for CTA B – a significant reduction of 12.9%.

5.2 COMMON RISK-ADJUSTED PERFORMANCE RATIOS

As mentioned in Section 5.1, the first step in performing a hedge fund analysis is to measure and rank the absolute performance of each hedge

---

[9] M/E is usually defined as the average amount of margin required by the FCM (M) divided by the un-notionalised management account size of the CTA (P), thus, average $M/E\% = (M \times 100)/P$.

fund in the risk-adjusted sense, so the higher the M1/M2 ratio the better. In this section, we will describe the main risk-adjusted return metrics currently used within the industry and use an example to show how each can be calculated for 10 different hedge funds (see Box 5.1) and to present a conclusion on the final results and the differences expected between each approach.

Box 5.1   Ten Hypothetical Hedge Funds

The table below shows 10 hypothetical hedge monthly returns between 2005 and 2010[*] classified as follows:

- commodity trading advisors CTA1, CTA2 and CTA3;
- global macro funds GM1 and GM2;
- long/short funds LS1, LS2 and LS3;
- market neutral funds MN1 and MN2.

	A	B	C	D	E	F	G	H	I	J	K	L
1		CTA1	CTA2	CTA3	GM1	GM2	LS1	LS2	LS3	MN1	MN2	Average
2	M1	12.82	6.86	14.21	11.81	5.52	9.84	9.57	6.91	4.65	3.32	8.55
3	M2	8.74	5.27	12.69	14.14	15.16	7.31	11.51	10.64	5.60	5.86	9.69
4	M3	0.07	0.35	-0.55	-0.02	0.13	0.89	0.11	0.23	0.10	0.11	0.14
5	M4	0.04	-0.85	1.71	-0.11	0.36	0.61	-0.57	-0.01	-0.29	0.23	0.11
6												
7			CTA		Global Macro		Long Short			Market Neutral		
8	Month	CTA1	CTA2	CTA3	GM1	GM2	LS1	LS2	LS3	MN1	MN2	
9	Jan-05	4.68	0.10	-2.69	0.89	-6.66	0.37	5.80	2.36	-3.09	2.81	
10	Feb-05	-0.18	1.79	3.61	-0.90	2.93	-1.06	4.27	0.32	-0.87	-3.51	
11	Mar-05	0.66	2.04	-0.28	-5.38	6.68	0.62	-3.11	-0.44	0.19	-1.56	
12	Apr-05	-1.45	1.34	2.95	1.33	2.26	-0.62	-4.67	4.89	0.56	-0.07	
13	May-05	3.11	-0.16	-4.83	0.88	2.21	-1.40	4.12	-1.54	-0.82	0.38	
14	Jun-05	1.10	-1.40	5.01	-1.02	-6.26	1.36	-0.31	1.02	0.97	-0.07	
15	Jul-05	-5.11	1.15	8.03	-2.88	6.66	2.02	6.87	1.12	1.50	-2.85	
16	Aug-05	4.91	-1.20	3.25	3.81	-0.72	0.74	0.31	4.32	2.41	0.62	
17	Sep-05	-0.70	-1.99	-1.96	5.93	0.38	0.54	-6.94	-0.10	2.23	-0.46	
18	Oct-05	1.33	2.20	-0.75	-6.20	1.30	1.77	1.97	-6.56	0.51	-0.33	
78	Oct-10	-0.31	-0.69	3.89	6.19	-6.24	-0.45	3.36	-2.65	1.87	1.38	
79	Nov-10	-0.85	1.27	1.42	-4.46	-5.71	0.78	7.45	-0.01	-0.74	-0.14	
80	Dec-10	0.45	0.10	-1.33	0.59	2.48	0.10	-0.54	1.27	-0.75	0.50	

CTA3 is seen to be the best performer in terms of the first moment (M1) with a return of 14.21%, closely followed by CTA1 at 12.82%. The clear poorest performer based on return is MN2 with a value of 3.32%.

The 10 hypothetical hedge funds will be used to demonstrate how the various metrics and asset pricing models can be used to investigate hedge fund performance. The results will also highlight the key differences in the approaches as each technique often produces different rankings for each fund.

The VAMIs for each hypothetical hedge fund are shown below:

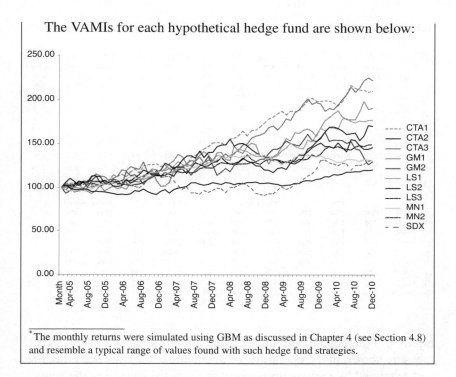

Table 5.2 shows the 10 hypothetical hedge funds and various absolute risk-adjusted return metrics. Most risk-adjusted return metrics are generalised using the following formulation:

$$\text{Risk-adjusted returns} = \frac{R_P - R_F}{\text{Risk}}. \qquad (5.3)$$

Usually the numerator does not change, i.e. it is the measured ex-post annualised return for the hedge fund less the annualised risk-free rate or some minimum acceptable rate of return. What does make each metric unique is the composition of the denominator, i.e. the risk measure. What constitutes the nature of risk is one of the biggest headaches for investor and academics alike – with many different measures emerging in recent decades. The most basic (and most widely used) method of calculating risk for the denominator is the volatility of returns. The good thing about volatility is that it *parsimoniously* captures the normal nature of market risk so that most investors and traders can intuitively understand it. However, it has drawbacks due to its simplicity, e.g. higher moments such as skewness and kurtosis are neglected, the distribution could be

Table 5.2   The 10 hypothetical hedge funds and risk-adjusted return metrics

	A	B	C	D	E	F	G	H	I	J	K	L
1		CTA1	CTA2	CTA3	GM1	GM2	LS1	LS2	LS3	MN1	MN2	Average
2	M1	12.82	6.86	14.21	11.81	5.52	9.84	9.57	6.91	4.65	3.32	8.55
3	M2	8.74	5.27	12.69	14.14	15.16	7.31	11.51	10.64	5.60	5.86	9.69
4	M3	0.07	0.35	-0.55	-0.02	0.13	0.89	0.11	0.23	0.10	0.11	0.14
5	M4	0.04	-0.85	1.71	-0.11	0.36	0.61	-0.57	-0.01	-0.29	0.23	0.11
6												
7	M1/M2	1.47	=B2/B3	1.12	0.84	0.36	1.35	0.83	0.65	0.83	0.57	0.93
8	Sharpe	1.12	=(B2-3)/B3	0.88	0.62	0.17	0.94	0.57	0.37	0.29	0.05	0.58
9	MSR	1.86	=fncMSR(B15:B86,3,0.05)			0.32	1.43	1.02	0.67	0.53	0.10	1.00
10	Sortino	2.98	=fncSORTINO(B15:B86,3)			0.50	2.19	1.60	0.97	0.52	0.10	1.48
11	DD Ratio	1.13	=(B2-3)/fncDDOWNMAX('10 VAMIs'!B13:B85)					0.39	0.15	0.13	0.03	0.43
12												
13			CTA		Global Macro		Long Short			Market Neutral		
14	Month	CTA1	CTA2	CTA3	GM1	GM2	LS1	LS2	LS3	MN1	MN2	
15	Jan-05	4.68	0.10	-2.69	0.89	-6.66	0.37	5.80	2.36	-3.09	2.81	
16	Feb-05	-0.18	1.79	3.61	-0.90	2.93	-1.06	4.27	0.32	-0.87	-3.51	
17	Mar-05	0.66	2.04	-0.28	-5.38	6.68	0.62	-3.11	-0.44	0.19	-1.56	
18	Apr-05	-1.45	1.34	2.95	1.33	2.26	-0.62	-4.67	4.89	0.56	-0.07	
19	May-05	3.11	-0.16	-4.83	0.88	2.21	-1.40	4.12	-1.54	-0.82	0.38	
20	Jun-05	1.10	-1.40	5.01	-1.02	-6.26	1.36	-0.31	1.02	0.97	-0.07	
85	Nov-10	-0.85	1.27	1.42	-4.46	-5.71	0.78	7.45	-0.01	-0.74	-0.14	
86	Dec-10	0.45	0.10	-1.33	0.59	2.48	0.10	-0.54	1.27	-0.75	0.50	

highly irregular and it does not measure drawdowns. As a result, the risk measure shown in the denominator in equation (5.3) has been modified and redefined by various researchers and practitioners over the years to encompass more complex and meaningful measures as demanded by sophisticated investors. These metrics will be described and modelled in the following subsections.

5.2.1   The Sharpe Ratio

The Sharpe ratio[10] is defined by Sharpe (1994) as

$$\text{Sharpe} = \frac{R_P - R_F}{\sigma_P}. \tag{5.4}$$

Where R_P is the annualised return, R_F is the annualised risk-free rate (e.g. using the T-bill as a proxy) and σ_P is the volatility of the returns. As can be seen, the only difference between equation (5.4) and the M1/M2 measure introduced in Section 5.1 is the existence of the risk-free rate

---

[10] William Sharpe (1934–) is famous for the development of the capital asset pricing model (CAPM).

Table 5.3 Ranked results for M1/M2 and the
Sharpe ratio for the 10 hypothetical hedge funds

	M1/M2		Sharpe
CTA1	1.47	CTA1	1.12
LS1	1.35	LS1	0.94
CTA2	1.30	CTA3	0.88
CTA3	1.12	CTA2	0.73
GM1	0.84	GM1	0.62
LS2	0.83	LS2	0.57
MN1	0.83	LS3	0.37
LS3	0.65	MN1	0.29
MN2	0.57	GM2	0.17
GM2	0.36	MN2	0.05

which is subtracted from the annualised first moment in the numerator.
As such, the Sharpe ratio introduces the concept of a static *benchmark*
to the numerator. In other words, the investor wants to earn at least
the risk-free rate and since they want the highest Sharpe ratio, this will
begin to penalise hedge funds whose returns are low. Also, any fund
with annualised returns less than the risk-free rate will have a negative
Sharpe ratio regardless of the fund volatility. The M1/M2 and Sharpe
ratios were calculated for the 10 hypothetical hedge funds and the results
ranked from the highest to the lowest in descending order using the **Sort**
dialog box in the **Data** menu in Excel. The results are shown in Table 5.3.

As can be seen, both methods rank the managers similarly, with some
differences noticed. The first two funds, CTA1 and LS1, both score
highest. Then the Sharpe method differs for the third and fourth funds,
i.e. CTA3 and CTA2 are the inverse of the M1/M2 ratio method. This
is because whilst CTA2 has a better absolute risk-adjusted return than
CTA3, the returns are lower – so when the Sharpe ratio is calculated with
$R_F = 3.0\%$, CTA2 is penalised and CTA3 takes its place in the ranked
order. So, we are starting to see the shine come off the previously top-
ranked funds as some degree of benchmarking is introduced – albeit a
static measure of a mere 3.0%. This effect continues as LS3 is preferred
over MN1 and GM2 is preferred over MN2 for similar reasons.

5.2.2   The Modified Sharpe Ratio

The Modified Sharpe Ratio (MSR) as developed by Gregoriou and Gueyie (2003) is defined as

$$MSR = \frac{R_P - R_F}{MVaR_p}. \tag{5.5}$$

The MSR takes the Sharpe ratio one stage further in complexity, taking into account the higher moments of the distribution – the skewness (S) and the excess kurtosis (K). The MSR was developed to capture higher moments in the risk measure of the denominator using the Cornish–Fisher expansion. The Cornish–Fisher expansion is given by

$$\tilde{z}_\alpha = z_\alpha + \frac{1}{6}\left(z_\alpha^2 - 1\right)S + \frac{1}{24}\left(z_\alpha^3 - 3z_\alpha\right)(K - 3) - \frac{1}{36}\left(2z_\alpha^3 - 5z_\alpha\right)S^2. \tag{5.6}$$

And the modified VaR $(MVaR_p)$ measure used as the denominator of equation (5.5) is written as[11]

$$MVaR_P(1 - \alpha) = \text{abs}\left(-\left(\mu + \tilde{z}_\alpha\sigma\right)\right). \tag{5.7}$$

Where z_α is the critical value for probability $1-\alpha$ (e.g. $z=-2.33$ at 99% confidence). For the Gaussian case, $S = 0$ and $K = 0$ so $\tilde{z}_\alpha = z_\alpha$. Source 5.1 shows a user-defined VBA function to calculate the MSR.

Source 5.1   User-defined VBA function to calculate modified Sharpe ratio for a series of returns

```
'function to calculate MODIFIED SHARPE RATIO
for a series of returns
Function fncMSR(list, Rf, alpha)

'count the no. of returns in the list
n = WorksheetFunction.Count(list)

'the average return in the list
m1 = WorksheetFunction.Average(list)

'the sample standard deviation of the
returns in the list
m2 = WorksheetFunction.StDev(list)
```

---

[11] MVaR will be discussed in further detail in Chapter 7.

```
'the skewness of the returns in the list
m3 = WorksheetFunction.Skew(list)

'the kurtosis of the returns in the list
m4 = WorksheetFunction.Kurt(list)

'the one-sided Z value corresponding to the CI
or alpha value supplied in the list of
arguments to the function eg. Z=2.33 for CI=99%
(alpha=0.01)

Z = WorksheetFunction.NormSInv(1 - alpha)

'the modified Cornish Fisher Z value
ZCF = Z + (1 / 6) * (Z ^ 2 - 1) * m3 + (1 / 24) *
(Z ^ 3 - 3 * Z) * m4 - (1 / 36) * (2 * Z ^ 3 -
5 * Z) * m3 ^ 2

'the modified Value at Risk (positive valued)
ModVar = m1 + ZCF * m2

'the Modified Sharpe Ratio (MSR) function
fncMSR = (m1 * 12 - Rf) / ModVar

End Function
```

Table 5.4 shows the results for the ranked MSR when applied to the 10 hypothetical hedge funds versus the M1/M2 and Sharpe ratios. As can be seen, there is now another change in the first two rankings, with CTA3 taking the preferred place over LS1 which was the second preferred choice for both the M1/M2 and Sharpe ratio. This is explained by the inclusion of higher moments in the denominator and, according to the MSR, CTA3 is preferred in this respect.

5.2.3 The Sortino Ratio

The Sortino[12] ratio is defined as

$$\text{Sortino} = \frac{R_P - MAR}{\sqrt{\frac{1}{T} \sum_{\substack{t=0 \\ R_P < MAR}}^{T} (R_{P,t} - MAR)^2}}.$$ (5.8)

---

[12] Initially defined by Brian M. Rom in 1986 but later developed in the 1990s by Frank Sortino.

Table 5.4   Ranked results for MSR, M1/M2 and Sharpe ratio for
10 hypothetical hedge funds

	M1/M2		Sharpe		MSR
CTA1	1.47	CTA1	1.12	CTA1	1.86
LS1	1.35	LS1	0.94	CTA3	1.72
CTA2	1.30	CTA3	0.88	LS1	1.43
CTA3	1.12	CTA2	0.73	CTA2	1.18
GM1	0.84	GM1	0.62	GM1	1.14
LS2	0.83	LS2	0.57	LS2	1.02
MN1	0.83	LS3	0.37	LS3	0.67
LS3	0.65	MN1	0.29	MN1	0.53
MN2	0.57	GM2	0.17	GM2	0.32
GM2	0.36	MN2	0.05	MN2	0.10

The Sortino ratio is another variant of the Sharpe ratio. The problem
with the Sharpe ratio is that it uses volatility as a measure of risk for
the entire time series of monthly returns. As a result, both large up
and downswings are penalised as they translate into higher volatility
and a lower Sharpe ratio. The Sortino ratio differentiates itself from the
Sharpe ratio by making the distinction between good (desirable upside)
volatility and bad (undesirable downside) volatility. As can be seen
from equation (5.8), the denominator uses the concept of the minimum
acceptable return (MAR) to set a reference point for the measurement
of returns. Basically the MAR is a fixed value, e.g. 3.0%, which sets
a minimum acceptable rate of return for the investor and in doing so
divides the returns into two categories, i.e. those returns greater than or
equal to MAR (the *upside semi-deviation*) and those returns less than
MAR (the *downside semi-deviation*). The Sortino ratio uses a measure
of standard deviation in the denominator which only uses the downside
returns in the calculation. Therefore the higher the Sortino ratio, the
better the manager is at controlling downside returns whilst not being
penalised for producing high upside returns. As such it is good metric
for assessing the effectiveness of risk management and profit generation
for a hedge fund manager.

The user-defined VBA function to calculate the Sortino ratio is shown
in Source 5.2.

Source 5.2   User-defined VBA function to calculate the Sortino ratio for a series of returns

```
'function to calculate the SORTINO RATIO
for a series of returns
Function fncSORTINO(list, MAR)

'initialise variables
Count = 0
DSdelsum = 0
Retsum = 0

 For Each Item In list

 'add all returns for the portfolio for the final
average return calculation
 Retsum = Item + Retsum

 'if the return is less than the MAR, then count
it as a downside return, otherwise don't

  If Item < MAR Then Item = Item
  If Item >= MAR Then Item = 0

 'calculate the downside semi-deviation
 Dsdel = (Item - MAR) ^ 2

 'sum them for all items in the list
 DSdelsum = Dsdel + DSdelsum

 'create a cumulative sum of the no. of points
 Count = Count + 1

 Next Item

'calculate the annualised portfolio return
Portret = (Retsum / Count) + 12
```

```
'calculate the denominator for the Sortino
ratio assuming the population version of this
standard deviation
Sordem = (DSdelsum / (Count)) ^ 0.5

'calculate the Sortino
fncSORTINO = (Portret - MAR) / Sordem

End Function
```

The ranked results are shown in Table 5.5, which shows that there seems to be a clear contender emerging from the risk-adjusted measures, namely CTA1 since it has been ranked top for all four methods so far. CTA3 is also favoured over LS1 due to the MSR result – showing that the high kurtosis of CTA3 must be associated with good kurtosis, i.e. high returns in the upside semi-deviation. Whilst having a negative skew, the returns in the downside semi-deviation below the MAR are milder than those associated with the downside semi-deviation in LS1. As we go down the Sortino ranking, we also notice that GM1 is preferred over CTA2. In a nutshell, it shows how the estimates of skewness and kurtosis can be misleading since CTA2 has a higher skewness (0.35 vs. –0.02

Table 5.5 Ranked Sortino ratio compared to other risk-adjusted return metrics

	M1/M2		Sharpe		MSR		Sortino
CTA1	1.47	CTA1	1.12	CTA1	1.86	CTA1	2.98
LS1	1.35	LS1	0.94	CTA3	1.72	CTA3	2.69
CTA2	1.30	CTA3	0.88	LS1	1.43	LS1	2.19
CTA3	1.12	CTA2	0.73	CTA2	1.18	GM1	1.96
GM1	0.84	GM1	0.62	GM1	1.14	LS2	1.60
LS2	0.83	LS2	0.57	LS2	1.02	CTA2	1.30
MN1	0.83	LS3	0.37	LS3	0.67	LS3	0.97
LS3	0.65	MN1	0.29	MN1	0.53	MN1	0.52
MN2	0.57	GM2	0.17	GM2	0.32	GM2	0.50
GM2	0.36	MN2	0.05	MN2	0.10	MN2	0.10

for GM1) and a lower kurtosis (-0.85 vs. -0.11 for GM1), while the Sortino ratio ranks GM1 higher than CTA2.

5.2.4   The Drawdown Ratio

The drawdown ratio (DD ratio) is given by

$$\text{DD ratio} = \frac{R_P - R_F}{|\text{max DD}|}. \tag{5.9}$$

The DD ratio is yet another variant of the Sharpe ratio, but this time the measure of risk in the denominator is determined by the absolute value of the *maximum historical drawdown*. The maximum drawdown is defined as the maximum amount lost in VAMI (or NAV) terms from the highest preceding high to the lowest low during the period that the hedge fund remains under water (it has not recuperated its value to that above the last highest high or high water mark). Once the hedge fund has recuperated its losses and has achieved a net new high, it is said to be *out-of-its* drawdown. The duration of this maximum drawdown period is called the *maximum drawdown duration*, and the difference between the highest high and the lowest low VAMI during this period is the magnitude of the maximum drawdown. Note that the DD ratio uses the absolute value of the maximum drawdown so that it is always a positive number since it is usually reported as a negative value (i.e. a loss).

A user-defined VBA function to calculate the maximum absolute drawdown is shown in Source 5.3. Note that the input range is not monthly returns but the VAMIs constructed from the monthly returns.

In Source 5.3 we use the maximum historical drawdown, whereas other variants such as the *Sterling ratio* use an average of the most significant drawdowns, and as such will not penalise a manager with one major drawdown and some smaller ones compared to a manager with several bad drawdowns. The *Burke ratio* uses the square root of the sum of the squares of each drawdown, again with the idea in mind of penalising more significant extended drawdowns compared with several milder ones.

The ranking results are shown in Table 5.6. There is another change of placing in the top three funds, whilst CTA1 retains its place at the top of the ranking, CTA2 is now second choice and LS1 third.

Source 5.3   User-defined VBA function to calculate the maximum absolute drawdown for a series of VAMIs

```
'function returns the MAXIMUM ABSOLUTE
DRAWDOWN for a series of VAMIs
Function fncDDOWNMAX(list)

'Initialise any variables

'maxDDregister is the running serial maximum
drawdown variable used to store its value
maxDDregister = 0

Count = 0
DDmin = 0

'start the serial counting process

 For Each Item In list

'DDmaxreg is the ongoing maximum or start value
of the DD, DDmin is the ongoing lowest value
or DD minimum

'find the max point

  If Item < previtem Then DDmax = previtem
  If DDmax < DDmaxreg Then DDmax = DDmaxreg
  DDmaxreg = DDmax

'find the min point

  If Item < previtem And DDmin < DDmaxreg Then
DDmin = Item

'calculate the DD

  DD = DDmaxreg - DDmin
```

```
'in % form DD = (DDmaxreg - DDmin) * 100/DDmaxreg

'create a one value delay for looking back one
value and comparing it to the current value
in the list

  previtem = Item

'a counter for each item in list

  Count = Count + 1

'keep a register of the maximum drawdown recorded
so far so that later smaller drawdowns do not
dominate

  If DD >= maxDDregister Then maxDDregister = DD

  Next Item

'the greatest absolute drawdown is calculated
as the maximum drawdown recorded so far

fncDDOWNMAX = maxDDregister

End Function
```

To conclude on the risk-adjusted results as shown in Table 5.6, it can be seen that there is no *one-size-fits-all* measure for the investor. Each method gives a different set of rankings. The general rankings are somewhat similar, however, with CTA1 being the obvious best performer and MN2 the worst. In between CTA1 and MN2, we can see that it is up to the investor to choose which metrics to apply, depending on their investment requirements. These metrics are therefore tools in a toolbox (Géhin, 2007) and offer the investor various ways of looking at the relative performance of hedge funds measured absolutely. An investor who wants to set up a managed account with high notional funding may indeed wish to look at the DD ratio, for example, since their concern may be focused on how much the CTA could lose from the outset of

Table 5.6 The DD ratio ranked with other risk-adjusted return metrics

	M1/M2		Sharpe		MSR		Sortino		DD Ratio
CTA1	1.47	CTA1	1.12	CTA1	1.86	CTA1	2.98	CTA1	1.13
LS1	1.35	LS1	0.94	CTA3	1.72	CTA3	2.69	CTA2	0.88
CTA2	1.30	CTA3	0.88	LS1	1.43	LS1	2.19	LS1	0.74
CTA3	1.12	CTA2	0.73	CTA2	1.18	GM1	1.96	CTA3	0.40
GM1	0.84	GM1	0.62	GM1	1.14	LS2	1.60	LS2	0.39
LS2	0.83	LS2	0.57	LS2	1.02	CTA2	1.30	GM1	0.37
MN1	0.83	LS3	0.37	LS3	0.67	LS3	0.97	LS3	0.15
LS3	0.65	MN1	0.29	MN1	0.53	MN1	0.52	MN1	0.13
MN2	0.57	GM2	0.17	GM2	0.32	GM2	0.50	GM2	0.07
GM2	0.36	MN2	0.05	MN2	0.10	MN2	0.10	MN2	0.03

their investment. As such the investor seeks to minimise *margin call-at-risk*.[13] On the other hand, a sophisticated pension fund investor may be more worried about the effects of higher moments and the asymmetry of the returns with respect to a minimum acceptable return. As such, their interests may be better served using the MSR or the Sortino ratio. Finally, it must be noted that these results only hold in an absolute environment, i.e. where the only benchmark is a static risk-free rate (which sometimes can be ignored and set equal to zero – especially if the investor is living in a period of economic stagnation where interest rates are very low, e.g. Japan during the 1990s and 2000s). As such, the results could turn out to be misleading especially if the managers have a high correlation to various benchmarks or indices, as discussed in the following sections and in Chapter 6.

5.3 COMMON PERFORMANCE MEASURES IN THE PRESENCE OF A MARKET BENCHMARK

In Section 5.2 we looked at a range of common risk-adjusted metrics with the sole objective of measuring and ranking the performance of a set of hedge funds in a world where the manager says they are not benchmarked and where the investor actually believes this. In reality this is not the case except for producers of *exotic alpha* through highly specialised trading techniques, e.g. arbitrage strategies. Otherwise most managers use trend-following or methods of forecasting so that they

---

[13] *Margin call-at-risk* is the probability of having margin calls on the managed account over a specified time, e.g. a year, calculated using the value-at-risk methodology for capital budgeting purposes.

take bets on the direction of a range of markets and underlying instruments. This is the case for most CTAs, global macro, market neutral and long/short hedge funds. As such, they are producing returns from a combination of underlying positions that offer dynamic risk premia on getting the direction right for the trade (e.g. if a manager believes crude oil is trending upwards they will take a long position in the commodity and hold it until their expectation is that the trend is over). As long as the manager is correct about their directional forecasts, they will generate positive average returns with a volatility dependent on that of the individual markets used and their respective covariances (from Markowitz's portfolio variance).

These risk-premia returns, however, are not strictly speaking true *alpha* but are better described as being *alternative beta*. That is, they are returns generated from having a directional exposure over a certain time period to various markets or instruments. Any return then emerges as a return borne out of *directional risk*.[14] This follows the general argument that return cannot exist without risk. In other words, the generation of positive average returns over time is an *emergent property* of taking risk. If you are receiving returns in excess of the risk-free rate from a manager, then the manager is taking risks in some form or another which are not necessarily mutually exclusive. As such, most hedge fund managers do not operate in an absolute world but instead in a complex adaptive relativistic world.

Before the science of hedge funds was understood and tools for analysis were fully developed, it was easy for a hedge fund manager to pretend that their returns were alpha and that they had a magic formula or mystical powers of foresight. This allowed them to produce a time series of returns which were considered absolute and as such investors were quite happy and willing to pay full fees, e.g. 2% and 20%. This arrangement was an accepted industry norm until the concept of alternative beta was defined in the early 2000s by Fung and Hsieh (2000b). Sophisticated investors then began questioning the entire hedge fund industry since they could in theory replicate a sizeable portion of the returns themselves. In other words, were hedge fund managers really providing extra returns due to their skill, or guilty of simply packaging opaque alternative betas into a fund as some kind of elaborate conjuring trick to reap hefty fees from the uninformed gullible investor?

---

[14] The *directional* risk is the loss inherent with having a directional exposure to an underlying market or instrument over a certain period of time.

We will now discuss performance measures in the presence of a benchmark. The 10 hypothetical hedge funds remain the same, but a market benchmark has been added which could be for example the composite performance of the world's major stock markets during the period.

5.3.1   The Information Ratio

The information ratio, as described by Goodwin (1998), is similar to the Sharpe ratio in that it uses the first two moments of the return distribution (and as such is built on the Markowitz mean–variance paradigm). However, where the Sharpe ratio uses a risk-free rate as a benchmark for the numerator, the information ratio goes one step further and uses a *market reference benchmark*. If $R_{P,t}$ is the return on a hedge fund in period t and $R_{B,t}$ is the return on a benchmark portfolio in period t, then the excess return Δ_t can be written as

$$\Delta_t = R_{P,t} - R_{B,t}. \tag{5.10}$$

The arithmetic average of excess returns from $t = 1$ to T is given by

$$\bar{\Delta} = \frac{1}{T} \sum_{t=1}^{T} \Delta_t. \tag{5.11}$$

Where σ_Δ is the standard deviation of the excess returns from the benchmark (or tracking error – see Section 3.4.1), written as

$$\sigma_\Delta = TE = \sqrt{\frac{1}{T} \sum_{t=1}^{T} (\Delta_t - \bar{\Delta})^2}. \tag{5.12}$$

The information ratio is then given by

$$\text{Information} = \frac{\bar{\Delta}}{TE}. \tag{5.13}$$

Table 5.7 shows the information ratio using a hypothetical global equity benchmark compared to the Sharpe ratio. The rankings change once again. CTA1 is still ranked highest and MN2 still lowest. However, CTA3 is in second place and GM1 has risen from the middle rankings to third. MN1 and MN2 have negative values, indicating that their excess returns are in fact negative when compared to the benchmark. LS1 and LS2 are in fourth and fifth place respectively, and CTA2 has dropped

Table 5.7 The information ratio compared to the Sharpe ratio

	Sharpe		**Information**
CTA1	1.12	CTA1	7.04
LS1	0.94	CTA3	5.58
CTA3	0.88	GM1	4.59
CTA2	0.73	LS1	4.50
GM1	0.62	LS2	3.32
LS2	0.57	CTA2	1.59
LS3	0.37	LS3	1.19
MN1	0.29	GM2	0.10
GM2	0.17	MN1	-0.69
MN2	0.05	MN2	-1.85

to sixth place although it was ranked second for the DD ratio. In other words, some funds are starting to look better than before in the presence of a benchmark, and some which had looked better are starting to slip down the rankings.

5.3.2   The M-Squared Metric

The M-squared (or M^2) metric was developed to be more easily interpreted by an average investor once the hedge funds have been volatility-adjusted for their average returns and ranked (Modigliani and Modigliani, 1997; Modigliani, 1997). The ratio uses a benchmark with an estimated volatility and each fund is leveraged or de-leveraged so that their volatility matches that of the benchmark. The leveraged or de-leveraged return of each fund is then ranked. As such, the fund's return can be interpreted as the return that would have been produced had the fund's volatility been equivalent to that of the market benchmark. When hedge funds are processed in this way and ranked, it is easier for the less sophisticated investor to see how they outperform the benchmark return to which they have had their risk profile matched. For the 10 hypothetical hedge funds, the benchmark has an annualised return of 5.36% and a volatility of 10.9% for matching purposes. M^2 is

Table 5.8   The M-squared ranked versus the Sharpe and information ratios

	Sharpe		Information		5.36% Rm M squared
CTA1	1.12	CTA1	7.04	CTA1	9.26
LS1	0.94	CTA3	5.58	LS1	7.20
CTA3	0.88	GM1	4.59	CTA3	6.63
CTA2	0.73	LS1	4.50	CTA2	4.98
GM1	0.62	LS2	3.32	GM1	3.79
LS2	0.57	CTA2	1.59	LS2	3.23
LS3	0.37	LS3	1.19	LS3	1.01
MN1	0.29	GM2	0.10	MN1	0.20
GM2	0.17	MN1	-0.69	GM2	-1.19
MN2	0.05	MN2	-1.85	MN2	-2.40

given by

$$M^2 = \frac{\sigma_M}{\sigma_P}(R_P - R_F) - R_F. \qquad (5.14)$$

The ranked results are shown in Table 5.8. The rankings are identical to those of the Sharpe ratio. However, the main point of the M^2 metric is that it is easy to interpret the rankings since they represent returns corresponding to volatilities that have been matched to that of the benchmark. Since the benchmark return is 5.36%, it follows that any fund with a return higher than 5.36% outperforms the market in the risk-adjusted sense, i.e. CTA1, LS1 and CTA3 (which is not instantly obvious from the Sharpe ratio rankings). Also, it is intuitively comforting for investors to know by how many percentage points their returns would be greater or less than the market for volatility-matched hedge funds.

5.3.3   The Treynor Ratio

The Treynor ratio, as introduced by Treynor (1962), is again of the same form as the generalised risk-adjusted return given by equation (5.3), but now risk is defined as the *beta* of the fund relative to a benchmark:

$$\text{Treynor} = \frac{R_P - R_F}{\beta_P}. \qquad (5.15)$$

The beta of the portfolio β_P can be calculated in two ways. The first method uses ordinary least squares (OLS) to estimate the slope of the regression line as discussed in Chapter 4. Box 5.2 provides a graphic explanation of beta and its estimation methods in Excel.

Box 5.2   Beta estimation

The denominator of equation (5.15) is estimated in Excel by

$\beta_P = \textbf{SLOPE}$(hedge fund excess returns, benchmark excess returns)

or

$\beta_P = \textbf{COVAR}$(benchmark excess returns, hedge fund excess returns)/$\textbf{VARP}$(benchmark excess returns)

Beta is a very common measure for estimating the extent to which the hedge fund excess returns are influenced by that of a benchmark or market excess returns. The beta of the portfolio is the gradient (m) of the OLS regression line where the market excess returns are plotted on the x-axis and the hedge fund excess returns on the y-axis. The fund's beta can be visualised as a measure of its relative directional exposure to the benchmark like a kind of relative elasticity as shown in the diagram below

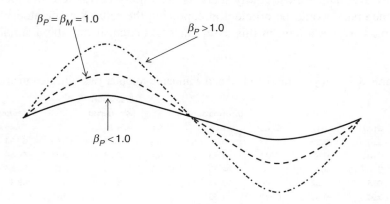

When the hedge fund's beta is greater than 1.0, it has tendency to exhibit greater moves in its returns (both positive and negative) than those of the benchmark. When the fund's beta is equal to 1.0, the fund is the benchmark held long (if the benchmark gains 1%, the hedge fund gains 1%). When the fund's beta is between zero and 1.0, the fund's returns are less than those of the benchmark (this is the region of beta usually occupied by long short funds). If the fund's beta is zero, the fund is technically market neutral and so whatever the benchmark does performance-wise, it has no impact on the returns of the fund. If the fund's beta is between zero and −1.0, then the fund's returns have a tendency to be opposite to those of the benchmark, but in a less volatile fashion. If the fund's beta is −1.0, the fund is the benchmark held short and so mimics exactly the benchmark performance-wise but in the opposite way (if the benchmark gains 1%, the fund loses 1% and vice versa).

The results for the Treynor ratio with a risk-free rate of 3.0% are shown in Table 5.9.

The Treynor ratio is a metric more commonly used for active traditional equity portfolios (like the information ratio). This is because if we were to use a benchmark for relative performance measurement, then the benchmark must be relevant. Since we are using a global equity market benchmark, it follows that the CTAs and global macro funds have little or no intuitive exposure to the benchmark and so to use it for any of the risk-adjusted metrics above would be practically meaningless. However, since most equity markets are highly correlated, the global benchmark would be efficient at capturing the returns associated with a passive investment in this asset class. As such, it may be a suitable

Table 5.9 Treynor ratio ranked and compared to other risk-adjusted metrics

	Sharpe		Information		5.36% Rm M squared		Treynor
CTA1	1.12	CTA1	7.04	CTA1	9.26	LS2	77.46
LS1	0.94	CTA3	5.58	LS1	7.20	CTA1	69.94
CTA3	0.88	GM1	4.59	CTA3	6.63	GM1	59.50
CTA2	0.73	LS1	4.50	CTA2	4.98	LS1	54.86
GM1	0.62	LS2	3.32	GM1	3.79	CTA2	49.13
LS2	0.57	CTA2	1.59	LS2	3.23	MN2	-3.42
LS3	0.37	LS3	1.19	LS3	1.01	CTA3	-32.39
MN1	0.29	GM2	0.10	MN1	0.20	MN1	-55.88
GM2	0.17	MN1	-0.69	GM2	-1.19	GM2	-75.20
MN2	0.05	MN2	-1.85	MN2	-2.40	LS3	-92.08

metric for the equity hedge funds LS1, LS2, LS3 and the market neutral hedge funds MN1 and MN2, all of which are assumed to be global equity hedge funds.

We are starting to see the limitations of using risk-adjusted returns with benchmarks for general hedge fund performance measurement. From Table 5.9 we see that LS2 is now ranked the highest and LS3 the lowest hedge fund. This is primarily because LS2 has a beta of 0.08 and LS3 has a beta of –0.04. In fact, the results can be highly misleading, since both betas may be statistically no different from zero if we apply a *hypothesis test* (see Box 5.3). In such a market neutral case, the Treynor ratio approaches infinity. The higher the maxima and minima of the ranks of the Treynor ratio the more market neutral the fund is and so the manager's returns are less influenced by the market, which is a sign of outperformance with respect to the market. Clearly, the Treynor ratio is difficult to interpret and obviously unsuitable for analysing non-equity hedge funds.

Box 5.3   Hypothesis testing for the significance of beta

As seen above, LS2 has an estimated beta of 0.08. But is this value of beta significantly different from zero? In other words, can we really believe the level of beta estimated at a 95% confidence? To find out, we need to perform a *hypothesis test*. The common approach to testing the strength of a beta estimate is by using the *t*-test statistic as already discussed in Chapter 4 and given by

$$t = \frac{\hat{b}_1 - b_1}{s_{\hat{b}_1}}.$$

Since two parameters were estimated in the regression (the intercept and the gradient), the *t*-statistic has two degrees of freedom. The denominator $s_{\hat{b}_1}$ is the *standard error*. The hypothesis test is usually carried out by determining a *critical t* value t_c which corresponds to the confidence interval of choice (typically 95% or 99%) in order that we can reject the null hypothesis if $t > t_c$. In our example we want to know if the value of beta for LS2, which is estimated at 0.08 (the *alternative hypothesis*, H_1), is significantly different from 0 (the *null hypothesis*, H_0).

We test LS2 against the null hypothesis that its beta is no different from zero at 95% confidence, i.e. assuming that it is a market neutral hedge fund with a beta of zero until proven that it is not with only a 5% chance of being wrong. Here we are testing the hypothesis that $H_0 \neq H_1$ and we therefore use the *two-tailed* t test. In Excel the standard error can be calculated using the following function

$s_{\hat{b}_1} = $ **STEYX**(hedge fund excess returns, benchmark excess returns)

The critical two-tailed t-value is calculated using the following function

$$t_c = \textbf{TINV}(\text{probability, degrees of freedom})$$

where probability refers to the probability of the significance level of the test, e.g. 0.05 for 95% and 0.01 for 99% confidence. The degrees of freedom are the total number of observations minus 2. So, for our example, the degrees of freedom are $72 - 2 = 70$. For the LS2 fund the standard error is 3.36, and the critical t-value for 95% confidence and 70 degrees of freedom is 1.99 ($t_c = 1.99$). With $b_1 = 0$, the test statistic t can be calculated as follows

$$t = \frac{\hat{b}_1 - b_1}{s_{\hat{b}_1}} = \frac{0.08 - 0}{3.36} = 0.023.$$

Since $t < t_c$ we cannot be sure at 95% if the fund has a beta which is not different from zero. In other words, we cannot reject the null hypothesis and therefore must assume the fund is market neutral even though it is classed as long/short which would suggest that it had a beta somewhere between 0 and 1.0.

5.3.4 Jensen's Alpha

One of the key goals of quantitative manager selection is the computation of *alpha*. Alpha is essentially the residue return left over once all known factors and risk adjustments have been accounted for and deducted from a fund's excess return. As such, alpha is technically meant to measure the manager's absolute skill at using their *information set* to predict future prices in the various financial markets and instruments traded in the fund. Hedge fund managers are meant to be *active* position takers only and are not paid to hold passive investments unless they are uniquely available or very difficult to access (e.g. certain emerging or frontier market equities). Managing a hedge fund would be too easy otherwise and managers should not be remunerated for something an investor can easily access or replicate at low cost.

The first attempt at measuring the alpha of a manager was the CAPM developed by Sharpe (1963). Recall that the straight-line regression equation is given by

$$y = ax + b. \tag{5.16}$$

The CAPM is the financial equivalent written as

$$(R_P - R_F) = \alpha_P + \beta_P (R_M - R_F). \tag{5.17}$$

Rearranging for alpha gives

$$\alpha_P = R_P - [R_F + \beta_P (R_M - R_F)]. \tag{5.18}$$

Where α_P is Jensen's alpha[15] (Jensen, 1968). Clearly, Jensen's alpha is simply the sum of the risk-free rate and beta adjusted market excess returns subtracted from the fund's net return. It is a first attempt at trying to understand why hedge fund returns may exceed the risk-free rate and a constant beta exposure to a market benchmark. In theory, if the alpha is positive the manager is producing excess returns due to trading skill.

The equation helps to identify the three components of return usually found within hedge funds – the *alpha* (skill), the *beta continuum* as introduced by Anson (2008) (from skill to no skill) and the *risk-free rate* (no skill). Since managers of hedge funds usually charge high fees for their services (e.g. 2% and 20%), it is of interest to investors to know what exactly it is they are paying for. Since skill is something that is rewarded and no skill is an activity that is generally free, it follows that the investor should only be paying full or partial hedge fund fees for that part of performance associated with skilled outperformance.

Jensen's alpha is ranked and compared to other risk-adjusted metrics in Table 5.10. Interestingly, CTA1 has been toppled from its premier position in the rankings by CTA3. In other words, CTA1 has been found guilty of *free-riding* on the market to produce a percentage of its returns. This is generally something frowned upon in the industry since a

---

[15] Michael Jensen (1939–) is an American economist working in the area of financial economics and is a founder of SSRN.com.

Table 5.10   Ranked Jensen ratio compared to other risk-adjusted return metrics

	Sharpe		Information		5.36% Rm M squared		Treynor		Jensen
CTA1	1.12	CTA1	7.04	CTA1	9.26	LS2	77.46	CTA3	12.03
LS1	0.94	CTA3	5.58	LS1	7.20	CTA1	69.94	CTA1	9.49
CTA3	0.88	GM1	4.59	CTA3	6.63	GM1	59.50	GM1	8.46
CTA2	0.73	LS1	4.50	CTA2	4.98	LS1	54.86	LS1	6.55
GM1	0.62	LS2	3.32	GM1	3.79	CTA2	49.13	LS2	6.37
LS2	0.57	CTA2	1.59	LS2	3.23	MN2	-3.42	LS3	4.01
LS3	0.37	LS3	1.19	LS3	1.01	CTA3	-32.39	CTA2	3.67
MN1	0.29	GM2	0.10	MN1	0.20	MN1	-55.88	GM2	2.60
GM2	0.17	MN1	-0.69	GM2	-1.19	GM2	-75.20	MN1	1.72
MN2	0.05	MN2	-1.85	MN2	-2.40	LS3	-92.08	MN2	0.54

manager should not get paid for taking passive risk on an easily *replicable* asset class as the same exposure can usually be obtained cheaply using ETFs or futures positions held long and rolled as necessary. CTA3, which was third as ranked by Sharpe, is now in first place with a Jensen's alpha of 12.03%. Whilst CTA1 is still in second place, GM1 keeps its place in third with a similar ranking to the Treynor ratio, but LS1 has been demoted to fourth place from second in the Sharpe and *M*-squared rankings. MN2 is still the bottom-ranked fund. Table 5.11 shows the complete set of risk-adjusted return metrics.

Table 5.11   The complete set of risk-adjusted return metrics for the 10 hypothetical hedge funds

	A	B	C	D	E	F	G	H	I	J	K	L	M
1		CTA1	CTA2	CTA3	GM1	GM2	LS1	LS2	LS3	MN1	MN2	SDX	Average
2	M1	12.82	=AVERAGE(B16:B87)*12			5.52	9.84	9.57	6.91	4.65	3.32	5.36	8.55
3	M2	8.74	=STDEVP(B16:B87)*SQRT(12)			15.16	7.31	11.51	10.64	5.60	5.86	10.90	9.69
4	M3	0.07	=SKEW(B16:B87)		-0.02	0.13	0.89	0.11	0.23	0.10	0.11	-0.15	0.14
5	M4	0.04	=KURT(B16:B87)		-0.11	0.36	0.61	-0.57	-0.01	-0.29	0.23	-0.36	0.11
6	Correlation	0.18	=CORREL(B16:B87,$L16:$L87)			0.02	0.19	0.08	-0.04	-0.06	-0.17	-	0.01
7	Beta	0.14	=SLOPE(B16:B87,$L16:$L87)			-0.03	0.12	0.08	-0.04	-0.03	-0.09	-	0.00
8	Critical t	2.52	=STEYX(B16:B87,$L16:$L87)			4.44	2.10	3.36	3.11	1.64	1.69	-	-
9	Information	7.04	=AVERAGE('Info Del'!B15:B86)*12/STDEVP('Info Del'!B15:B86)*SQRT(12)						1.19	-0.69	-1.85	-	-
10	M squared	9.26	=($LS3/B3)*(B2-3)-3		3.79	-1.19	7.20	3.23	1.01	0.20	-2.40	-	-
11	Treynor	69.94	=(B2-3)/B7	12.39	59.50	-75.20	54.86	77.46	-92.08	-55.88	-3.42	-	-
12	Jensen	9.49	=B2-(3+B7*($L$2-3))		8.46	2.60	6.55	6.37	4.01	1.72	0.54	-	-
13													
14			CTA			Global Macro		Long Short			Market Neutral		The Market	
15	Month	CTA1	CTA2	CTA3	GM1	GM2	LS1	LS2	LS3	MN1	MN2	SDX	
16	Jan-05	4.68	0.10	-2.69	0.89	-6.66	0.37	5.80	2.36	-3.09	2.81	3.21	
17	Feb-05	-0.18	1.79	3.61	-0.90	2.93	-1.06	4.27	0.32	-0.87	-3.51	-0.20	
18	Mar-05	0.66	2.04	-0.28	-5.38	6.68	0.62	-3.11	-0.44	0.19	-1.56	0.54	
86	Nov-10	-0.85	1.27	1.42	-4.46	-5.71	0.78	7.45	-0.01	-0.74	-0.14	2.56	
87	Dec-10	0.45	0.10	-1.33	0.59	2.48	0.10	-0.54	1.27	-0.75	0.50	1.99	

5.4   THE OMEGA RATIO

The omega ratio, as defined by Keating and Shadwick (2002), is a non-parametric method so it does not rely upon calculating the moments of a distribution of returns for determining the ranking of each hedge fund versus a threshold level. Developed in the early 2000s, it has gained popularity with practitioners due to its inclusiveness of the full distribution of the returns in describing the relative ranking of a fund. As mentioned earlier, investors like high odd moments and low even moments, and the risks borne of holding an asset prone to fourth-moment risk may be rare but tend to have a high impact when they occur (e.g. a stock market correction or crash). Its popularity also stems from the fact that it inherently describes the risk–reward properties of the return distribution and so can be easily interpreted. The ratio considers returns below and above a specific loss *threshold* return level. In doing so, it places a threshold return on the unitised distribution of returns (the PDF with an area under the curve of one) which have been accumulated by summing (taking the integral) from the left-hand side of the distribution to form the CDF, $F(x)$. Instead of using the positive and negative infinity signs to signify the limits on either side of the integral, we use a for the *downside* limit and b for the *upside* limit. The omega ratio is written as

$$\Omega(L) = \frac{\int_L^b (1 - F(x))dx}{\int_a^L F(x)dx}. \tag{5.19}$$

The returns below a certain threshold are considered as losses, and the returns above are considered profits. It follows from equation (5.19) that a higher value of omega for a given threshold is preferred over a lower value for a rational investor. Accordingly, when the omega ratio takes a value of one, this represents the mean of the portfolio since it is the balancing point in terms of moments. The omega ratio is commonly used to create rankings based on various return thresholds. The rankings may change as a function of a perceived loss threshold which will vary from investor to investor (depending on their appetite for risk) which is interpreted here as the magnitude of return threshold.

Figure 5.3 shows the results of the omega function plotted against the return threshold. Clearly, the rankings change as a function of the threshold. The omega ratio rankings are shown in Table 5.12 for a range of threshold values between zero and 10 in increments of 2. CTA3 is confirmed to be the highest-ranked performer in general, except for thresholds at 4.0% and 6.0%. For these two thresholds, GM1 is ranked

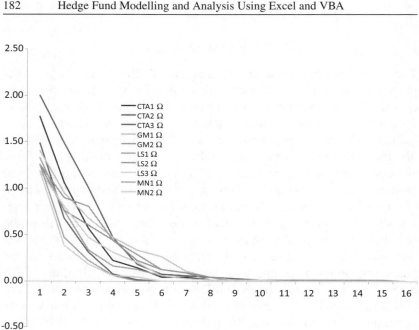

Figure 5.3 The omega functions for the 10 hypothetical hedge funds

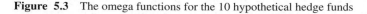

highest, followed by GM2 and then LS2. This result is interesting, and shows that the omega ratio is somewhat different from the other risk-adjusted return metrics depending on the threshold level chosen by the investor. This phenomenon is reinforced by the knowledge that the omega ratio is non-parametric and intrinsically reflects all moments of the distribution, so a hedge fund with a high excess kurtosis will be ranked lower than one with no excess kurtosis, assuming both hedge funds have the same return, volatility and skewness.

Table 5.12 Ranked omega ratios for thresholds ranging from zero to 10

Threshold	0.00		2.00		4.00		6.00		8.00		10.00
CTA3	2.00	CTA3	1.00	GM1	0.33	GM1	0.11	CTA3	0.03	CTA3	0.01
CTA1	1.77	GM2	0.80	GM2	0.29	GM2	0.09	GM2	0.01	GM2	0.01
CTA2	1.48	GM1	0.67	LS2	0.22	GM1	0.09	GM1	0.01	GM1	0.01
GM1	1.40	LS2	0.60	LS3	0.20	LS3	0.06	CTA2	0.01	CTA2	0.00
LS1	1.32	CTA1	0.57	CTA3	0.18	CTA1	0.04	LS2	0.00	LS2	0.00
GM2	1.25	LS3	0.47	CTA1	0.14	LS3	0.03	LS3	0.00	LS3	0.00
LS2	1.25	LS1	0.33	LS3	0.13	CTA1	0.03	CTA1	0.00	CTA1	0.00
MN1	1.25	CTA2	0.31	MN2	0.04	CTA2	0.00	LS1	0.00	LS1	0.00
LS3	1.18	MN1	0.22	CTA2	0.01	MN1	0.00	MN1	0.00	MN1	0.00
MN2	1.18	MN2	0.18	MN1	0.00	MN2	0.00	MN2	0.00	MN2	0.00

The risk-adjusted return metrics described in this chapter are the ones most commonly used within the hedge fund industry. Others have emerged in recent times, such as the Stutzer index (Stutzer, 2000), the Sharpe-Omega ratio (Gupta *et al.*, 2003), AIRAP (Sharma, 2004), kappa (Kaplan and Knowles 2004) and Rachev ratio. Lo (2002) also reports a modified risk-adjusted ratio adjusted for autocorrelation. This chapter nonetheless gives a broad introduction to the subject of risk-adjusted returns and demonstrates that when appraising hedge fund performance, returns must be risk-adjusted to be meaningful.

6
Asset Pricing Models

In Chapter 5, we looked at a range of risk-adjusted return metrics which were both absolute and relative to a benchmark. As such we were trying to answer the question *which*? In this chapter we will try to answer the question *why*? Asset pricing models allow us to delve deeper into the structure of hedge fund returns in an attempt to explain them as a complex mix of various exposure factors. In doing so, we look beyond the superficial gloss of the beauty contest associated with the array of risk-adjusted return metrics already described. For sophisticated investors, asset pricing models are very useful in the hedge fund selection process since they allow them to figure out if a hedge fund is really producing skill-based returns worth paying for, or whether the hedge fund could easily be replicated at low cost.

6.1 THE RISK-ADJUSTED TWO-MOMENT CAPITAL ASSET PRICING MODEL

In Section 5.3.4, we introduced Sharpe's CAPM market model, given by

$$(R_P - R_F) = \alpha_P + \beta_P (R_M - R_F). \qquad (6.1)$$

On rearranging, the alpha term can be written as

$$\alpha_P = R_P - [R_F + \beta_P (R_M - R_F)]. \qquad (6.2)$$

Where α_P is Jensen's alpha. Equation (6.2) can be broken down into two terms

Term 1: fund return
$$\alpha_p = R_p.$$

Term 2: risk-free rate and market return
$$- [R_F + \beta_P (R_M - R_F)]. \qquad (6.3)$$

Equation (6.3) has until recently been widely used for the calculation of alpha within the asset management industry. It states that the excess return on a hedge fund is simply the return on the fund minus the risk-free rate minus the market excess returns adjusted for the fund's beta coefficient. However, equation (6.3) is somewhat inadequate for measuring the alpha associated with hedge funds. It may be useful in the world of traditional investing where managers usually do not use leverage and are constrained to take only long positions using the same basket of stocks as the market portfolio. For hedge funds, however, it is not very well suited. There are two main reasons for this.

Firstly, imagine a hedge fund that is market neutral and so has a beta of zero. Inserting a value of zero for beta into equation (6.3) gives us a measure of Jensen's market neutral alpha, such that

$$\alpha_P = R_P - R_F. \tag{6.4}$$

The main problem with equation (6.4) is that the manager can stay market neutral but use *leverage* to increase returns (e.g. they can double the exposure of their long and short positions but still remain market neutral). Equation (6.4) does not take the leverage effect into account since there is no leverage neutralisation term and, as a result, Jensen's alpha is seen to be a function of leverage which would show up in higher fund returns. This should not be the case since alpha is meant to represent trading skill or superior security selection and the use of leverage is not strictly skill since it also entails taking a directly proportional increased market risk. As mentioned earlier, a mediocre manager could simply leverage up to achieve high returns – their volatility and chances of blow-up might be unacceptably high as a result. For this reason, alpha should be a risk-adjusted quantity.

Secondly, since hedge fund managers are by definition supposed to take long and short positions within a fund, the hedging effect of mixing such positions has a significant *volatility reduction effect* on the fund. The outcome is the tendency towards producing a higher Sharpe ratio for the hedge fund since the denominator is significantly reduced due to having short positions. Once again, such a *free-lunch* volatility reduction effect is not adequately captured by Jensen's alpha.

Sharpe's CAPM is therefore not suitable for use in hedge fund analysis since it relies solely on a first-moment regression model. In an attempt to improve Sharpe's CAPM to overcome the two deficiencies mentioned above, Hampton (2009) extended the single-factor CAPM

reasoning to the second moment (volatility) and second-moment covariance (long–short correlation) and, by using a leverage-invariant identity,
derived a two-moment CAPM model. Accordingly the Hampton CAPM
is thought to be more suitable for measuring the alpha of hedge funds
and, in particular, long/short and market neutral equity hedge fund portfolios which are selected from and benchmarked against a defined basket
or index of stocks. The approach used by Hampton was to create a hedge
fund CAPM for the first moment for all betas between -1.0 and 1.0
(the beta space where most long/short and market neutral equity funds
exist) in order to get an expression for the expected return of the fund as
a function of alpha, beta and the risk-free rate. The result was an equation exactly the same as Sharpe's CAPM, yet derived in a different way
using the reasoning of a hedge fund manager engaged in statistical arbitrage within a basket of equities. Building on this successful outcome,
the same approach was then applied to model the hedge fund variance
in order to obtain a second-moment CAPM. The two terms were then
associated using the risk-adjusted invariance argument as follows

$$\frac{R_P}{\sigma_P} = \frac{\alpha_P + \beta_P R_M + (1 - \beta_P) R_F}{\sigma_M \sqrt{\dfrac{(\beta_P^2 - 1)(1 - \bar{\rho}_{LS})}{2} + 1}}. \tag{6.5}$$

From which we obtain the following risk-adjusted equilibrium identity

$$R_P \sigma_M \sqrt{\frac{(\beta_P^2 - 1)(1 - \bar{\rho}_{LS})}{2} + 1} = \sigma_P \left(\alpha_P + \beta_P R_M + (1 - \beta_P) R_F\right). \tag{6.6}$$

Simplifying and rearranging for alpha, we finally obtain

$$\alpha_P = R_P \times \frac{\sigma_M}{\sigma_P} \times H - [R_F + \beta_P (R_M - R_F)]. \tag{6.7}$$

Where H is defined as

$$H = \left[0.5 \left(\beta_P^2 + 1\right) - 0.5 \bar{\rho}_{LS} \left(\beta_P^2 - 1\right)\right]^{0.5}. \tag{6.8}$$

$\bar{\rho}_{LS}$ is the average estimate of the correlations between all the long and
short positions in the hedge fund during the relevant time period.

Clearly, this two-moment CAPM has a general form identical to
the Sharpe CAPM but with two additional multiplicative terms which
correct for the leverage and long/short volatility reduction effects,

that is

Term 1: fund return adjusted for leverage and volatility reduction

$$\alpha_p = R_p \times \frac{\sigma_M}{\sigma_P} \times H.$$

Term 2: risk-free rate and market return

$$- \left[R_F + \beta_P (R_M - R_F) \right]. \tag{6.9a}$$

The two new additions to Term 1 are a leverage factor given by σ_M/σ_P (which incidentally is the same as that encountered in the M^2 risk-adjusted metric), and a volatility reduction factor due to long–short correlations, H. The latter is a scaling term that accounts for the reduction in a fund's volatility due to the correlation effect of the returns associated with the long and short positions. It has been shown from empirical studies by Hampton (2009) that for a typical equity index, e.g. Dow Jones, the global average correlation between the longs and shorts is typically in the range -0.7 to -0.6. Due to the existence of the H-function, a new set of benchmarks must be developed for the industry which represent average long/short correlations for each major market index.[1]

Example 6.1 Jensen's versus Hampton's alpha for a market neutral fund

Consider a truly market neutral fund which has a beta of zero i.e. $\beta_P = 0$. Substituting this value into equation (6.7) gives an estimate for Hampton's alpha for the market neutral hedge fund such that

$$\alpha_P = R_P \times \frac{\sigma_M}{\sigma_P} \times \sqrt{\frac{1}{2}(1 + \bar{\rho}_{LS})} - R_F.$$

This equation takes into account both the leverage and the volatility reduction effect due to having negatively correlated long and short positions in the portfolio (second moment and co-moment) as opposed to the Sharpe CAPM for a market neutral hedge fund which does not, that is

$$\alpha_P = R_P - R_F.$$

---

[1] See www.darbyshirehampton.com for a detailed specification of the index design and regular updates.

It is likely that the two-moment Hampton CAPM is generally more suitable for measuring the alpha of hedge funds since it is more inclusive of the effects of leverage and volatility reduction caused by having short positions – the two effects which essentially define a hedge fund.

For example, let us assume a market neutral hedge fund manager does not use leverage and the volatility of the fund is the same as the market. Assuming $\sigma_P = \sigma_M = 15\%$ and $\bar{\rho}_{LS} = -0.75$, for example, we have

$$\alpha_P = 0.35 R_P - R_F.$$

For Hampton's alpha, compared to

$$\alpha_P = R_P - R_F.$$

For Jensen's alpha. Clearly, alpha is reduced as a consequence in Hampton's version but remains unaffected in Jensen's.

Now imagine that the manager doubles their leverage so that $\sigma_P = 30\%$. Here Hampton's alpha remains constant, that is

$$\alpha_P = 0.35 \times 2R_{P \times} \frac{15}{30} - R_F = 0.35 R_P - R_F.$$

For Jensen's alpha, on the other hand, we have

$$\alpha_P = 2R_P - R_F.$$

Which would be twice as big if the risk-free rate was zero.

Clearly, Hampton's alpha is leverage invariant whereas Jensen's is a function of leverage.

6.1.1   Interpreting H

Recall that H is given by

$$H = \left[0.5 \left(\beta_P^2 + 1\right) - 0.5 \bar{\rho}_{LS} \left(\beta_P^2 - 1\right)\right]^{0.5}.$$

H takes values between 0 and 1.0 as long as the fund's beta and $\bar{\rho}_{LS}$ take values between -1.0 and 1.0. H is defined as a function of the fund's beta and the average correlation estimate between the long and short returns in the portfolio (rolling estimates can be made, for example, by grouping all the long and short positions together in the fund at the end of each day for marking-to-market purposes and calculating the correlation between the daily average long and short sub-portfolio returns over the same time period). Assuming average periodic returns (or P&Ls) are available for each long and short sub-portfolio for estimation purposes, $\bar{\rho}_{LS}$ can be calculated using the CORREL() function for a rolling window length

$$\bar{\rho}_{LS} = \textbf{CORREL} \text{ (time series of average daily long returns,}$$
$$\text{time series of average daily short returns)}$$

In Figure 6.1, H values are shown plotted against $\bar{\rho}_{LS}$ and β_P for $-1.0 \leq \bar{\rho}_{LS} \leq 1.0$ and $-1.0 \leq \beta_P \leq 1.0$. As can be seen, H decreases with decreasing values of $\bar{\rho}_{LS}$ and decreasing absolute values of beta. What this means is that if you had a hedge fund which was market neutral (beta = 0) and if the average long and short returns over time were perfectly negatively correlated ($\bar{\rho}_{LS} = -1.0$), then you would achieve a volatility reduction for the portfolio of 100% i.e. $(1 - H) \times 100\%$. In reality, empirical studies performed by Hampton (2009) suggest that for major stock market indices, since the constituent stocks are mostly correlated (or co-integrated) over time, once randomly

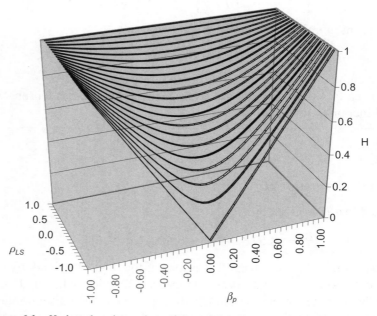

Figure 6.1 H plotted against values of β_P and $\bar{\rho}_{LS}$

separated into long and short portfolios, the average correlation between the long and short sub-portfolio returns over a time period tend to be significantly negatively correlated, typically between -0.60 and -0.70. Assuming $\bar{\rho}_{LS} = -0.70$ and a typical long/short hedge fund has a beta of 0.40, then $H = 0.53$. In other words, the typical long/short hedge fund manager can expect a volatility reduction of approximately 50% for their fund versus the market's volatility if they are unleveraged. It follows on rearranging (6.9a) that the fund's volatility is directly proportional to H, that is

$$\sigma_P = \frac{R_P \sigma_M H}{\alpha + R_F + \beta_M (R_M - R_F)}. \tag{6.9b}$$

So if the benchmark volatility is (say) 15%, the fund should have an expected volatility of around 7.5%. No wonder then, assuming the fund manager can produce some alpha per year, their Sharpe ratio would seem suspiciously high despite low returns since the denominator would be halved.

6.1.2 Static Alpha Analysis

Tables 6.1 and 6.2 show the results of Jensen's and Hampton's alpha applied to the 10 hypothetical hedge funds and their subsequent rankings, respectively. As seen from Table 6.2, where the S&P index is used

Table 6.1 Jensen and Hampton alpha estimates for 10 hypothetical hedge funds

	CTA1	CTA2	CTA3	GM1	GM2	LS1	LS2	LS3	MN1	MN2	S&P Index	Fund Averages
M1	12.82	6.86	14.21	11.81	5.52	9.84	9.57	6.91	4.65	3.32	9.91	8.55
M2	8.74	5.27	12.69	14.14	15.16	7.31	11.51	10.64	5.60	5.86	11.46	9.69
M3	0.07	0.35	-0.55	-0.02	0.13	0.89	0.11	0.23	0.10	0.11	-0.07	0.14
M4	0.04	-0.85	1.71	-0.11	0.36	0.61	-0.57	-0.01	-0.29	0.23	-0.21	0.11
Correlation	0.19	0.06	-0.18	0.03	-0.05	0.35	0.18	0.33	-0.01	-0.06	-	0.08
Beta	0.14	0.03	-0.20	0.04	-0.06	0.22	0.18	0.31	-0.01	-0.03	-	0.06
Information	2.68	-2.98	2.77	1.27	-2.71	-0.08	-0.28	-2.82	-4.93	-6.00	-	
M squared	9.89	5.39	7.13	4.14	-1.09	7.72	3.55	1.21	0.37	-2.37		
Treynor	68.99	129.53	-55.35	250.19	-39.78	31.00	36.43	12.67	-248.97	-10.18		
Jensen	8.84	=B2-(3+B7*($L$2-3))		8.57	2.96	5.32	5.33	1.78	1.69	0.54		
Hampton	8.03	=B2*($L$3/B3)*((0.5*(B7^2+1)-(0.5*0*(B7^2-1)))^0.5)-(3+B7*($L$2-3))							0.73	-0.26		
	NOTE: $\rho_{LS} = -0.7$ for LS and MN funds and $\rho_{ls} = 0.0$ for CTAs and GM funds											
	$R_f = 3.0\%$											

Table 6.2   Ranked Jensen's and Hampton's alpha

	Information		M squared		Treynor		Jensen		Hampton
CTA3	2.77	CTA1	9.89	GM1	250.19	CTA3	12.61	CTA1	8.03
CTA1	2.68	LS1	7.72	CTA2	129.53	CTA1	8.84	CTA3	7.66
GM1	1.27	CTA3	7.13	CTA1	68.99	GM1	8.57	CTA2	7.34
LS1	-0.08	CTA2	5.39	LS2	36.43	LS2	5.33	GM1	3.53
LS2	-0.28	GM1	4.14	LS1	31.00	LS1	5.32	LS1	2.22
GM2	-2.71	LS2	3.55	LS3	12.67	CTA2	3.65	MN1	0.73
LS3	-2.82	LS3	1.21	MN2	-10.18	GM2	2.96	GM2	0.40
CTA2	-2.98	MN1	0.37	GM2	-39.78	LS3	1.78	LS2	-0.23
MN1	-4.93	GM2	-1.09	CTA3	-55.35	MN1	1.69	MN2	-0.26
MN2	-6.00	MN2	-2.37	MN1	-248.97	MN2	0.54	LS3	-1.56

as a proxy for a benchmark, Jensen's alpha is quite close to the rankings witnessed for the information ratio, with the exception of CTA3 which is now ranked top. The results for the CTAs and global macro funds, however, will be erroneous since the S&P index is not a suitable benchmark as it is probably not representative of the exposures taken by these managers. The long/short managers are seen to outperform the market neutral managers, with LS2 being the top ranked LS fund and MN2 as usual being ranked last. On first comparison, what is striking is the extent to which Hampton's alpha is consistently lower than Jensen's alpha.

Long/short and market neutral hedge fund managers typically select a large number of stocks to long and short at any one time depending on their relative outperformance forecasts. A value for long–short correlation of −0.7 has been used for calculating Hampton's alpha for the long/short and market neutral funds – a figure representative of an average expectation. CTAs and global macro funds, however, tend to take positions over time across a number of uncorrelated markets such as bonds, money markets, commodities and foreign exchange. As a result, an average long–short correlation value of zero was used in the example above for the CTAs and global macro managers. From the H-function, it can be seen that the more negative the average long–short correlation, the more volatility reduction can be achieved by the hedge fund manager. To sum up, with Jensen's alpha, this effect is not accounted for and the risk reduction appears as a kind of *free-lunch* when calculating the alpha. In the risk-adjusted version proposed by Hampton this is accounted for, so Hampton's alpha is usually automatically lower than Jensen's alpha as seen in Table 6.2.

6.1.3 Dynamic Rolling Alpha Analysis

Of key interest to the investor is how stable the alpha estimate is likely to be over time. If alpha can be dynamically estimated using a *rolling window* technique, then its characteristics can be graphed over time and analysed for stability. Stable alpha generation is really the goal of hedge funds since lumpy alpha or alpha that is volatile is not a desired outcome for the rational risk-adverse investor. Rolling analysis is easily carried out with Excel, with the rolling period being facilitated by using the OFFSET() function. For example, if we want to calculate a moving average (or any other suitable statistical function) with a variable look-back window length of e.g. *winlen* (where winlen refers to a named cell with a user-defined integer value), this can be performed in Excel using the following function definition

```
Excel_function(OFFSET(value, -winlen+1,0,winlen))
```

In Table 6.3, the value for winlen represents a 12-month moving average of the hedge fund monthly return, e.g. AVERAGE(OFFSET(B17, −winlen+1,0,winlen))*winlen = −3.49. The OFFSET() function is very useful for creating dynamic models which can be user-adjusted for rolling *ex-post* window lengths. The value of winlen can be varied by changing cell value A2 in Table 6.3 with any associated formulae, recalculating automatically.

In the Table 6.3 spreadsheet column C represents the benchmark (in this case the S&P index), column D the risk-free rate and column E the hypothetical average long–short correlation index for the S&P index.

Table 6.3 Dynamic rolling alpha analysis for long short hedge fund LS2

	A	B	C	D	E	F	G	H	I	J	K	L	M	N	O	P	Q	R
1	winlen																	
2	12																	
3		Portfolio	Index	Rf	Rho LS	Rolling	Rolling	Rolling	Rolling	Rolling	Rolling	Rolling	Rolling	Rolling	Rolling	Rolling		
4	Month	LS2	S&P Index	Rf % pa	Rho LS	Rp	Rm	RAf	BetaP	RhoLP	VRAT	Rf	Term 1	Term 2	Hampton A	Jensen A		
5	Jan-05	5.80	2.33	5.15	-0.80	=AVERAGE(OFFSET(B17,-winlen+1,0,winlen))*winlen												
6	Feb-05	4.27	-0.57	5.23	-0.83	=AVERAGE(OFFSET(C17,-winlen+1,0,winlen))*winlen												
7	Mar-05	-3.11	0.63	5.34	-0.80		=STDEVP(OFFSET(C17,-winlen+1,0,winlen))/STDEVP(OFFSET(B17,-winlen+1,0,winlen))												
8	Apr-05	-4.67	0.53	5.24	-0.84		=SLOPE(OFFSET(B17,-winlen+1,0,winlen),OFFSET(C17,-winlen+1,0,winlen))												
9	May-05	4.12	-0.24	4.95	-0.87		=AVERAGE(OFFSET(E17,-winlen+1,0,winlen))											
10	Jun-05	-0.31	3.30	5.18	-0.87		=0.5*(I17^2+1)-0.5*J17*(I7^2-1)											
11	Jul-05	6.87	-3.41	5.24	-0.88		=AVERAGE(OFFSET(D17,-winlen+1,0,winlen))*winlen/12											
12	Aug-05	0.31	5.07	5.23	-0.92		=F17*H17*K17											
13	Sep-05	-6.94	2.32	5.11	-0.96		=(L17+I17*(G17-L17))											
14	Oct-05	1.97	-2.85	5.20	-0.93		=M17-N17											
15	Nov-05	-1.80	-0.44	5.21	-0.89		=F17-(L17+I17*(G17-L17))											
16	Dec-05	-3.75	4.25	5.35	-0.85	↓	↓	↓	↓	↓	↓	↓	↓	↓	↓		
17	Jan-06	-0.45	-2.73	5.20	-0.85	-3.49	5.87	0.68	-0.76	-0.87	0.60	5.20	-1.43	4.70	-6.13	-8.19		
76	Dec-10	-0.54	1.53	1.17	-0.80	9.20	1.91	0.67	0.17	-0.71	0.17	1.60	1.03	1.65	-0.62	7.54		

Columns F–P show the rolling estimates of each salient term defined as follows

F   Rolling return on the hedge fund
G   Rolling return on the market index
H   Rolling risk-adjustment term (the rolling market sigma divided by rolling hedge fund sigma as in the M^2 metric)
I   Rolling beta of the hedge fund compared to the market index
J   Rolling average long–short correlation index for the market index
K   Rolling H-function volatility risk-adjustment term
L   Rolling risk-free rate
M   Rolling Term 1 of equation (6.9a) for Hampton and (6.3) for Jensen
N   Rolling Term 2 of equation (6.9a) for Hampton and (6.3) for Jensen
O   Rolling Hampton's alpha
P   Rolling Jensen's alpha

Figure 6.2 shows that Hampton's alpha has an average value less than Jensen's alpha and is also more stable over time, as is evident towards the latter part of the plot. Since the stability of alpha over time, in addition to a high average, is an important measure of a manager's ability to produce alpha, alpha generation *persistence* could be measured directly from the rolling alpha measure by differencing the time series and calculating the average and standard deviation. In this way, a risk-adjusted

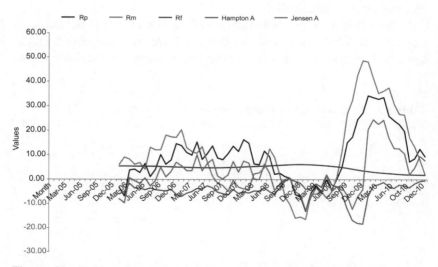

Figure 6.2   Rolling values for Hampton's and Jensen's alpha from Table 6.3

estimate could be calculated where higher values would correspond to managers with a high positive alpha which is reasonably constant over time and not very volatile. It is interesting to note for the LS2 hedge fund graphed in Figure 6.2 that Jensen's alpha has a positive value whereas Hampton's alpha has a negative value over time. As a consequence, the manager may well have been selected on the basis of their Jensen's alpha but would not have been selected if considering their Hampton alpha.

6.2   MULTI-FACTOR MODELS

Linear multi-factor models are a logical extension to the single-factor CAPM model. In Section 6.1 the Sharpe CAPM was introduced in its market form (i.e. using past data for estimation of the parameters). As can be seen from equation (6.3), the Sharpe CAPM would be better classified as a single-factor model, where the single factor is the market's excess returns over the risk-free rate. The Sharpe CAPM therefore models the most important factor – the market or benchmark from which the fund's portfolio is constructed. Jensen's alpha (and Sharpe's CAPM) can therefore be extended into a multi-factor version as follows

Term 1: fund return
$$\alpha_p = R_p.$$

Term 2: risk-free rate and market return
$$- [R_F + \beta_P (R_M - R_F)]. \tag{6.10}$$

Term 3: multi-factor exposure for K factors
$$- \sum_{i=1}^{K} \beta_i F_i.$$

In terms of Hampton's alpha, we have

Term 1: fund return adjusted for leverage and volatility reduction
$$\alpha_p = R_p \times \frac{\sigma_M}{\sigma_P} \times H.$$

Term 2: risk-free rate and market return
$$- [R_F + \beta_P (R_M - R_F)]. \tag{6.11}$$

Term 3: multi-factor exposure for K factors

$$-\sum_{i=1}^{K} \beta_i F_i.$$

As can be seen from equations (6.10) and (6.11), the multi-factor model extension consists of subtracting further aggregate sources of return from the hedge fund return which are attributable to other sources of easily available returns. The multi-factor extension accounts for up to K sources of return exposures from a range of F factors. From equation (6.11) we see that Hampton's alpha affects only Term 1 and so is valid within the multi-factor extended framework.

One can see that the zero alpha null hypothesis case strengthens ever further against the hedge fund manager. Having already exposed Jensen's alpha as usually being too generous when applied to hedge funds, alpha will further be eroded if factors other than the market can be found for inclusion in the aggregate measure in Term 3 of equation (6.11).

6.3 THE CHOICE OF FACTORS

As documented in Section 6.2, there exist in theory K factors which may explain the performance of a hedge fund over and above the market's excess returns and the risk-free rate. A *benchmark* is a reference portfolio which is closely representative of the risk factor exposures of a fund. An *index*, however, is a reference portfolio that is representative of one or more risk factors or styles, e.g. a style index or a sector index. Indices make good benchmarks if they are representative of the styles of the fund. A good set of benchmark qualities as proposed by Bailey (1990) include being

- Unambiguous;
- Investable;
- Measurable;
- Appropriate;
- Reflective of current investment opinions;
- Specified in advance.

Tables 6.4–6.7 list the 15 factors used in the factor analysis, subdivided into four subgroups (see Preface). The factors in subgroup 1 (Table 6.4) are indicative of global passive indices and as such are

Table 6.4 Subgroup 1: Beta factors

No.	Abbreviation	Factor
1	PSDX	Passive Global Stock Index
2	S&P 500 Index	S&P 500 Equity Index
3	PBond DX	Passive Global Bond Index
4	PCom DX	Passive Long Global Commodity Index
5	PUSD DX	Passive Long USD Index
6	Rf	Risk-Free Rate

classed as *beta factors*. Many indices exist in reality for which this set is a proxy and which are easily investable at low cost through ETFs and futures (e.g. Wiltshire, MSCI, Dow Jones, Barclays).

Subgroup 2 (Table 6.5) is representative of typical indices based on the reported returns from the various managers within each style group. This is a hypothetical proxy group representing two main styles, namely long/short equity hedge and CTAs. These indices exist in investable (e.g. EDHEC Investable Hedge Fund Indices, Lyxor Investable Strategies) and non-investable forms (e.g. Eurekahedge, IASG – actual recorded past month and historical non-traded index reporting agencies). Since the indices we use are assumed to be investable and the exposures to underlying markets are by definition active since they are composed of hedge funds, subgroup 2 could be classed as *sophisticated alternative beta*.

Subgroup 3 (Table 6.6) shows the three classic factors introduced by Fama and French (1992) and later by Carhart (1997). These factors differ from the others since they are not directly investable. They remain a reasonably valid method for explaining the increased returns experienced by investing in long value and short growth stocks, long small cap and short large cap (the difference reflects largely taking higher credit risks with the small cap companies, hence it reflects additional risk premia earned from endogenous risk factors). Momentum measures the

Table 6.5 Subgroup 2: Industry reference alternative beta factors

No.	Abbreviation	Factor
7	CTA Index	Commodity Trading Advisor Index
8	LS Index	Long Short Equity Index

Table 6.6 Subgroup 3: Fama–French–Carhart factors

No.	Abbreviation	Factor
9	Val – Gr	Value minus Growth
10	SC – LC	Small Cap minus Large Cap
11	Mom	Momentum

abnormal returns borne from holding long certain stocks within a stock market basket and shorting others depending on their recent performance.

Subgroup 4 (Table 6.7) is representative of *alternative beta* indices which are either available commercially or which could be replicated in-house using a transparent systematic trading approach, e.g. a trend-following scheme applied to futures markets. Four indices are proposed which cover the main financial markets within the managed futures/CTA industry, namely stock indices, bonds, commodities and foreign exchange. The question now is: how do they fit in to our assessment of hedge fund performance? To start to answer this question, the available factor set is best visualised in terms of a *beta continuum* (Anson, 2008) versus hedge fund fees, as shown in Figure 6.3.

It could be argued that alpha is in fact a cleverly disguised complex *alternative beta* and so could in theory be replicated. According to hedge fund managers, however, they have unique proprietary trading algorithms, pricing models and skill which allow them to generate alpha. Up to the last decade or so, most investors did not have the analysis tools available to find out who was bluffing whom. In fact, it could be argued that most of the hedge fund theory which properly explains active hedge fund returns did not even exist until 2001.[2] Both hedge fund

Table 6.7 Subgroup 4: Active alternative beta factors

No.	Abbreviation	Factor
12	ASDX	Active Global Stock Futures Index
13	ABDX	Active Global Bond Futures Index
14	ACDX	Active Global Commodity Futures Index
15	AFDX	Active Global Foreign Exchange Futures Index

[2] Fung and Hsieh defined the concept and coined the phrase *alternative beta* around 2000.

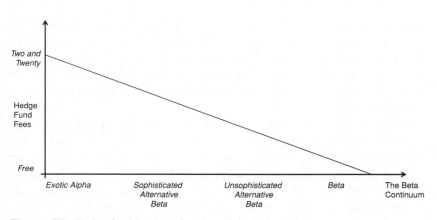

Figure 6.3   Hedge fund fees as a function of the beta continuum

managers (or traders) and informed investors now know that the vast bulk of hedge fund returns are derived from taking either long or short positions in underlying markets and keeping those positions open for a certain time period (ranging from months for the global macro strategy to seconds for the high-frequency CTA). Since time is involved, the hedge fund manager is said to be earning a *premium* for taking a risk over a defined time period (there is no return without risk). If the trader gets the directional forecast of the underlying market right more times than not, they expect to earn a series of daily marked-to-market cash flows with a positive average return over time. The trader who is better at forecasting will be better at producing higher risk-adjusted returns.

The mathematician Benoît Mandelbrot (1964, 1982) postulated that markets exhibit *fracticality* with trends (*or memory*) effects at all frequencies and gave birth to the hypothesis that it is the breakdown of this heterogeneous fractal structure in markets which causes market crashes and fat tails as all traders panic and become short-term traders (e.g. the Flash Crash of 2010[3]). Many hedge fund managers, for example, tend to be trend followers at diverse heterogeneous frequencies

---

[3] The Flash Crash of 2010 was believed to have been caused by a *fat-finger* trader error involving the sale of too may S&P minis at the market which forced other high-frequency traders to react to unexpected price declines that ultimately led to a snowball effect, wiping the entire value off several multi-billion market cap companies momentarily until prices rectified themselves some minutes later when market players realised there was no bad news apart from the apparent *animal spirits* (Keynes) of the market or a *touch of the endogenous* (Mandelbrot).

since public information tends to affect market prices over different time horizons, depending on its severity. These kinds of managers are seen to be primarily producers of alternative beta. It can be argued that it is the level of sophistication of this alternative beta which defines whether the manager is producing alpha. In this sense, alpha is defined as *exotic alternative beta*.

Hedge funds often offset long positions with short positions in different underlying instruments, depending on the manager's style. This will happen naturally from time to time for the CTA and global macro manager, but long/short and market neutral managers are mandated to do this all the time. They typically adjust the betas of their portfolios in a dynamic fashion and engage in leverage. As seen from the Hampton-analysis, this has a tendency to significantly decrease the hedge fund volatility.

In any case, however the hedge fund returns are classified, they are almost always borne of active position-taking by definition and in theory earn *risk premia* over time. The vast majority of bona-fide hedge fund returns could therefore be classed as alternative beta. Hedge fund returns can therefore be classed as *alternative beta* as opposed to *beta* which is the return gained from holding a passive exposure. After all, a hedge fund manager should not get paid for holding passive positions since this can be just as easily done very cheaply by the investor. This effect is seen in Figure 6.3 where true beta is virtually costless and the continuum of alternative beta as it goes from the unsophisticated (basic mechanical trend following trading rules) to the sophisticated is met with higher skill levels required of the hedge fund manager. As such, the fees charged by the hedge manager should be commensurate with their degree of skill in producing better-quality alternative beta returns over time – possibly measured by the stability of their alpha as defined in equation (6.11) or absolute alpha once all other components have been correctly specified versus a benchmark. *Alpha* can be defined as the residual percentage return per year that remains after the net hedge fund returns have been risk-adjusted, correlation-adjusted, adjusted for the risk-free rate, adjusted for the market excess return component and, finally, adjusted for any other factor exposures. If alpha is statistically positive and acceptably stable over time, then the manager may well deserve to get well remunerated and chosen as the preferred manager since they have demonstrated how to add value to a sophisticated alternative portfolio as a result of demonstrably significant market forecasting or security selection skills.

It was decided to include several factors in the factor set as investable proxies spanning the beta continuum as described below

- The factors in subgroup 1 are beta and virtually costless to access via ETFs and futures markets.
- The factors in subgroup 2 represent sophisticated alternative beta and the average industry performance for hedge funds, depending on the style.
- The factors in subgroup 3 are included for completion and remain relevant to mainly long/short performance analysis but do not represent true investable indices.
- The factors in subgroup 4 are unsophisticated alternative beta and have been generated from a basic systematic trend-following rule. They can be accessed via low-cost funds or easily replicated.

Amenc *et al.* (2003) document four types of factors models, namely

1. *Implicit factor model.* Principal component analysis (PCA) is used to derive the inherent or implicit factors identified for the hedge fund by calculating eigenvalues. This is the underlying approach to the EDHEC pure indices, i.e. taking a statistical extraction of the extent of each underlying hedge fund performance index to form a kind of consensus as to what must statistically be the true (*or pure*) index.
2. *Explicit macro factor model.* In this factor model, macroeconomic variables are either computed as predictive variables or used ex-post to gauge major market sensitivities to macroeconomic variables such as GDP expectations versus actual reported GDP (i.e. modelling the effect of the surprise), inflation etc.
3. *Explicit micro factor model.* Microeconomic predictive variables are estimated and forecast, in much the same way as the explicit macro factor model.
4. *Explicit index factor model.* The alternative beta continuum where each factor is investable and so represents some fund or index available as an ETF or future contract.

Model 4 describes the investment universe which is behind factor replication and has been the main focus in this chapter. Models 1–3 may be useful for hedge fund managers themselves as a means of trying to improve forecasting, particularly by using economic factors which if properly forecast usually lead directly to accurate directional forecasts in the associated or underlying traded financial markets as they adjust to fundamental information over time.

The next section will detail the steps necessary to estimate risk-adjusted alpha (RALPH) – the *residual term* once all factor exposures have been identified, quantified, risk-adjusted and removed from the fund's net return using either the Jensen or Hampton framework.

6.3.1 A Multi-Factor Framework for a Risk-Adjusted Hedge Fund Alpha League Table

It is now clear that hedge funds must be appraised in a risk-adjusted sense if any results are to be meaningful. The framework adopted for creating an *alpha league table* for hedge funds must therefore be carried out in a risk-adjusted fashion. The idea behind multi-factor analysis is to identify key factors responsible for driving a proportion of the returns of each hedge fund. These factors are then simulated and their returns subtracted from the hedge fund return. What is left over should be a term closely resembling alpha. What makes the approach adopted in this book different from traditional fund appraisal is that once the factor portfolio has been identified and simulated, it is then risk-adjusted by multiplying by a *scaling factor* to give it a volatility equal to the hedge fund itself. This risk-adjustment process is necessary if the factor portfolio returns are to be appraised on the same basis as the hedge fund, i.e. with equivalent risk in the form of portfolio volatility. By doing so, it will be possible to calculate the percentage of the hedge fund that could be replicated. It will also be possible to allocate percentage impact weights per beta continuum class – showing the impact of each beta continuum sector as a percentage of the overall hedge fund return. The investor will then be able to simulate a revised cost structure and to decide whether or not to pursue a lower-cost replication approach. Of course, the results presented are ex-post or *in-sample*. It would be necessary in reality to split the data set into in- and out-of-sample periods. The results from the in-sample period would then need to be simulated out-of-sample and the results tested against the null hypothesis that there would be no meaningful factors out-of-sample. If sufficient proof existed that the chosen factors were indeed significantly meaningful, then they may be acceptable candidates for inclusion in the investor's revised allocation strategy.

The standard approach to finding factors which empirically drive returns in the hedge fund is to find the beta of each factor and estimate each coefficient of determination, R^2. It was decided to choose only the factors with R^2 values greater than 0.05 since it was assumed that factors with R^2 values less than 0.05 would probably be spurious. The R^2 statistic shows the proportion of the variance in the fund's excess returns attributable to the variance in the factor excess returns using the following Excel function

R-squared $=$ **RSQ**(hedge fund excess returns factor excess returns)

This function is suitable for deciding which factor is meaningful or not as a return driver for the hedge fund. In the subsequent analysis, *r2lim* is the value that controls the R^2 cut-off point and set equal to 0.05. Each factor chosen is simulated and marked-to-market monthly to derive the associated return and risk of the final factor portfolio, such that

$$r_{FP,t} = \sum_{i=1}^{L} \beta_{i,t} F_{i,t}. \qquad (6.12)$$

Where there exist L factors chosen out of a possible K factors. The factor returns are then summed to create the final factor portfolio which will have a return given by

$$R_{FP} = \sum_{t=1}^{T} r_{FP,t}. \qquad (6.13)$$

The factor return time series will also have an associated volatility of σ_{FP}. In order to adjust the factor portfolio so that it has the same volatility as the hedge fund, it is necessary to multiply each period value by a scaling factor S such that

$$S = \frac{\sigma_P}{\sigma_{FP}}. \qquad (6.14)$$

In Table 6.8, column S shows the risk-adjusted factor portfolio (which gives the same volatility as the hedge fund MN2). Then

$$R_{RFP} = S \times R_{FP}. \qquad (6.15)$$

Table 6.8　Risk-adjusted calculations for hedge fund MN2

	Q	R	S	T	U	V	W	X	Y	Z	AA	AB	AC	AD
1	M1	8.29	4.58	3.32		Scaling Factor	0.55	=IF(R1=0,1,T2/R2)	Risk Adjusted FP	0.78	=S1/S2	I alpha	-0.38	=W2*100/T1
2	M2	10.59	5.86	5.86		Jensens Alpha	-1.26	=T1-S1	Risk Adjusted Beta	0.00	=W5/S2	I sAB	0.00	=W7*100/T1
3	M1/M2	0.78	0.78	0.57		RAMFA	-0.22	=W2/T2	Risk Adjuted uAB	0.78	=W6/S2	I uAB	1.38	=W6*100/T1
4	M3	-0.56	-0.56	0.11		Rep Efficiency	137.99	=S1*100/T1	Risk Adjusted sAB	0.00	=W7/S2	I beta	0.00	=W5*100/T1
5	M4	1.74	1.74	0.23		Total Beta	0.00	=SUM(B2:F2)*S1/SUM(B2:P2)				Sum	1.00	=SUM(AC1:AC4)
6	Total Factor	Risk Adjusted	Hedge Fund			Total uAB	4.58	=SUM(J2:P2)*S1/SUM(B2:P2)						
7	Portfolio	Factor Portfolio	MN2			Total sAB	0.00	=SUM(H2:I2)*S1/SUM(B2:P2)						
8	-2.61	-1.44	2.81											
9	2.66	1.47	=R9*$W$1											
10	-0.61	-0.34	-1.56											
11	2.10	1.16	-0.07											
12	-4.38	-2.42	0.38											
13	3.83	2.12	-0.87											
77	3.15	1.74	1.38											
78	1.10	0.61	-0.14											
79	-1.19	-0.66	0.50											

Jensen's alpha can therefore be calculated in a relative reference framework, such that

$$\alpha_J = R_P - R_F - \left(S \sum_{i=1}^{L} \beta_i F_i \right). \tag{6.16}$$

For L factors chosen out of a possible K factors. Hampton's alpha can also be calculated in a similar two-moment risk-adjusted sense such that

$$\alpha_H = R_P \frac{\sigma_M}{\sigma_P} H - R_F - \left(S \sum_{i=1}^{L} \beta_i F_i \right). \tag{6.17}$$

We will focus on Jensen's alpha for the remainder of the chapter since it is a standard, well-documented measure used widely within the industry. It is up to the investor's discretion to use Hampton's alpha which is more meaningful for equity long/short and market neutral managers and so constitutes a rather specialised add-on approach not particularly suitable for every kind of hedge fund. As can been seen from Table 6.8, we have classified the beta continuum into four subgroups of returns: alpha (α), sophisticated alternative beta (sAB), unsophisticated alternative beta (uAB) and beta (β). Hence, the rescaled factor portfolio return can be defined as

$$R_{RFP} = \omega_\beta R_\beta + \omega_{uAB} R_{uAB} + \omega_{sAB} R_{sAB}. \tag{6.18}$$

Where

$$\omega_\beta + \omega_{uAB} + \omega_{sAB} = 1.0. \tag{6.19}$$

The various risk-adjusted components of the hedge fund return are given as follows the risk-adjusted multi-factor alpha (RAMFA)

$$RAMFA = \frac{\alpha_J}{\sigma_P}. \tag{6.20}$$

The risk-adjusted sophisticated alternative beta

$$sAB = \frac{R_{sAB}}{\sigma_P}. \tag{6.21}$$

The risk-adjusted unsophisticated alternative beta

$$uAB = \frac{R_{uAB}}{\sigma_P}. \tag{6.22}$$

The risk-adjusted beta

$$\beta = \frac{R_\beta}{\sigma_P}. \tag{6.23}$$

The total sophisticated alternative beta

$$R_{sAB} = \frac{\sum_{m=1}^{Y} \sigma_{sAB_m}}{\sum_{j=1}^{L} \sigma_{FP_j}} R_{RFP}. \tag{6.24}$$

For Y sAB factors and L out of a total of K factors
the total unsophisticated alternative beta

$$R_{uAB} = \frac{\sum_{k=1}^{X} \sigma_{uAB_k}}{\sum_{j=1}^{L} \sigma_{FP_j}} R_{RFP}. \tag{6.25}$$

For X uAB factors and L out of a total of K factors
and finally, the total beta

$$R_\beta = \frac{\sum_{i=1}^{M} \sigma_{\beta_i}}{\sum_{j=1}^{L} \sigma_{FP_j}} R_{RFP}. \tag{6.26}$$

For M beta factors and L out of a total of K factors.

It is of interest to know not only the absolute values of each return as defined in equations (6.20)–(6.23), but also the percentage 'impact' of each subgroup factor on the fund's return. As such, an impact factor of zero indicates no effect on the hedge fund return, whereas an impact factor of 1.0 indicates that beta continuum group accounts for 100% of the returns of a portfolio with the same volatility as the hedge fund. In

this case we define the following estimates
the alpha impact factor

$$I_\alpha = \frac{\alpha_J}{R_P}. \qquad (6.27)$$

The sophisticated alternative beta impact factor

$$I_{s_{AB}} = \frac{R_{sAB}}{R_P}. \qquad (6.28)$$

The unsophisticated alternative beta impact factor

$$I_{u_{AB}} = \frac{R_{uAB}}{R_P}. \qquad (6.29)$$

And the beta impact factor

$$I_\beta = \frac{R_\beta}{R_P}. \qquad (6.30)$$

Where

$$I_\alpha + I_{sAB} + I_{uAB} + I_\beta = 1.0. \qquad (6.31)$$

Table 6.8 confirms that the sum of all beta continuum factor impacts equal the sum of hedge fund returns after being *unitised*. Each impact factor multiplied by 100 will therefore give the *efficiency* of the fund's return explained by returns from that beta continuum subgroup.

From Table 6.9 it is clear that after the risk-adjusted multi-factor analysis, the rankings have changed significantly compared to those generated in Chapter 5. This shows the superficiality of the approach of using risk-adjusted return metrics without a thorough investigation of underlying risk factors.

Table 6.9   Rankings after risk-adjusted multi-factor analysis

	RAMFA		Net Jensens Alpha		Total Replication Efficiency		Beta Efficiency		Lo AB Efficiency		Hi AB Efficiency
CTA2	1.30	CTA2	6.86	CTA2	0.00	CTA2	0.00	CTA2	0.00	CTA2	0.00
CTA1	0.69	CTA1	5.99	CTA1	53.32	LS2	0.00	GM1	6.14	CTA1	14.39
LS1	0.56	CTA3	4.28	LS1	58.14	CTA1	2.96	CTA3	8.29	MN2	14.82
CTA3	0.34	LS1	4.12	CTA3	69.87	MN2	3.59	GM2	25.87	LS1	18.24
GM1	0.05	GM1	0.75	GM1	93.68	LS1	10.48	LS1	29.42	MN1	20.05
LS2	0.05	LS2	0.57	LS2	94.04	LS3	17.26	CTA1	30.00	CTA3	24.25
MN1	0.05	MN1	0.26	MN1	94.34	MN1	23.58	LS2	40.59	GM1	38.48
LS3	-0.13	MN2	-1.26	LS3	120.49	CTA3	37.33	MN1	50.71	LS3	46.62
MN2	-0.22	LS3	-1.42	MN2	137.99	GM1	49.06	LS3	56.61	LS2	53.45
GM2	-0.42	GM2	-6.34	GM2	214.87	GM2	106.79	MN2	108.15	GM2	82.21

Table 6.10   The unchosen CTA index factor for the MN2 hedge fund

	A	B	C	D	E	F	G	H	I	J	K	L	M	N	O	P
1	M1					0.00			0.00		0.80	7.52	-0.03			
2	M2					0.00			0.00		1.02	9.61	0.04			
3	M1/M2					-			-		0.78	0.78	-0.78			
4	M3					-			-		-0.56	-0.56	0.56			
5	M4					-					1.74	1.74	1.74			
6	Choose?	1	1	1	1	0	1	1	0	1	1	1	1	1	1	1
7	Month	SDX	S&P Index	Bond DX	Com DX	USD DX	Rf % pa	LS Index	CTA Index	Val - Gr	SC - LC	Mom	ASDX	ABDX	ACDX	AFDX
8	Jan-05					0.00			0.00		-0.25	-2.37	0.01			
9	Feb-05					0.00			0.00		0.26	2.41	-0.01			
10	Mar-05					0.00			0.00		-0.06	-0.55	0.00			
11	Apr-05					0.00			0.00		0.20	1.91	-0.01			
12	May-05					0.00			0.00		-0.42	-3.98	0.02			
13	Jun-05					0.00			0.00		0.37	3.48	-0.01			
77	Oct-10					0.00			0.00		0.30	2.86	-0.01			
78	Nov-10					0.00			0.00		0.11	1.00	-0.00			
79	Dec-10					0.00			0.00		-0.12	-1.08	0.00			

A final step was deemed necessary so that only relevant factors were chosen for the multi-factor analysis even though initially they may have had a R^2 value greater than 0.05. For example, the MN2 fund showed the CTA index was a possible factor. Yet this is a market neutral fund and as such should have no link to the CTA index. This factor was then unchosen by putting a zero in the relevant cell as is shown in Table 6.10.

As can be seen from Table 6.11, CTA2 is the clear leader with an acceptable RAMFA level of 1.30 and a net Jensen's alpha of 6.86%. CTA1 follows with a RAMFA of 0.69 and a net Jensen's alpha of 5.99% (not far behind CTA2 but with a higher volatility, hence the lower RAMFA). LS1 and CTA3 follow in the ranking order, with MN2 and GM2 at the bottom. GM2 has obviously been caught out as a *free-rider* and, whilst producing positive returns, the returns do not merit the manager charging the 2/20 fee – in fact they can be more than replicated as seen by the replication efficiency value of 214%. This means that an ex-post replication strategy could have produced returns more than

Table 6.11   Hedge fund alpha league table relative to RAMFA rankings

	RAMFA		Net Jensens Alpha		Total Replication Efficiency		Beta Efficiency		Lo AB Efficiency		Hi AB Efficiency
CTA2	1.30	CTA2	6.86	CTA2	0.00	CTA2	0.00	CTA2	0.00	CTA2	0.00
CTA1	0.69	CTA1	5.99	CTA1	53.32	LS2	0.00	GM1	6.14	MN1	0.00
LS1	0.56	CTA3	4.28	LS1	58.14	MN1	0.00	CTA3	8.29	MN2	0.00
CTA3	0.34	LS1	4.12	CTA3	69.87	MN2	0.00	CTA1	14.10	LS1	18.24
GM1	0.05	GM1	0.75	GM1	93.68	CTA1	6.68	GM2	25.87	CTA3	24.25
LS2	0.05	LS2	0.57	LS2	94.04	LS1	10.48	LS1	29.42	CTA1	32.53
MN1	0.05	MN1	0.26	MN1	94.34	LS3	17.26	LS2	40.59	GM1	38.48
LS3	-0.13	MN2	-1.26	LS3	120.49	CTA3	37.33	LS3	56.61	LS3	46.62
MN2	-0.22	LS3	-1.42	MN2	137.99	GM1	49.06	MN1	94.34	LS2	53.45
GM2	-0.42	GM2	-6.34	GM2	214.87	GM2	106.79	MN2	124.79	GM2	82.21

double those of the hedge fund, for the same volatility. Note that a risk-free rate of zero was used for the above analysis.

6.3.2 Alpha and Beta Separation

Identification of the impact of various subgroups in the beta continuum is important for the separation of alpha and beta as documented by Clarke *et al.* (2009). Separation of alpha and beta is important for two main reasons:

1. Alpha is skill-based and is therefore justifiably costly (perhaps 2/20 or even more[4]), whereas the various declines in skills needed per subgroup of the beta continuum should be less and less costly, with passive beta exposure being virtually costless (e.g. 10 basis points management fee and no incentive fee). The decision whether to instigate a replication programme may therefore be swayed depending on the outcome of a revised cost analysis.
2. The implementation of a core–satellite investment programme. The core–satellite paradigm (Singleton, 2005) is based around the intuitive concept of figuring out which parts of an investment portfolio are passive or active, irrespective of what the manager of the fund might claim. The various factors are divided as shown in Table 6.12 and managed as a core–satellite portfolio which is cheaper, i.e. the core is generally passive (composed of the beta factors) and

Table 6.12 Impact per beta continuum subgroup for hedge fund MN2

AB	AC	AD
I alpha	-0.38	=W2*100/T1
I sAB	0.00	=W7*100/T1
I uAB	1.38	=W6*100/T1
I beta	0.00	=W5*100/T1
Sum	1.00	=SUM(AC1:AC4)

---

[4] SAC Advisors, run by Steve Cohen, apparently used to charge 5% and 50%. They were, however, producing annualised gross returns of around 100% with a single-digit maximum drawdown using high-frequency trading, and despite their excessive fee structure, were highly successful at raising assets.

the satellite is generally active (composed of the range of sophisticated and unsophisticated alternative beta factors plus alpha). The
core–satellite method of portfolio construction is a least-cost method
of achieving an investment result largely in line with the theory and
findings of this chapter. Core–satellite investments are also known to
be stable over time in terms of performance persistence and expli-
cation, and exhibit more desirable characteristics in terms of transparency. It is of course desirable to know that an advisor is not
overcharging for a return generation effect which could be achieved
at a lower cost and perhaps with less counterparty and liquidity risk
via an ETF or future.

Example 6.2   Cost reduction from separation of alpha and beta

For the analysis below, the various impact factors were calculated
for the CTA1 fund. Without going into detail as to the source of each
beta continuum impact factor, let us consider the potential reduction
in management and incentive fees which could arise if we were able
to replicate the same return as the hedge fund only using the range
of the beta continuum for the same volatility.

Z	AA
I alpha	0.47
I sAB	0.33
I uAB	0.14
I beta	0.07
Sum	1.00

Assume a linear cost reduction function versus the various subgroups in the beta continuum as shown in the figure

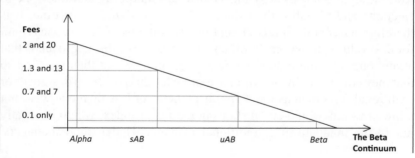

If we assume a linearly decreasing cost function for the fee structure associated with each subgroup, we are in a position to calculate the total fees for the partially replicated hedge fund. The total fee cost for the replicated hedge fund as shown in the table above is the total revised management fee given by

$$\text{Mgt Fee} = I_\alpha \times 2 + I_{sAB} \times 1.3 + I_{uAB} \times 0.7 + I_\beta \times 0.1$$
$$= 0.47 \times 2 + 0.33 \times 1.3 + 0.14 \times 0.7 + 0.07 \times 0.1 \approx 1.4\%,$$

and the total revised performance fee is written as

$$\text{Perf Fee} = I_\alpha \times 20 + I_{sAB} \times 13 + I_{uAB} \times 07 + I_\beta \times 0$$
$$= 0.47 \times 20 + 0.33 \times 13 + 0.14 \times 7 + 0.07 \times 0 \approx 14\%.$$

Therefore, the total risk-adjusted fee structure associated with implementing such a replicating factor portfolio could be reduced from 2% and 20% to 1.4% and 14% – a significant saving in management and incentive fees.

Of further interest would be the availability of each of the factor components in the partial replicating portfolio, their implementation cost and the variability of the factor components over time. An in- and out-of sample study would then need to be undertaken before the investor would be convinced of the merits of a partial replication approach versus investing fully in the hedge fund chosen and trying to negotiate a fee reduction directly with the fund manager.

6.4 DYNAMIC STYLE BASED RETURN ANALYSIS

Rolling style analysis was introduced by Sharpe as a framework to calculate and visualise the extent of beta sensitivities over time. It is therefore a dynamic approach and involves the use of *rolling windows* for past value estimation. The interesting feature of this approach is that at any one time the individual betas are summed and then rescaled so that they equal one. In the original approach (Sharpe, 1992) designed for traditional fund management appraisal, betas of less than one were not allowed as this would entail shorting the factor index, which is usually not in the mandate of a traditional manager. Hedge fund managers,

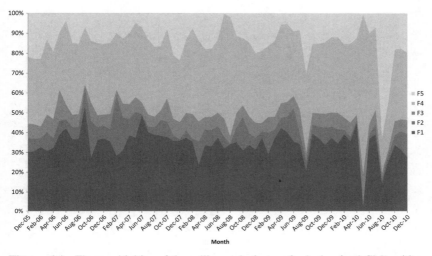

Figure 6.4 The sensitivities of the rolling style factors for hedge fund GM1 with a rolling window of 3 months

however, are paid for shorting – hence the term *hedge*[5] fund. As a consequence, the version of Sharpe's style based return analysis used in this chapter allows for negative betas. In this case, the absolute values are summed and rescaled so that for any one time interval the sum of the absolute betas equals one. As such, the variability of the fund under examination is unitised to the sum of all known factors, as shown in Figures 6.4 and 6.5.

For the hedge fund GM1, the style factor sensitivities seem to be reasonably stable over time for the 12-month rolling version of Figure 6.5 (year-on-year annualised) versus the more noisy and volatile version of Figure 6.4 with only a three-month rolling period (quarter-to-quarter annualised). The stability of these rolling style factors is not surprising, considering the hypothetical nature of the data used for the 10 hedge funds and 15 factors. Real-life data have a tendency to be more wild, varied and complex. The use of hypothetical data and factors, however, provides a good null hypothesis for benchmarking the same approaches used with industry data. The approach in Excel is demonstrated in Tables 6.13–6.15.

---

[5] The term is said to have emerged in the Victorian era in England, when bets were placed with bookmakers through hedges, thus obscuring the face of the better. Nowadays it means shorting out any exposure so that an investment is partially or fully protected with respect to risk.

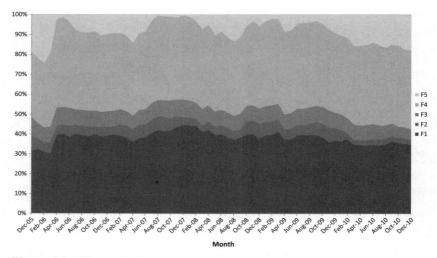

Figure 6.5 The sensitivities of the rolling style factors for hedge fund GM1 with a rolling window of 12 months

Table 6.13 The five factors

	A	B	C	D	E	F	G
1							
2		**Hedge Fund**			**The Five Factors**		
3		**Rm**	**F1**	**F2**	**F3**	**F4**	**F5**
4	**Month**	**GM1**	**PBond DX**	**PCom DX**	**PUSD DX**	**CTA Index**	**ABDX**
5	Jan-05	0.89	-1.60	-12.95	-6.08	-0.74	-3.24
6	Feb-05	-0.90	0.58	4.24	3.34	1.45	2.50
7	Mar-05	-5.38	-0.41	-1.97	-3.85	0.74	0.34
67	Mar-10	2.24	-1.13	-10.52	-2.72	0.13	-2.30
68	Apr-10	1.86	0.23	8.82	0.98	0.75	2.69
69	May-10	-3.57	-0.55	-4.12	-3.24	0.15	-0.15
70	Jun-10	-1.70	-0.19	-1.38	0.34	0.53	1.55
71	Jul-10	-0.13	1.24	9.35	7.44	1.87	-0.78
72	Aug-10	0.05	-1.99	-15.22	-11.29	-1.43	-2.77
73	Sep-10	5.06	0.78	5.27	1.96	1.35	2.31
74	Oct-10	6.19	-0.41	1.89	-3.73	0.57	-0.01
75	Nov-10	-4.46	-2.56	-6.35	-15.35	-1.67	-3.61
76	Dec-10	0.59	-0.02	-1.88	-4.97	0.46	0.08

Table 6.14 The five factor dynamic style analysis

	H	I	J	K	L	M	N	O	P	Q	R	S	T
1													
2													
3													
4	lookback							Absolute					
5	12							Values					
6		Rolling	Rolling	Rolling	Rolling	Rolling							
7		Beta F1	Beta F2	Beta F3	Beta F4	Beta F5		Beta F1	Beta F2	Beta F3	Beta F4	Beta F5	
8													
9													
10		=SLOPE(OFFSET($B19,-lookback+1,0,lookback),OFFSET(C19,-lookback+1,0,lookback))											
11													
12			=SLOPE(OFFSET($B19,-lookback+1,0,lookback),OFFSET(D19,-lookback+1,0,lookback))										
13													
14				=SLOPE(OFFSET($B19,-lookback+1,0,lookback),OFFSET(E19,-lookback+1,0,lookback))									
15													
16					=SLOPE(OFFSET($B19,-lookback+1,0,lookback),OFFSET(F19,-lookback+1,0,lookback))								
17						=SLOPE(OFFSET($B19,-lookback+1,0,lookback),OFFSET(G19,-lookback+1,0,lookback))							
18		↓	↓	↓	↓	↓							
19		0.59	0.14	0.19	0.61	0.35		0.59	0.14	0.19	0.61	0.35	=ABS(M19)
20		0.97	0.17	0.23	0.97	0.66		0.97	0.17	0.23	0.97	0.66	
78		1.66	0.13	0.26	1.83	0.82		1.66	0.13	0.26	1.83	0.82	
79		1.42	0.10	0.22	1.63	0.73		1.42	0.10	0.22	1.63	0.73	

Table 6.15 The unitised five factor beta coefficients

	U	V	W	X	Y	Z	AA
1							
2							
3							
4	As a fraction of 1						
5							
6							
7	Beta F1	Beta F2	Beta F3	Beta F4	Beta F5		
8							
9							
10	=O19/(SUM($O19:$S19))						
11							
12		=P19/(SUM($O19:$S19))					
13							
14			=Q19/(SUM($O19:$S19))				
15							
16				=R19/(SUM($O19:$S19))			
17					=S19/(SUM($O19:$S19))		
18	↓	↓	↓	↓	↓		
19	0.31	0.07	0.10	0.33	0.19		
20	0.32	0.06	0.08	0.33	0.22		
78	0.35	0.03	0.06	0.39	0.18		
79	0.35	0.02	0.05	0.40	0.18		

6.5 THE MARKOWITZ RISK-ADJUSTED EVALUATION METHOD

The Markowitz model allows the calculation of the volatility of a fund if the covariances (or correlations) are known or anticipated for the N assets. The model was a breakthrough in its day, as already noted, and gives an exact answer for the portfolio variance or volatility if the various historical returns, variances and covariances are correctly estimated. Knowing this, it can be used in a forward-looking sense (i.e. ex-ante) if we use predictions instead of historical estimations for the inputs. It has been used widely within the industry since its inception and remains one of the key pillars of modern-day portfolio theory – hence its key role in the study and analysis of hedge fund performance. It can be shown that as N gets bigger, the variance of an equally weighted portfolio will equal the average covariance of the assets in the portfolio. In other words, when there are many assets, the individual variance of each asset does not affect the portfolio variance – only covariance (and correlation) matters for portfolios composed of a large number of positions. The general finding of Markowitz is that individual manager volatility does not affect the portfolio volatility of a FoHFs if there are many heterogeneous funds in the investment portfolio. Instead the key drivers of the volatility of a FoHFs are the individual correlations of each asset within the portfolio.

As a final stage in the hedge fund analysis process, a mean–variance analysis is usually attempted so that the correlations can be measured for each fund and their impacts modelled for various target portfolios as a variance–covariance (VCV) matrix. Up to now we have analysed hedge funds in terms of their risk-adjusted performance and risk-adjusted multi-factor performance. Now we shall model them in terms of their overall risk-adjusted performance, taking correlations into account. Assume that we do not want to allocate capital to any more than five funds. From Table 6.11, the top performing five funds in terms of RAMFA are CTA2, CTA1, LS1, CTA3 and GM1. It is interesting to note that these are the five top funds according to the omega ratio rankings with a threshold of zero (see Table 5.12) and the Sharpe ratio rankings (see Table 5.10). Let us consider three cases in which we may want to proceed in order to create a final portfolio:

(1) Unconstrained mean–variance optimisation for five funds only (unconstrained satellite portfolio);

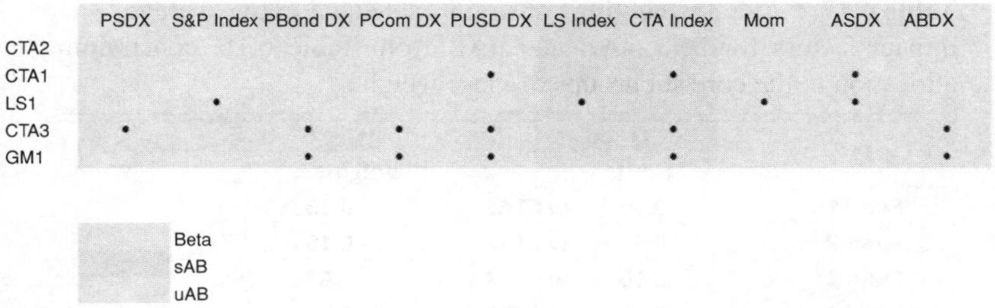

	PSDX	S&P Index	PBond DX	PCom DX	PUSD DX	LS Index	CTA Index	Mom	ASDX	ABDX
CTA2										
CTA1					•		•		•	
LS1		•			•			•	•	
CTA3	•		•	•	•		•			•
GM1			•	•	•		•			•

Beta
sAB
uAB

Figure 6.6   Factor impact matrix for the five funds

(2) Unconstrained mean–variance optimisation for the five funds and ten salient factors (unconstrained core-satellite portfolio);
(3) Constrained mean–variance optimisation for the five funds and ten salient factors (constrained core-satellite portfolio).

As can be seen in Figure 6.6, the five funds are assumed to have the various underlying factor exposures as shown by the dot matrix. For the impact factors shown in Table 6.16, an average is taken so that the final portfolio weights may be constrained by this amount per beta continuum subgroup exposure. Table 6.17 shows the approach for Case 3 to constrain the weights of each subsector and actual set up using the **Solver** function shown in Figure 6.7. The optimiser is now set to solve for a maximum Sharpe ratio (assuming a risk-free interest rate of 3%). Since each subgroup's overall weights are constrained, the optimiser will come up with the optimal intra-group weights to achieve an overall maximum Sharpe ratio for the portfolio as a whole.

Table 6.16   Average impact factors per beta continuum subgroup exposure

	Alpha	sAB	uAB	Beta	Sum
CTA2	1.00	0.00	0.00	0.00	1.00
CTA1	0.47	0.33	0.14	0.07	1.00
LS1	0.42	0.18	0.29	0.10	1.00
CTA3	0.30	0.24	0.08	0.37	1.00
GM1	0.06	0.38	0.06	0.49	1.00
Total/5	0.45	0.23	0.12	0.21	1.00

Table 6.17 Case 3 weighting constraints set equal to the average impact factors for beta, sAB and uAB from Table 6.16, constraining allocation to the core subgroups of these weights

	A	B	C	D	E
21		Limits		Weights	
22	Fund 1	0.50	w CTA1	0.13	
23	Fund 2	0.50	w CTA2	0.18	
24	Fund 3	0.50	w CTA3	0.07	
25	Fund 4	0.50	w GM1	0.04	
26	Fund 5	0.50	w LS1	0.14	
27	Beta Factor 1	0.50	w PSDX	0.02	
28	Beta Factor 2	0.50	w S&P	0.05	
29	Beta Factor 3	0.50	w PBondDX	0.00	
30	Beta Factor 4	0.50	w PComDX	0.00	
31	Beta Factor 5	0.50	w PUSDDX	0.00	
32	sAB Factor 1	0.50	w LS Index	0.08	
33	sAB Factor 2	0.50	w CTA Index	0.15	
34	uAB Factor 1	0.50	w Mom	0.09	
35	uAB Factor 2	0.50	w ASDX	0.03	
36	uAB Factor 3	0.50	w ABDX	0.00	
37	Constraint 1		Total	1.00	=SUM(D22:D36)
38	Constraint 2		Total Beta	0.08	=SUM(D27:D31)
39	Constraint 3		Total sAB	0.23	=SUM(D32:D33)
40	Constraint 4		Total uAB	0.12	=SUM(D34:D36)
41					
42	Portfolio Mean	9.93			
43	Portfolio Sigma	2.58			
44	Sharpe Ratio	2.69			

Table 6.18 shows the ranked weighting scheme for each case. For Case 1 the investor wants to know the optimal mean–variance ex-post ranked weighting for the five top chosen hedge funds. CTA2 has the optimal weight at 0.28, followed by CTA1 with 0.25, LS1 with 0.25 (these three dominate), CTA3 with 0.14 and GM1 with 0.08.

For Case 2 the investor has decided to set up a core–satellite portfolio and is interested in knowing what the optimal unconstrained ex-post mean–variance rankings would be for all five funds and ten factors. From Table 6.18 it is seen that the factors dominate – probably due to favorable correlation effects reducing the portfolio variance. We see that the CTA index would be weighted at 0.21, momentum at 0.19, LS index

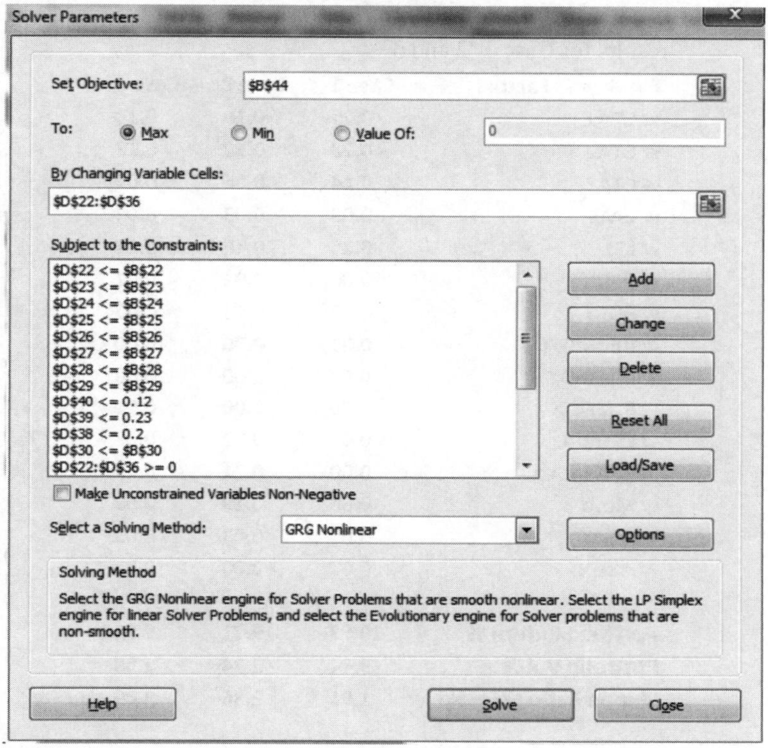

Figure 6.7 The **Solver** dialogue box

at 0.12, CTA at 0.12, LS1 at 0.1, CTA1 at 0.1, CTA3 at 0.06, ASDX at 0.03, S&P at 0.03 and PSDX at 0.01. The ex-post Sharpe ratio of such an unconstrained core-satellite portfolio has risen considerably to 2.86, as shown in Table 6.18.

Finally, for Case 3, where we have constrained the impact factors of each beta continuum subgroup to the ex-post estimated amounts calculated above, we see that CTA2 is 0.18, CTA index 0.15, LS1 0.14, CTA1 0.13, momentum 0.09, LS index 0.08, CTA3 0.07, S&P 0.05, GM1 0.04, ASDX 0.03 and PSDX 0.02. The Sharpe ratio is calculated at 2.69, as shown in Table 6.18.

If ranked amongst the factors in the constrained portfolio, the final ranking of each fund is therefore CTA2, LS1, CTA1, CTA3 and GM1 – interestingly the same as the basic M1/M2 ratio of Table 5.6, but probably a coincidence. Table 6.19 shows ranked weights for each fund and factor for Case 1, 2 and 3.

Table 6.18 Mean–variance optimised ex-post results for Case 1, 2 and 3

Funds and Factors	Case 1	Case 2	Case 3
w CTA1	0.25	0.10	0.13
w CTA2	0.28	0.12	0.18
w CTA3	0.14	0.06	0.07
w GM1	0.08	0.03	0.04
w LS1	0.25	0.10	0.14
w PSDX	0.00	0.01	0.02
w S&P	0.00	0.03	0.05
w PBondDX	0.00	0.00	0.00
w PComDX	0.00	0.00	0.00
w PUSDDX	0.00	0.00	0.00
w LS Index	0.00	0.12	0.08
w CTA Index	0.00	0.21	0.15
w Mom	0.00	0.19	0.09
w ASDX	0.00	0.03	0.03
w ABDX	0.00	0.00	0.00
Portfolio Return %	10.52	9.71	9.93
Portfolio Vol %	3.84	2.34	2.58
Sharpe Ratio (RF=3%)	1.96	2.86	2.69

Table 6.19 Ranked weights for each fund and factor for Case 1, 2 and 3

Funds and Factors	Case 1	Funds and Factors	Case 2	Funds and Factors	Case 3
w CTA2	0.28	w CTA Index	0.21	w CTA2	0.18
w CTA1	0.25	w Mom	0.19	w CTA Index	0.15
w LS1	0.25	w LS Index	0.12	w LS1	0.14
w CTA3	0.14	w CTA2	0.12	w CTA1	0.13
w GM1	0.08	w LS1	0.10	w Mom	0.09
w PSDX	0.00	w CTA1	0.10	w LS Index	0.08
w S&P	0.00	w CTA3	0.06	w CTA3	0.07
w PBondDX	0.00	w ASDX	0.03	w S&P	0.05
w PComDX	0.00	w S&P	0.03	w GM1	0.04
w PUSDDX	0.00	w GM1	0.03	w ASDX	0.03
w LS Index	0.00	w PSDX	0.01	w PSDX	0.02
w CTA Index	0.00	w PComDX	0.00	w PComDX	0.00
w Mom	0.00	w PBondDX	0.00	w PBondDX	0.00
w ASDX	0.00	w PUSDDX	0.00	w PUSDDX	0.00
w ABDX	0.00	w ABDX	0.00	w ABDX	0.00

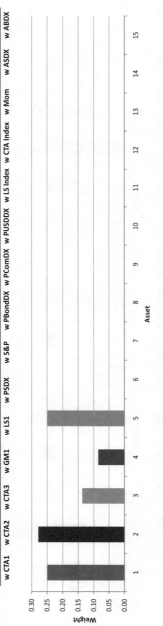

Figure 6.8 Final portfolio weights for case 1 – unconstrained satellite portfolio

| 0.10 | 0.12 | 0.06 | 0.03 | 0.10 | 0.01 | 0.03 | 0.00 | 0.00 | 0.00 | 0.00 | 0.12 | 0.21 | 0.19 | 0.03 | 0.00 |
| w CTA1 | w CTA2 | w CTA3 | w GM1 | w LS1 | w PSDX | w S&P | w PBondDX | w PComDX | w PUSDDX | w LS Index | w CTA Index | w Mom | w ASDX | w ABDX |

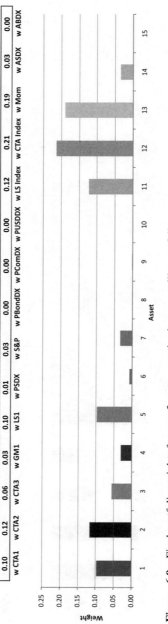

Figure 6.9 Final portfolio weights for case 2 – unconstrained core–satellite portfolio

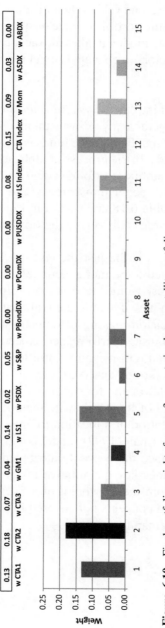

Figure 6.10 Final portfolio weights for case 3 – constrained core–satellite portfolio

The final rankings of the five chosen hedge funds were seen to be CTA2, LS1, CTA1, CTA3 and GM1 when mean–variance optimised in a constrained core–satellite portfolio. Since mean–variance optimisation is based on the Markowitz model, it takes into account the correlations of each hedge fund and factor – a concept critical for hedge fund portfolio analysis.

This chapter has looked into the *whys and wheres* of hedge fund return structures using multi-factor analysis in an attempt to estimate true measures of alpha for each fund. Five hedge funds were finally chosen out of the ten initial hedge funds. In the process of alpha and beta separation, it was shown how core–satellite portfolios could be constructed offering lower fee structures with better transparency and benchmarking. This was demonstrated in Table 6.18 and shown in Figures 6.8–6.10 with a significantly higher Sharpe ratio versus the original for the five hedge fund portfolio.

Of course this analysis is the just the end of the beginning for the investor. Fees would need to be more accurately modelled and an *out-of-sample* hypothesis test would have to be performed. The investor would need to ascertain how dynamic the reallocation and adjustments would be and what decision-making parameters would need to be included into the model. Further performance expectations would have to be evaluated for expected returns and volatilities. Other approaches in the literature would need to be analysed, e.g. the conditional approach of Kat and Miffre (2002) or the four-moment extension of Favre and Ranaldo (2005). Instead of the Markowitz method, known to produce an impractical concentration of allocation to only a few funds in practice, the Black and Litterman (1992) model could be employed which has a tendency to produce more evenly attributed allocation weights. Lhabitant (2004) provides key quantitative insights into the world of hedge funds as seen from the viewpoint of a FoHFs manager and introduces other advanced concepts not covered in this text such as style cluster analysis and Kalman filtering.

7
Hedge Fund Market Risk Management

We have encountered throughout this book the problems associated with the risk that the value of a hedge fund will decrease due to the impact of various market factors, such as changes in interest and foreign currency rates. Moreover, with the heightened publicity surrounding recent financial events, hedge fund managers have come under increased pressure from investors and regulators to efficiently manage, monitor, measure and report such market risks inherent in their investment strategies. Indeed, experience has clearly shown that the measurement and management of extreme market conditions is of paramount importance for hedge funds.

This chapter provides an introduction to market risk management for hedge funds and presents the fundamentals of quantitative risk measures and models used in the industry today. The chapter also covers some of the more advanced risk measures available that can more effectively manage risk in light of the limitations encountered with traditional market risk measures.

7.1 VALUE-AT-RISK

The value-at-risk (VaR)[1] for a portfolio of assets is the worst estimated loss over a given time horizon (e.g. daily or monthly) at a specified level of confidence (e.g. 95% or 99%). VaR is often based on the assumption that asset returns follow a normal distribution and that the performance of the hedge fund portfolio is affected by a set of linear market factors. As discussed in Chapter 4, under such assumptions it is possible to describe the distribution of hedge fund returns by just two statistical parameters, μ and σ. That is, assuming that a set of monthly hedge fund returns (or P&Ls) are characterised by a normal distribution, then, at a confidence level of $c\%$ there is an expected loss for the hedge fund no worse than z_α

---

[1] VaR is an example of a *downside risk* measure, i.e. the likelihood that an investment will decline in value, or the amount of loss that could result from such a potential decline.

Box 7.1   Quantiles

Quantiles (already encountered in Chapter 4) are points taken at regular intervals from a probability distribution. More formally, the quantile function for any probability distribution is the inverse of the cumulative distribution function (CDF). Some q-quantiles have special names:

- 4-quantiles are called quartiles;
- 100-quantiles are called percentiles.

For an ordered (or *ranked*) set of data, the percentile is a value that represents the number below which a certain percentage of the data fall, e.g. the 95th percentile is the value below which 95% of all the observations fall. Sometimes, when trying to find a particular percentile of a distribution of ordered values, a problem can be encountered when there is no perfect division of the distribution due to the number of data points. In this case, a *linear interpolation* is applied to two adjacent percentiles in order to determine the best value that divides the distribution exactly. Consider a distribution of ordered returns. A linear interpolation can be performed between two adjacent returns using the following

$$r_p = r_1 + \frac{r_2 - r_1}{w_2 - w_1} \times (w_p - w_1).$$

Where r_p is the linearly interpolated return, r_1 and r_2 are the lower and upper returns; w_1 and w_2 are the lower and upper cumulative weights around the required percentile, and w_p is the required percentile weight.

---

standard deviations (i.e. $z_\alpha \sigma$) below the mean (see Box 7.2) over the next month.

For example, at a 95% confidence level (95th percentile), 95% of the time the loss is expected to be no worse than 1.645σ. VaR does not give any information about the amount of loss expected in excess of VaR over this period but only indicates that 5% of the time the loss to the hedge fund is expected to be at least that bad (see Figures 7.1 and 7.2).

Box 7.2   Confidence levels and critical values for the standard normal distribution

The table below shows the two most common confidence levels at 95% and 99% along with their associated critical values z_α for the standard normal distribution. At a 95% confidence level, the critical value is −1.645 indicating that there is a 5% probability that a particular value will be at least 1.645 standard deviations below the mean (i.e. −1.645σ).

	A	B	C	D	E
1	c	$\alpha = (1-c)$	Critical Value (z_α)		
2	95%	5%	-1.645	=NORMSINV(B2)	
3	99%	1%	-2.326		

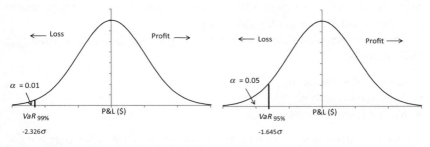

Figure 7.1   VaR at the 95% and 99% confidence levels

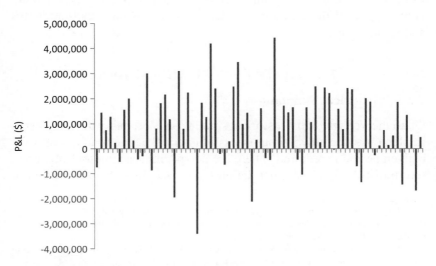

Figure 7.2   The estimated 5% worse case P&Ls

So, for a standard normal distribution (i.e. $\mu = 0$ and $\sigma = 1$), the VaR for a hedge fund at a confidence $c = 100(1 - \alpha)\%$, denoted by $VaR_{1-\alpha}$, is given by

$$VaR_{1-\alpha} = Z_\alpha. \qquad (7.1)$$

However, μ and σ are parameters[2] of the hedge fund return (or P&L) distribution and therefore $VaR_{1-\alpha}$ can be written more formally[3] as:

$$VaR_{1-\alpha} = \mu - Z_\alpha\sigma. \qquad (7.2)$$

Note that $VaR_{1-\alpha}$ scales with the volatility. VaR is usually reported on a monthly[4] basis in negative dollar terms, which further emphasises that it is a measure of loss, or as an *absolute* positive dollar amount. Some fund managers report VaR on a monthly basis in percentage terms so as to be consistent across measures.

There are generally three industry-accepted methods for estimating VaR, namely:

- historical simulation;
- parametric method;
- Monte Carlo simulation.

Each has a different approach in terms of how it describes the distribution of losses. Monte Carlo simulates data, historical simulation uses actual data, and the parametric approach utilises the data but only in order to generate the necessary parameters to characterise the distribution. However, all of these traditional measures of VaR have their strengths and weaknesses.

7.2 TRADITIONAL MEASURES

7.2.1 Historical Simulation

Of all the VaR methods, historical simulation is probably the simplest to implement since only a time series of historical hedge fund returns over a given period is required. There are no specific assumptions about the return distribution, only that the past is an accurate characterisation of

---

[2] Indeed, this is an example of the parametric method for calculating VaR.

[3] In equation (7.2), μ is used to centre the normal distribution, before subtracting the relevant number of σs to get the VaR figure.

[4] If a different time horizon for VaR is required (e.g. annual VaR) a similar square root rule to that used for the standard deviation can be applied, e.g. $VaR_{annual} = VaR_{monthly} \times \sqrt{12}$.

the future. It is important to be careful not to draw any conclusions from the data set if it is not large enough to be representative of the returns distribution looking forward. In this sense, the assumption that historic monthly hedge fund returns are an accurate representation of the future is a major disadvantage of this method since there is no certainty that the past will replicate the future.

Estimating VaR by historical simulation involves calculating a series of simulated P&L values based on a set of historical monthly hedge fund returns. A set of simulated P&Ls are generated for each hedge fund return and placed in ascending order (i.e. lowest to highest). An associated cumulative weight for each P&L value is then calculated whereby the lowest P&L corresponds to the 100% cumulative weight. For a $c\%$ confidence level, the cth percentile in the ordered P&L is used to estimate VaR. Dependent on the number of data points, it may be necessary to perform a *linear interpolation* on adjacent percentiles to obtain the required P&L that corresponds to the $c\%$ confidence level (see Box 7.1). Table 7.1 shows an implementation of a historical simulation to determine the VaR for the hypothetical CTA index of monthly returns with $100 million AuM. A user-defined VBA function is used to determine the linear interpolated P&L value for the 95th percentile (see Source 7.1). The historical monthly $VaR_{95\%}$ is estimated at $1,527,428 for a 95% confidence level, i.e. over the next month there is a 5% probability that

Table 7.1 Calculation of historical VaR at a 95% confidence level

	A	B	C	D	E	F	G	H	I	J
1	CTA Index AuM ($)	100,000,000								
2	Confidence Level	95%								
3	Critical Value (z_a)	1.645	=NORMSINV(B2)							
4	Monthly VaR$_{95\%}$ ($)									
5	-1,539,199	=PERCENTILE(D11:D82,(1-B3))								
6	-1,527,428	=H14							Min. P&L ($)	-3,395,043
7									Max. P&L ($)	4,435,435
8			CTA Index	Simulated		Cumulative	Confidence		Bin Interval	250,000
9	Date	RoR (%)	Count	P&L ($)	Ordered P&L ($)	Weight	Level		P&L Bins ($)	Frequency
10	Jan-05	-0.74	1	-737,997	-3,395,043	100.00%			-4,500,000	0
11	Feb-05	1.45	2	=$B$1*(B11/100)	2,103,537	98.61%			-4,250,000	0
12	Mar-05	0.74	3	745,844	1,939,201	97.22%			-4,000,000	0
13	Apr-05	1.29	4	1,286,621	-1,668,682	95.83%	95%	-1,527,428	-3,750,000	0
14	May-05	0.24	5	240,482	-1,433,258	94.44%			-3,500,000	0
15	Jun-05	-0.51	6	-514,206	-1,344,620	93.06%	=fncLNRINTERP(E15,E14,F15,F14,G14)			
16	Jul-05	1.57	7	1,570,757	=SMALL($D$11:$D$82,C16)					
17	Aug-05	2.01	8	2,010,515					-2,750,000	0
18	Sep-05	0.33	9	330,329	-737,997	88.89%			-2,500,000	0
19	Oct-05	-0.42	10	-421,613	-698,638	=F20+1/$C$83			-2,250,000	0
20	Nov-05	-0.29	11	-293,985	-628,098				-2,000,000	1
81	Dec-10	0.46	72	458,882	4,435,435	1.39%				
82		# Data Points	72							

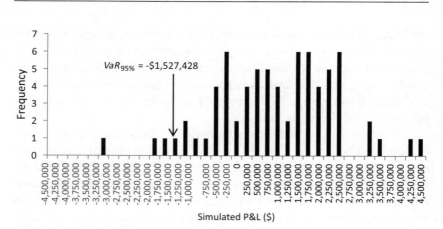

Figure 7.3   Historical VaR at a 95% confidence level

the CTA will lose $1,527,428 in value.[5,6] Figure 7.3 shows the distribution of monthly simulated P&L values and the $VaR_{95\%}$ depicting a loss in the *left tail* of the distribution.

Source 7.1   User-defined VBA function to perform linear interpolation between two values

```
'function to perform LINEAR INTERPOLATION between
two values
Function fncLNRINTERP(r1 As Double, r2 As
Double, w1 As Double, w2 As
Double, wp As Double) As Double

fncLNRINTERP = r1 + ((r2 - r1) / (w2 - w1)) *
(wp - w1)

End Function
```

---

[5] It is also possible (as shown in Table 7.1) to calculate the P&L value for the required confidence level using the PERCENTILE() function. The two values are slightly different, which reflects the *non-normality* of the simulated P&L distribution and approximations when using linear interpolation.

[6] With historical simulation, since *actual* monthly returns are used, the distribution is already assumed to be centred, so there is no need to subtract the relevant number of σs from μ in order to get the VaR figure.

7.2.2 Parametric Method

From Chapter 4 (see Section 4.11.1), for a hedge fund made up of N risky assets, $i = 1,\ldots, N$, the portfolio variance is given by the matrix equation

$$\sigma_p^2 = W^T \Sigma W. \tag{7.3}$$

Where W^T is the matrix transpose of W which contains all the individual asset weights, w_i, and Σ is the variance–covariance matrix for the individual assets i and j:

$$W = \begin{pmatrix} w_1 \\ w_2 \\ w_3 \\ \vdots \\ w_N \end{pmatrix}. \tag{7.4}$$

$$W^T = \begin{pmatrix} w_1 & w_2 & w_3 & \cdots & w_N \end{pmatrix}. \tag{7.5}$$

$$\Sigma = \begin{pmatrix} \sigma_1^2 & \mathrm{cov}_{12} & \mathrm{cov}_{13} & \cdots & \mathrm{cov}_{1n} \\ \mathrm{cov}_{21} & \sigma_2^2 & \mathrm{cov}_{23} & \cdots & \cdots \\ \mathrm{cov}_{31} & \mathrm{cov}_{32} & \sigma_3^2 & \cdots & \cdots \\ \vdots & \vdots & \vdots & \vdots & \vdots \\ \mathrm{cov}_{n1} & \cdots & \cdots & \cdots & \sigma_N^2 \end{pmatrix}. \tag{7.6}$$

If the portfolio standard deviation σ_P is given by

$$\sigma_p = \sqrt{W^T \Sigma W}. \tag{7.7}$$

Then the estimated VaR is written as follows

$$VaR_{1-\alpha} = P \times z_\alpha \times \sigma_p. \tag{7.8}$$

Where P is the market value of the portfolio. In Chapter 4 (see Section 4.11.2), the mean–variance optimisation problem was solved for the FoHFs (10 hedge funds) which produced the results (note that no short sales were allowed) as shown in Table 7.2.

For a FoHFs with \$100 million AuM the minimum variance gives us a monthly VaR of \$4,766,094 at the 95% confidence level, as shown in Table 7.3. That is, there is only a 5% chance that the value of the

Table 7.2 Optimised weights for the fund of hedge funds (10 hedge funds) and minimum variance

	A	B	C	D	E
88	**Return Matrix (R)**		**Weight Matrix (W)**		
89	**Fund**	**Return (%)**	**Fund**	**Weight**	**Limit**
90	1	12.82	1	0.16	0.50
91	2	6.86	2	0.22	0.50
92	3	14.21	3	0.09	0.50
93	4	11.81	4	0.06	0.50
94	5	5.52	5	0.02	0.50
95	6	9.84	6	0.17	0.50
96	7	9.57	7	0.07	0.50
97	8	6.91	8	0.05	0.50
98	9	4.65	9	0.10	0.50
99	10	3.32	10	0.06	0.50
100			TOTAL	1	
101					
102			Target Return (%)	9.00	
103					
104			Portfolio		
105			Return (%)	9.00	
106			Min. Variance	8.40	

FoHFs will fall by more than \$4,766,094 over the next month. The parametric method suffers from the fact that linear relationships[7] are assumed between risk variables and that hedge fund returns are assumed to be normally distributed.

7.2.3 Monte Carlo Simulation

The Monte Carlo (MC) method assumes that monthly hedge fund returns can be characterised by a *stochastic* model. MC methods are a widely used class of computational algorithms for simulating the behaviour of various physical and mathematical systems, having been popularised

---

[7] Such linear relationships are clearly an oversimplification of the model when considering the fact that more and more hedge funds are utilising sophisticated trading strategies involving derivatives (e.g. options) which are known to possess non-linear characteristics.

Table 7.3 Parametric VaR for the FoHF (10 hedge funds)

	A	B	C	D	E	F	G	H	I
1		Optimal Weights	Fund	Allocation ($)					
2		0.16	CTA1	16,298,776					
3		0.22	CTA2	22,013,720					
4		0.09	CTA3	8,824,360					
5		0.06	LS1	5,619,446					
6		0.02	LS2	2,166,291					
7		0.17	LS3	17,441,831		FoHF AuM ($)	100,000,000		
8		0.07	GM1	6,544,046		Variance (Min.)	8.40		
9		0.05	GM2	5,089,250		St. Dev.	2.90%		
10		0.10	MN1	10,272,473		Confidence Level	95%		
11		0.06	MN2	5,729,804		Critical Value (z_α)	1.645	=NORMSINV(G10)	
12	Total	1		100,000,000		$VaR_{95\%}$ ($)	4,766,094		
13							=G7*G11*G9		
14									

by John von Neumann[8] and Nicholas Metropolis[9] among others. MC methods are distinguished from other simulation-based methods by being of a stochastic nature, i.e. the MC model includes a non-deterministic component that introduces a degree of uncertainty or randomness into the process through the use of random number generators.[10] The fundamental idea behind the technique involves simulating thousands of trials (or *paths*) that a series of hedge fund returns are likely to follow over a certain time period in the future based on a specific mathematical (i.e. stochastic) model. Each trial leads to a terminal value for the hedge fund return (or P&L) at the end of each simulation period. After thousands of such runs, a simulated P&L distribution is obtained from which a VaR can be estimated at a preferred confidence level in much the same way as the historical simulation, i.e. ordering the P&L values and locating the relevant confidence percentile P&L value (or loss).

A drawback (although not a restrictive one) to the MC method is that the simulated P&L distribution relies on a particular stochastic model or process that a series of hedge fund returns are expected to be governed by in the future. Such a model is primarily driven by the μ and σ of the hedge fund return distribution determined from historical data as well

[8] John von Neumann (1903–1957) was a Hungarian-American mathematician who made major contributions to a vast range of fields, including set theory, functional analysis, quantum mechanics, economics, game theory, computer science and numerical analysis.
[9] Nicholas Metropolis (1915–1999) was a Greek-American physicist.
[10] MC simulations rely heavily on the *sampling method* and *stability* of the random number generator. For this reason, many financial houses spend a great deal of time, money and effort developing better and more robust random number generators.

as the inclusion of a degree of subjective knowledge (i.e. market experience) into the model where necessary. The material covered in Chapter 4 on the geometric Brownian motion (see Section 4.8) gives a classic example of a typical stochastic model that can be used to implement an MC simulation. The stochastic model is the fundamental building block to many MC simulations being used extensively throughout the financial markets. The MC method is a very powerful and much used technique for estimating VaR within the hedge fund community. Not only is the method robust and probabilistically strong, it is also an excellent way of building non-linearity into the return distribution and facilitating a better understanding of the characteristics of the use of derivatives within the portfolio with greater confidence. However, the MC method can easily become mathematically challenging and computationally expensive especially when dealing with the inherent complexities of a particular hedge fund portfolio and strategy.

Table 7.4 gives a brief summary of the advantages and disadvantages of the three traditional measures of VaR.

In addition to the estimation of VaR through either of the traditional methods, hedge fund managers will also carry out a variety of *stress tests* on the hedge fund portfolio. That is, the parameters and risk factors that

Table 7.4 Comparison of traditional VaR measures

Method	Advantages	Disadvantages
Historical simulation	No assumptions about the return distributions.	Assumes data used in the simulation are representative of the future.
Parametric	Mathematically simple to understand and implement through matrix equations.	Strong assumptions about the hedge fund return distribution in terms of μ and σ. Less accurate for non-linear instruments used within the hedge fund portfolio and strategy.
Monte Carlo	Flexibility in terms of choosing the stochastic process, and allows for the inclusion of subjective judgements into the model.	Most demanding in terms of computational resources. Can become mathematically complex and challenging.

affect hedge fund performance will be greatly magnified, for example raising the volatility over a particular period (e.g. by 100% or 200%) of the original value so as to cause a serious risk to the hedge fund of losing a catastrophic amount of money. This helps the fund manager understand where problems may be concentrated and allows them to be prepared for such events should they arise (however unlikely). Similarly, fund managers may run *scenario analyses* using a set of historical data and related parameters that cover a specific turbulent period in the financial markets, such as the stock market crash of 1987 or the recent financial crisis of 2008. This will also help the manager identify potential areas of large losses and allow them to develop strategic measures to mitigate against such problems in the event of a similar financial disaster.

7.3   MODIFIED VaR

Despite the use of stress tests and scenario analysis, the most erroneous (and potentially damaging) assumption when using traditional VaR methods is that of hedge fund returns following a normal distribution. Clearly, this is invalid since it is well known that hedge fund returns generally have fatter tails and an asymmetric return distribution, i.e. negative skewness and positive excess kurtosis. In order to address this issue many extensions to the traditional VaR methods have been put forward as better estimators of hedge fund market risk. Such methods either explicitly incorporate skewness and kurtosis into the model or focus primarily on the left tails of the returns distribution where most of the extreme negative returns (i.e. large losses) occur.[11] One such extension already touched upon in Chapter 5 (see Section 5.2.2) when discussing the modified Sharpe ratio (MSR) is modified VaR (MVaR). MVaR explicitly takes into account the standardised third and fourth central moments of the return distribution, namely skewness and kurtosis. Indeed, there is a branch of mathematics that is involved with power series expansions of quantile functions (see Box 7.1) such as those related to VaR. The higher moments of the distribution (M3 and M4) are incorporated into the VaR measure using the celebrated Cornish–Fisher expansion (Cornish and Fisher, 1937), such that the following power

---

[11] Many other methods exist that offer better estimations of the distribution hedge fund returns, e.g. Johnson distributions and simulated skewed Student's *t* distributions.

series can be obtained for the first few terms:

$$z_{cf} \approx z_\alpha + \tfrac{1}{6}\left(z_\alpha^2 - 1\right)S + \tfrac{1}{24}\left(z_\alpha^3 - 3z_\alpha\right)K - \tfrac{1}{36}\left(2z_\alpha^3 - 5z_\alpha\right)S^2.$$
(7.9)

Where z_{cf} is the Cornish–Fisher critical value from the normal distribution at the respective confidence level, S is the sample skewness and K is the sample excess kurtosis. Note that when the return distribution is normally distributed, S and K will both be zero and therefore

$$z_{cf} \approx z_\alpha.$$
(7.10)

The modified VaR is given by

$$MVaR_{1-\alpha} = \mu - Z_{cf}\sigma.$$
(7.11)

where $MVaR_{1-\alpha}$ is the estimated VaR at a confidence $c = 100(1-\alpha)\%$, μ is the mean of the hedge fund returns and z_α is the critical value from the normal distribution for the respective confidence level (see Box 7.2). It turns out that using equation (7.11) leads to a more accurate measure of the VaR. However, there are limitations to this estimation. A higher required confidence (e.g. 99%) will take us further into the left tail of the distribution and lead to inaccurate results. The MVaR is also unreliable when the returns (or P&L) distribution is highly skewed and fat-tailed. Table 7.5 shows that the monthly MVaR at a 95% confidence is $2,717,148 and clearly higher when compared to the historical VaR estimate of $1,527,428 for the hypothetical CTA index over the period 2005–2010. A user-defined VBA implementation of the MVaR calculation is shown in Source 7.2 using the VBA functions developed in Chapter 4; this further extends the implementation covered in Section 5.2.2.

Source 7.2   User-defined function to calculate MVaR for a simulated P&L distribution

```
'function to calculate MVAR for a simulated
P&L distribution
Function fncMVAR(PL As Range, CI As Double)
As Double

    'the mean, st. dev., skewness and xskurtosis of
simulated P&L distribution
    mean = fncMEAN(PL) / 12 'monthly
```

```
std = fncSTDEV(PL) / Sqr(12) 'monthly
skew = fncSKEWNESS(PL)
xsKurt = fncXSKURTOSIS(PL)

z= Application.WorksheetFunction.NormSInv(1 -
(CI / 100))

a = (1 / 6) * (z ^ 2 - 1) * skew
b = (1 / 24) * ((z ^ 3) - (3 * z)) * xsKurt
c = (1 / 36) * ((2 * z ^ 3) - (5 * Z)) *
(skew * 2)

fncMVAR = mean - ((z + a + b - c) * std)

End Function
```

Table 7.5   Calculation of MVaR at a 95% confidence level

	A	B	C	D
1	CTA Index AuM ($)	100,000,000		
2	Mean P&L ($)	853,771		
3	St. Dev. P&L ($)	1,475,497		
4	Confidence Level	95%		
5	$VaR_{95\%}$ ($)	-1,527,428		
6	$MVaR_{95\%}$ ($)	-2,717,148	=fncMVAR(D10:D81,B4)	
7				
8		CTA Index		Simulated
9	Date	RoR (%)	Count	P&L ($)
10	Jan-05	-0.74	1	-737,997
11	Feb-05	1.45	2	1,450,798
12	Mar-05	0.74	3	743,844
13	Apr-05	1.29	4	1,286,621
14	May-05	0.24	5	240,482
15	Jun-05	-0.51	6	-514,206
16	Jul-05	1.57	7	1,570,757
17	Aug-05	2.01	8	2,010,515
18	Sep-05	0.33	9	330,329
19	Oct-05	-0.42	10	-421,613
20	Nov-05	-0.29	11	-293,985
21	Dec-05	3.00	12	3,003,202
81	Dec-10	0.46	72	458,882

7.4 EXPECTED SHORTFALL

Apart from the assumption that the P&L distribution is normal, VaR also fails to satisfy one of the concepts of a *coherent risk measure*. Artzner *et al.* (1999) have stated that a desirable measure of risk should satisfy four basic properties or axioms, namely:

1. It must be *monotonic*: if asset $X \geq 0$, $VaR(X) \leq 0$, i.e. positive returns should not increase risk.
2. It must be *sub-additive*: for assets X_1 and X_2, $VaR(X_1 + X_2) \leq VaR(X_1) + VaR(X_2)$, i.e. the risk of a portfolio of two assets should not be larger than the risk of the sum of the individual assets. If this were the case then adding assets to a portfolio to reduce risk through diversification would not be possible.
3. It must possess *positive homogeneity*, so that, for any positive real number a, $VaR(aX) = a.VaR(X)$, i.e. increasing the size of the port-folio by a times should increase the risk by a multiple of a, assum-ing all the assets within the portfolio remain the same in terms of weighting.
4. It must be *translationally invariant*, so that, for any real number a, $VaR(X + a) \leq VaR(X) - a$, i.e. adding an amount of cash (or risk-free asset) to the portfolio should result in a reduction of the risk by an amount a.

Unfortunately VaR only satisfies three of the axioms, i.e. it fails to satisfy the sub-additivity rule. For this reason, an alternative (and often complementary) measure of VaR was developed known as expected shortfall (ES),[12] which is discussed in detail in Rockafellar and Uryasev (2000). ES does satisfy all of the above axioms and is thus considered a coherent risk measure. ES is the conditional expectation of loss given that the value is beyond VaR, i.e. the loss conditional on the value exceeding the VaR

$$ES_{1-\alpha} = E\left[X \mid X > VaR_{1-\alpha}\right]. \tag{7.12}$$

Where $ES_{1-\alpha}$ is the estimated ES at a confidence $c = 100(1 - \alpha)\%$. If we consider ES as the average loss in the area beyond VaR, i.e. the extreme left tail of the distribution, it is possible to give a more mathematical interpretation of ES, such that:

$$ES_{1-\alpha} = E\left[L \mid L > 1 - \alpha\right] = \int_{\infty}^{1} \frac{1}{\alpha} q_c dc. \tag{7.13}$$

---

[12] Also known as conditional VaR, mean excess loss, beyond VaR or tail VaR.

Table 7.6 ES at 95% and 99% confidence levels

	A	B	C	D	E	F	G	H
1	c	$\alpha = (1-c)$	Critical Value (z_α)	$ES_{1-\alpha}$				
2	95%	5%	-1.645	-2.063	=-NORMDIST(NORMSINV(A2),0,1,)/(1-A2)			
3	99%	1%	-2.326	-2.665				

Where L is the expected loss in the left tail of the return (or P&L) distribution and q_c is the percentile relating to the required confidence level c. The formulation in equation (7.13) gives us a better understanding of how we can use the NORMDIST() and NORSMINV() built-in functions in Excel to estimate ES. Table 7.6 shows a similar analysis for ES to that of the critical values for the 95% and 99% confidence levels determined above for VaR. The ES in the left tail of the P&L distribution with 95% confidence beyond the VaR at 1.645σ, is 2.063σ. That is, conditional on the loss exceeding 1.645σ, the expected value (or *average*) of the left tail is 2.063σ.[13] This gives the information on the expected loss in the left tail, but of course it is only the average of the left tail; the loss could be further along, i.e. greater than 2.063σ. Since ES is by definition more than VaR, ES is a more conservative estimate, and this is why it is often used as a complement to traditional VaR measures.

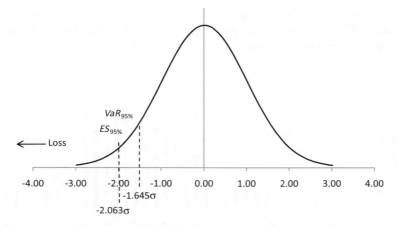

Figure 7.4 Comparison of ES and VaR at the 95% confidence level

---

[13] The NORMDIST() function returns the normal distribution for a specified mean and standard deviation, i.e. for the standard normal distribution the mean is zero and standard deviation is one.

Table 7.7 Computation of ES at the 95% confidence level

	A	B	C	D	E	F	G	H
1	CTA Index AuM ($)	100,000,000						
2	Mean P&L ($)	853,771						
3	St. Dev. P&L ($)	1,475,497	=STDEV(D9:D80)					
4	Confidence Level	95%						
5	ES$_{95\%}$ ($)	-3,043,527	=B3*NORMDIST(NORMSINV(B4),0,1,)/(1-B4)				Min. P&L ($)	-3,395,043
6							Max. P&L ($)	4,435,435
7			CTA Index		Simulated		Cumulative	Bin Interval	250,000
8	Date	RoR (%)	Count	P&L ($)	Ordered P&L ($)	Weight	P&L Bins ($)	Frequency
9	Jan-05	-0.74	1	-737,997	-3,395,043	100.00%	-4,500,000	0
10	Feb-05	1.45	2	1,450,798	-2,103,537	98.61%	-4,250,000	0
11	Mar-05	0.74	3	743,844	-1,939,201	97.22%	-4,000,000	0
12	Apr-05	1.29	4	1,286,621	-1,668,682	95.83%	-3,750,000	0
13	May-05	0.24	5	240,482	-1,433,258	94.44%	-3,500,000	0
14	Jun-05	-0.51	6	-514,206	-1,344,620	93.06%	-3,250,000	1
15	Jul-05	1.57	7	1,570,757	-1,027,152	91.67%	-3,000,000	0
16	Aug-05	2.01	8	2,010,515	-866,476	90.28%	-2,750,000	0
17	Sep-05	0.33	9	330,329	-737,997	88.89%	-2,500,000	0
18	Oct-05	-0.42	10	-421,613	-698,638	87.50%	-2,250,000	0
19	Nov-05	-0.29	11	-293,985	-628,098	86.11%	-2,000,000	1
20	Dec-05	3.00	12	3,003,202	-514,206	84.72%	-1,750,000	1
80	Dec-10	0.46	72	458,882	4,435,435	1.39%		
81		# Data Points	72					

Table 7.7 shows the comparison between the monthly VaR and ES at the 95% confidence level for the hypothetical CTA index. ES, as a much more conservative value than the traditional VaR, is much larger, and as such offers a greater insight into the actual loss that could be faced by the CTA over the next month. Figure 7.5 shows the simulated P&L distribution and the ES estimated at $3,043,527.

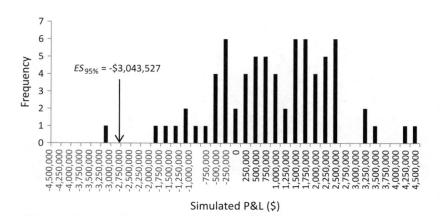

Figure 7.5 ES at the 95% confidence level

Although ES is a more conservative and useful indicator of the esti-mated VaR at a particular confidence level, it is important to note that ES does not give any information of the *severity* of loss by which VaR is exceeded, only the expected (or average) loss. Moreover, when con-sidering a 99% confidence in the left tail then, for 100 P&L values, only one value will be used to determine the average of the tail loss. In this case, it is necessary to investigate further the area of extreme losses with a deeper analysis of the left tail of the P&L distribution.

7.5   EXTREME VALUE THEORY

We have already stated and discussed the fact that hedge fund return distributions have negative skewness and positive excess kurtosis, i.e. the distribution does not adequately capture the probability where losses are severe. This is where the branch of mathematics known as *extreme value theory*[14] (EVT) becomes a very useful tool in estimating VaR. The theoretical foundations of EVT were first developed heuristically by Fisher and Tippett (1928) and have since been applied to insurance and finance by Embrechts *et al.* (1999). In general, EVT is the theory of modelling and measuring events which occur with very small prob-ability. Clearly this is useful for analysing the extreme losses (i.e. left tail) in the return (or P&L) distribution. Indeed, EVT is really the only method of extracting an accurate measure of the estimated loss given the limited data around an extreme event. Figure 7.6 shows the 'parent' distribution characterised by the first two moments (i.e. μ and σ) and a separate 'child' distribution that specifically characterises the distri-bution of losses in the left tail of the parent distribution, i.e. the extreme tail losses. Interpreting the main distribution in terms of the parent and then a child distribution within the parent gives us some qualitative understanding of how EVT is applied.

Consider Figure 7.7, which shows a hypothetical plot of the losses for a particular hedge fund over a 100-day period. Given such information, the next step is to try to characterise the losses over this period in some mathematical way. EVT offers two fundamental methods for such characterisations, namely the *block maxima* and *peaks over threshold* methods.[15]

---

[14] Some hedge fund managers prefer to use stress testing and scenario analysis rather than EVT to estimate their exposures to tail events.

[15] Both methods are mathematically challenging and beyond the scope of this book, and the reader should consult the references cited for more detailed explanations.

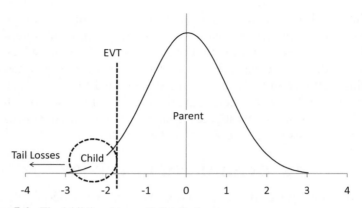

Figure 7.6   The 'child' and 'parent' distributions

7.5.1   Block Maxima

The block maxima (BM) method is based on subdividing the time period into a set of buckets (or *blocks*) of equal size. For example, Figure 7.8 reproduces the loss data given in Figure 7.7 for the hypothetical hedge fund over the 100-day period but divides the time into 10 blocks, i.e. each block is a 10-day period that will contain a certain number of losses. Taking the maximum loss in each of the 10-day blocks gives us 10 local *maxima*, i.e. 10 data points which can be used to characterise (or fit) a probability distribution. The distribution is known as a *generalised extreme value distribution*. Within the hedge fund community, the block maxima method is the less preferred method of estimating VaR using EVT.

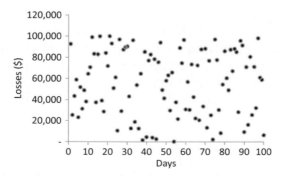

Figure 7.7   Hypothetical hedge fund losses over 100 days

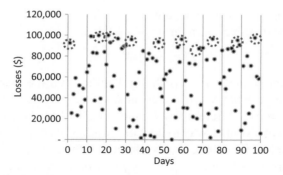

Figure 7.8   The largest losses in each 10-day block

7.5.2   Peaks over Threshold

The peaks over threshold (POT) method is a more modern and widely
accepted method for estimating VaR, although mathematically demand-
ing. The basic idea behind the method is to choose a numerical *threshold*
so that every loss over that threshold is considered an extreme loss. The
number of data points over the threshold can be used to characterise
(or fit) a probability distribution, in this case known as the *generalised
Pareto*[16] *distribution*. Figure 7.9 shows an example of a typical threshold in which only those losses exceeding $90,000 will be considered
extreme relative to the value of the portfolio.

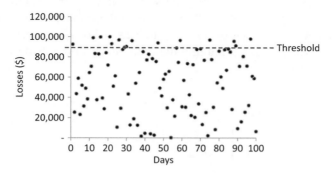

Figure 7.9   Losses over a threshold

---

[16] Vilfredo Pareto (1848–1923) was an Italian engineer, sociologist, economist, and philosopher and made several important contributions to economics, particularly in the study of income
distribution.

We have already seen in Chapter 4 (see Section 4.4) how to consider
a probability distribution in terms of a CDF, i.e.

$$F(x) = P(X \leq x). \tag{7.14}$$

For a given value x, $F(x)$ is the probability that the observed value
of a random variable X will be at most x, i.e. less than or equal to x.
For EVT there is a different function to consider based on a conditional
probability (in a similar way to how the conditional expectation models
the ES). That is, for an excess distribution of the return variable X over
a certain threshold u, the *conditional probability distribution* of $y = X$
$- u$ such that $X > u$ can be written as

$$F_u(y) = P\,(X - u \leq y\,|X > u\,). \tag{7.15}$$

The CDF is now the probability that $y = X - u$, i.e. the excess loss (or
exceedance) over the threshold is less than or equal to y conditional on X
exceeding the threshold u (see Figure 7.10). One of the main theorems
of EVT, developed by Pickands (1975), states that for a reasonably
high threshold u, $F_u(y)$ can be approximated by the generalised Pareto
distribution written as

$$G(X) = \begin{cases} 1 - \left(1 + \frac{\xi y}{\beta}\right)^{-1/\xi} & \text{if} \quad \xi \neq 0 \\ 1 - \exp\left(-\frac{y}{\beta}\right) & \text{if} \quad \xi = 0. \end{cases} \tag{7.16}$$

Where $y = X - u$, $\xi = 1/\alpha$ is the shape parameter, α the tail index and β
a simple scaling parameter. There are several approaches to estimating
the parameters in equation (7.16), such as maximum likelihood, the
elemental percentile method and the method of moments described in

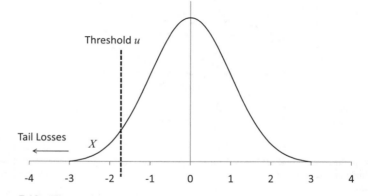

Figure 7.10   The random variable X and threshold u

the studies by Hosking and Wallis (1987), Grimshaw (1993) and Castillo and Hadi (1997).

An estimate of the VaR using the generalised Pareto distribution approach described above can be written as

$$VaR_{1-\alpha} = u + \frac{\beta}{\xi}\left(\left(\tfrac{N}{n_u}\alpha\right)^{-\xi} - 1\right). \tag{7.17}$$

Where N is the total number of data points, and n_u the number of data points that exceed the threshold u. Furthermore, the method can be extended so that the expected shortfall $ES_{1-\alpha}$ can be stated in terms of $VaR_{1-\alpha}$, that is

$$ES_{1-\alpha} = \frac{VaR_{1-\alpha}}{1-\xi}\frac{\beta - \xi u}{1-\xi}. \tag{7.18}$$

For hedge funds, the amount of data in the tail of the returns distribution is often small and therefore leads to broad confidence intervals and weak significance estimates. Both the BM and POT methods suffer from the problem of limited data, although it is possible to reduce the time division in the BM method or lower the threshold for the POT technique to produce more data points to fit to the desired distribution.

In this chapter we have provided an introduction to the main quantitative risk measures, from the traditional VaR approaches to some of the more advanced and challenging theoretical hedge fund market risk models. We have seen throughout this book that hedge fund returns usually have fatter tails and an asymmetric return distribution which clearly violates the assumption of a normal distribution that underlies traditional measures. In order to address such limitations many extensions to the traditional VaR methods have been developed as better estimates of hedge fund market risk. Such methods either explicitly incorporate skewness and kurtosis into the model or focus primarily on the left tails of the return distribution where most of the large losses occur. Despite the availability of more robust and potentially accurate market risk models, it must be made clear that the analysis in this chapter covers only one component of the risks associated with hedge funds. A more complete treatment would involve incorporating other equally important risks into the analysis. For example, the monitoring, management and reporting of credit, liquidity and operational risk should also be considered alongside market risk within a robust and effective hedge fund risk management process.

References

Amenc, N. and Martellini, L. (2003) Desperately seeking pure style indices. Working Paper, EDHEC Risk and Asset Management Research Centre.

Amenc, N., Sfeir, D. and Martellini, L. (2003) An integrated framework for style analysis and performance measurement, *Journal of Performance Measurement*, 7(4), 35–41.

Anson, M. (2008) The beta continuum: From classic beta to bulk beta. *Journal of Portfolio Management*, 34(2), 53–64.

Artzner, P., Delbaen, F., Eber, J.M. and Heath, D. (1999) Coherent measures of risk. *Mathematical Finance*, 3(9), 203–228.

Bailey, J.V. (1990) Some thoughts on performance-based fees. *Financial Analysts Journal*, 46(4), 31–40.

Black, F. and Litterman, R. (1992) Global portfolio optimization. *Financial Analysts Journal*, 48(5), 28–43.

Carhart, M.M. (1997) On persistence in mutual fund performance. *Journal of Finance*, 52(1), 57–82.

Castillo, E. and Hadi, A. (1997) Fitting the generalised Pareto distribution to data. *Journal of the American Statistical Association*, 92(440), 1609–1620.

Clarke, R.C., de Silva, H. and Thorley, S. (2009) *Investing separately in alpha and beta*. Research Foundation of CFA Institute.

Cornish, E.A. and Fisher, R.A. (1937) Moments and cumulants in the specification of distributions. *Review of the International Statistical Institute*, 5(4), 307–320.

Embrechts, P. Klüppelberg, C. and Mikosch, T. (1999) *Modelling Extremal Events*. Berlin: Springer-Verlag.

Fama, E. and French, K.R. (1992) The cross-section of expected stock returns. *Journal of Finance*, 47(2), 427–465.

Favre, L. and Ranaldo A. (2005) Hedge fund performance and higher-moment market models. *Journal of Alternative Investments*, 8(3), 38–51.

Fisher, R.A. and Tippett, L.H.C. (1928) Limiting forms of the frequency distributions of the largest or smallest member of a sample. *Proceedings of the Cambridge Philosophical Society*, 24, 180–190.

Fung, W. and Hsieh, D.A. (2000a) Performance characteristics of hedge funds and commodity funds: Natural versus spurious biases. *Journal of Financial and Quantitative Analysis*, 35(3), 291–307.

Fung, W. and Hsieh, D.A. (2000b) The risk in hedge fund strategies: Theory and evidence from trend followers. *Review of Financial Studies*, 14, 313–341.

Fung, W. and Hsieh, D.A. (2004) Hedge fund benchmarks: A risk-based approach. *Financial Analysts Journal*, 60(5), 65–80.

Géhin, W. (2007) The challenge of hedge fund performance measurement: A toolbox rather than a Pandora's box. EDHEC Risk Institute, January.

Goodwin, T.H. (1998) The information ratio. *Financial Analysts Journal*, 54(4), 34–43.

Gregoriou, G.N. and Gueyie, J.P. (2003) Risk-adjusted performance of funds of hedge funds using a modified Sharpe ratio. *Journal of Wealth Management*, 6(3), 77–83.

Grimshaw, S.D. (1993) Computing maximum likelihood estimates for the generalised Pareto distribution. *Technometrics*, 35, 185–191.

Gupta, R.H., Kazemi, H. and Schneeweis, T. (2003) Omega as a performance measure. CISDM Research Paper, June.

Hampton, D.E. (2009) A mean-variance capital asset pricing model for long short equity portfolios. SSRN Working Paper, http://ssrn.com/author=837926.

Hosking, J.R.M. and Wallis, J.R. (1987) Parameter and quantile estimation for the generalised Pareto distribution. *Technometrics*, 29(3), 339–349.

Jarque, C.M. and Bera, A.K. (1987) A test for normality of observations and regression residuals. *International Statistical Review*, 55(2), 163–172.

Jensen, M.C. (1968) The performance of mutual funds in the period 1945–1964. *Journal of Finance*, 23(2), 389–416.

Kaplan, P.D. and Knowles, J.A. (2004) Kappa, a generalized downside risk-adjusted performance measure. *Journal of Performance Measurement*, 8(3), 42–54.

Kat, H. and Miffre, J. (2002) Performance evaluation and conditioning information: The case of hedge funds. Working Paper, University of Reading.

Keating, C. and Shadwick, W. (2002) A universal performance measure. *Journal of Performance Measurement*, 6(3), 59–84.

Lo, A.W. (2002) The statistics of Sharpe ratio. *Financial Analyst Journal*, 58(4), 36–52.

Lhabitant, F.-S. (2004) *Hedge Funds: Quantitative Insights*. Chichester: John Wiley & Sons, Ltd.

Malkiel, B.G. (1995) Returns from investing in equity mutual funds 1971 to 1991. *Journal of Finance*, 50(2), 549–572.

Mandelbrot, B. (1964) The variation of certain speculative prices. In P. Cootner (ed.), *The Random Character of Stock Prices*. Cambridge, MA: MIT Press.

Mandelbrot, B. (1982) *The Fractal Geometry of Nature*. New York: WH Freeman.

Markowitz, H. (1952) Portfolio selection. *Journal of Finance*, 7(1), 77–91.

Modigliani, F. and Modigliani, L. (1997) Risk-adjusted performance. *Journal of Portfolio Management*, 23(2), 45–54.

Modigliani, L. (1997) Yes, you can eat risk-adjusted returns. *Morgan Stanley U.S. Investment Research 1997* (17 March), 1–4.

Pickands, J. (1975) Statistical inference using extreme order statistics. *Annals of Statistics*, 3(1), 119–131.

Rockafellar, R.T. and Uryasev, S. (2000) Optimisation of conditional value-at-risk. *Journal of Risk*, 2(3), 21–41.

Sharma, M. (2004) A.I.R.A.P. – alternative risk-adjusted performance measures for alternative investments. *Journal of Investment Management*, 2(4).

Sharpe, W. (1963) A simplified model for portfolio analysis. *Management Science*, 9(2), 277–293.

Sharpe, W.F. (1992) Asset allocation: Management style and performance measurement. *Journal of Portfolio Management*, 18(2), 7–19.

Sharpe, W.F. (1994) The Sharpe ratio. *Journal of Portfolio Management*, 21(1), 49–58.

Singleton, J.C. (2005) *Core-Satellite Portfolio Management – A Modern Approach to Professionally Managed Funds*. New York: McGraw-Hill.

Stutzer, M. (2000) A portfolio performance index. *Financial Analysts Journal*, 56(3), 52–61.

Treynor, J.L. (1962) Toward a theory of market value of risky assets. Unpublished manuscript printed in 1991 as Chapter 2 in Robert A. Korajczyk (ed.), *Asset Pricing and Portfolio Performance*. London: Risk Books.

Xu, X.E., Liu, J. and Loviscek, A.L. (2009) Hedge fund attrition, survivorship bias, and performance: Perspectives from the global financial crisis. Working Paper, Seton Hall University.

Important Legal Information

Please refer to Box 3.1 on page 71 for associated material. This material has been prepared by Credit Suisse Asset Management, LLC ("Credit Suisse") on the basis of publicly available information, internally developed data and other third party sources believed to be reliable. Credit Suisse has not sought to independently verify information obtained from public and third party sources and makes no representations or warranties as to accuracy, completeness or reliability of such information. All opinions and views constitute judgments as of the date of writing without regard to the date on which the reader may receive or access the information, and are subject to change at any time without notice and with no obligation to update. This material is for informational and illustrative purposes only and is intended solely for the information of those to whom it is distributed by Credit Suisse. No part of this material may be reproduced or retransmitted in any manner without the prior written permission of Credit Suisse. Credit Suisse does not represent, warrant or guarantee that this information is suitable for any investment purpose other than as specifically contemplated by a written agreement with Credit Suisse and it should not be used as a basis for investment decisions. This material does not purport to contain all of the information that a prospective investor may wish to consider. This material is not to be relied upon as such or used in substitution for the exercise of independent judgment. **Past performance does not guarantee or indicate future results.**

This material should not be viewed as a current or past recommendation or a solicitation of an offer to buy or sell any securities or investment products or to adopt any investment strategy. The securities identified and described do not represent all of the securities purchased, sold or recommended for client accounts. The reader should not assume that any investments in companies, securities, sectors, strategies and/or markets identified or described herein were or will be profitable and no representation is made that any investor will or is likely to achieve results comparable to those shown or will make any profit or will be able to avoid incurring substantial losses. This informational report does not constitute research and may not be used or relied upon in connection with any offer or sale of a security or hedge fund or fund of hedge funds. Performance differences for certain investors may occur due to various factors, including timing of investment and eligibility to participate in new issues. Investment return will fluctuate and may be volatile, especially over short time horizons. **Investing entails risks, including possible loss of some or all of the investor's principal.** The investment views and market opinions/analyses expressed herein may not reflect those of Credit Suisse AG as a whole and different views may be expressed based on different investment styles, objectives, views or philosophies.

Investments in hedge funds are speculative and involve a high degree of risk. Hedge funds may exhibit volatility and investors may lose all or substantially all of their investment. A hedge fund manager typically controls trading of the fund and the use of a single advisor's trading program may result in a lack of diversification. Hedge funds also may use leverage and trade on foreign markets, which may carry additional risks. Investments in illiquid securities or other illiquid assets and the use of short sales, options, leverage, futures, swaps, and other derivative instruments may create special risks and substantially increase the impact of adverse price movements. Hedge funds typically charge higher fees than many other types of investments, which can offset trading profits, if any. Interests in hedge funds may be subject to limitations on transferability. Hedge funds are illiquid and no secondary market for interests typically exists or is likely to develop. The incentive fee may create an incentive for the hedge fund manager to make investments that are riskier than it would otherwise make.

In addition, the investment strategy described herein relies on proprietary models and predictions with regard to the performance of an asset class or particular investment generated by these models and may not be accurate because of imperfections in the models, their deterioration over time, or other factors, such as the quality of the data input into the model, which involves the exercise of judgment. Even if the model functions as anticipated, it cannot account for all factors that may influence the prices of the investments, such as event risk. The asset management business of Credit Suisse Group AG is comprised of a network of entities around the world. Each legal entity is subject to distinct regulatory requirements and certain asset management products and services may not be available in all jurisdictions or to all client types. There is no intention to offer products or services in countries or jurisdictions where such offer would be unlawful under the relevant domestic law. The charts, tables and graphs contained in this document are not intended to be used to assist the reader in determining which securities to buy or sell or when to buy or sell securities. Benchmarks are used solely for purposes of comparison and the comparison does not mean that there will necessarily be a correlation between the returns described herein and the benchmarks. There are limitations in using financial indices for comparison purposes because, among other reasons, such indices may have different volatility, diversification, credit and other material characteristics (such as number or type of instrument or security).

Certain information contained in this document constitutes "Forward-Looking Statements" (including observations about markets and industry and regulatory trends as of the original date of this document), which can be identified by the use of forward-looking terminology such as "may", "will", "should", "expect", "anticipate", "target", "project", "estimate", "intend", "continue" or "believe", or the negatives thereof or other variations thereon or comparable terminology. Due to various risks and uncertainties beyond our control, actual events, results or performance may differ materially from those reflected or contemplated in such forward-looking statements. Readers are cautioned not to place undue reliance on such statements. Credit Suisse has no obligation to update any of the forward-looking statements in this document. The only legally binding terms of this investment product including risk considerations, objectives, charges and expenses are set forth in the private placement memorandum and subscription documents which are available upon request. This document does not constitute an offer or invitation to enter into any type of financial transaction. The issuer has no obligation to issue this investment product. Where not explicitly otherwise stated, the issuer has no duty to invest in the underlying assets. Before deciding to invest, prospective investors must carefully read the relevant private placement memorandum and subscription documents and pay particular attention to the risk factors contained therein and determine if this investment product suits the investor's particular circumstances and should independently assess (with the investor's tax, legal and financial advisers) the specific risks (maximum loss, currency risks, etc.) and the legal, regulatory, credit, tax and accounting consequences. Prospective investors should have the financial ability and willingness to accept the risk characteristics of this investment product. This investment product is intended only for investors who understand and are capable of assuming all risks involved. Credit Suisse makes no representation as to the suitability of this investment product for any particular investor or as to the future performance of this investment product.

Important Information Regarding Hypothetical, Back-Tested or Simulated Performance

The hypothetical performance shown is for illustrative purposes only and does not represent actual performance of the index. Credit Suisse Asset Management, LLC. ("Credit Suisse") does not represent that the hypothetical returns would be similar to actual performance had the firm actually managed the index or accounts in this manner.

Simulations for the Credit Suisse Liquid Alternative Beta Index, the Credit Suisse Long/Short Liquid Index, the Credit Suisse Global Macro Liquid Index, the Credit Suisse Global Strategies Liquid Index and the Credit Suisse Event Driven Liquid Index were conducted to measure how a portfolio of securities and security indices designed to track hedge fund indices would have performed in the period beginning December 31, 1997. Returns were simulated assuming no transaction costs for execution at daily closing prices. Any invested or borrowed cash earned or paid interest at market rates. Monthly index portfolio weights were computed on the day that the Dow Jones Credit Suisse Hedge Fund Index data was updated, which has typically occurred on the first US business day on or after the 15th day of each month. Index rebalancing occurred on the first day after the portfolio weights were computed and for which all instruments involved in the rebalancing process were available to be traded. The platform on which this testing was performed is a proprietary system developed at Credit Suisse. All simulations were conducted by Credit Suisse Asset Management, LLC.

Simulations for the Credit Suisse Merger Arbitrage Liquid Index were conducted to measure how a portfolio of securities designed to mimic a merger arbitrage strategy would have performed in the period beginning December 31, 1997. Returns were simulated assuming no transaction costs for execution at daily closing prices. Any invested or borrowed cash earned or paid interest at market rates. Index portfolio weights were computed daily and index rebalancing occurred on the day after the portfolio weights were computed and for which all instruments involved in the rebalancing process were available to be traded. The platform on which this testing was performed is a proprietary system developed at Credit Suisse. All simulations were conducted by Credit Suisse Asset Management, LLC.

Hypothetical, back-tested or simulated performances have many inherent limitations only some of which are described as follows: (i) It is designed with the benefit of hindsight, based on historical data, and does not reflect the impact that certain economic and market factors might have had on the decision-making process. No hypothetical, back-tested or simulated performance can completely account for the impact of financial risk in actual performance. **Therefore, it will invariably show positive rates of return.** (ii) It does not reflect actual asset trading and cannot accurately account for the ability to withstand losses. (iii) The information is based, in part, on hypothetical assumptions made for modeling purposes that may not be realized in the actual management of indices. No representation or warranty is made as to the reasonableness of the assumptions made or that all assumptions used in achieving the returns have been stated or fully considered. Assumption changes may have a material impact on the model returns presented. This material is not representative of any particular index's performance. **Investors should not assume that they will have an investment experience similar to the hypothetical, back-tested or simulated performance shown.** There are frequently material differences between hypothetical, back-tested or simulated performance results and actual results subsequently achieved by any investment strategy.

Unlike an actual performance record based on trading actual portfolios, hypothetical, back-tested or simulated results are achieved by means of the retroactive application of a back-tested model itself designed with the benefit of hindsight. Hypothetical, back-tested or simulated performance does not reflect the impact that material economic or market factors might have on an adviser's decision making process if the adviser were actually managing a portfolio. The back-testing of performance differs from performance because the investment strategy may be adjusted at any time, for any reason and can continue to be changed until desired or better performance results are achieved. The back-tested performance includes hypothetical results that do not reflect the reinvestment of dividends and other earnings or the deduction of advisory fees, brokerage or other commissions, and any other expenses that a client would have paid or actually paid. **No representation is made that any index will or is likely to achieve profits or losses similar to those shown.** Alternative modeling techniques or assumptions might produce significantly different results and prove to be more appropriate. Past hypothetical, back-test or simulated results are neither indicators nor guarantees of future returns. **In fact, there are frequently sharp differences between hypothetical, back-tested and simulated performance results and the actual results subsequently achieved.** As a sophisticated investor, you accept and agree to use such information only for the purpose of discussing with Credit Suisse your preliminary interest in investing in the strategy described herein.

Index

Compiled by Indexing Specialists Ltd., Hove, UK